DESTINY IS DEBATABLE

DESTINY IS DEBATABLE

A Memoir of Meningitis, Losing Sight,
and the Love I Didn't See Coming

JOHN B. GRIMES

Published by Cemblem LLC
PO Box 6013
Frisco, Texas 75035

Hardcover ISBN: 979-8-9939813-0-7
Paperback ISBN: 979-8-9939813-1-4
Digital ISBN: 979-8-9939813-2-1

Library of Congress Control Number: 2026904052

This is a work of nonfiction, drawn from my personal experiences and memories. Some names and identifying details have been changed to protect privacy. Medical details reflect my own experience and are not intended as medical advice.

First Edition

For Erin, Emma, Laurel, and Corinne

"When you come out of the storm, you won't be the same person who walked in. That's what the storm is all about."

— *Haruki Murakami*

CONTENTS

SECTION V: FINDING MYSELF IN THE DARK

SECTION VI: MY SO-CALLED ADULT LIFE

SECTION VII: ERIN

PREFACE

The story I am finally telling became possible on February 13, 1998, when I surfaced from a coma into darkness and my dad pried open my eye, letting light rush in. It has taken decades, and more than a few failed attempts, to get that moment onto this page. Most tries ended the same way: with more questions than answers and a blank page staring back at me.

Then I met Erin, and suddenly the words started to cooperate. Telling my story didn't feel like reopening a wound anymore. It felt like tending to something alive. With her, the pieces began to fit: love, faith, redemption. Eventually, our lives grew into something I never saw coming, a family of five with hearts far bigger than our house.

I wanted this book for them, for Erin, for our girls who taught me to grow brave and true, so they'd know why their dad is a little eccentric and a lot determined. Why our family tree sprouted a wild branch. Why possibility will always be part of their inheritance.

Life has taught me that experts can predict outcomes, but they can't measure hope. Mine took faith, family, and an endless string of small, stubborn choices to keep believing in what could be.

Somewhere along the way, I realized that while my story, like yours, is still being written, it has also become far fuller than it could have been more than twenty years ago. Back then, survival was the goal. Now, it's life itself that feels abundant. It's laughter at the dinner table, a house full of noise, the quiet moments when gratitude sneaks in and stays awhile. The pages may still be unfolding, but the story already feels rich.

This book isn't just about what happened to me. It's about what can happen after, about the ordinary grace that meets us when everything else falls apart and about how faith holds the flashlight when logic has given up.

I'm still a work in progress, but so are you. Somewhere along the way, this stopped being my story and became ours, shaped by the love and faith that keep carrying it forward. My hope is that our story will light someone else's way, the same way so many others have lit mine.

Because if I've learned anything, it's that even the messiest chapters can still lead somewhere beautiful.

Destiny isn't written. It's lived.

—SECTION I—
Bacterial What?

BEFORE IT ALL
WENT DARK

I t began innocuously enough, with what I assumed was a mere cold or maybe a sinus infection. A sniffle, a bit of a headache, nothing unusual for the winter flu season. This minor annoyance was no match for me. As a nineteen-year-old sophomore at Texas Tech University, I was a typical student and, like most teenagers, felt like I was ten feet tall and bulletproof.

Driving home from an intramural basketball game on campus, I stopped off at a drugstore to get some over-the-counter cold medicine. I'd take it with dinner. At the apartment, I was greeted by my roommates Kevin and Ryan. We commiserated over the basketball game loss, poking fun at our teammate who'd air-balled a free throw, and then discussed weekend plans that included a big fraternity party.

Not feeling much worse and convinced the OTC meds were helping, I blew through my Thursday classes. Daydreaming while sitting in accounting, I remembered the sirloin steak stashed in the refrigerator at home. Hmm…were there any potatoes to go with that? I wondered. Maybe my favorite meal, steak and potatoes, was just what I needed to get over the hump and fuel my evening studies to end the week strong. As it turned out, we did have potatoes in the pantry, but they were in a box. Who needs a Michelin Star when you have a box of scalloped potatoes? Perfect! I prepared both on the stovetop and devoured them at our kitchen table while flipping through my political science notes.

I started feeling worse as Thursday evening dragged on. Maybe this was more than a cold, or maybe I was just tired and needed another dose of meds and a good night's sleep. My test wasn't until tomorrow afternoon, I thought. Yeah, that's it. Another dose and hit the rack. I'd finish studying in the morning.

Just after 3 a.m., my body was jolted awake by what felt like a volcano erupting from my stomach. What I considered a minor inconvenience just a few hours earlier had escalated into a full-blown, four-alarm disaster. In a matter of seconds, I found myself face down on the carpeted floor. The instant my feet touched down, my legs turned to Jell-O. As I attempted to stand up and make it to the bathroom just a few feet away, the sensation of vertigo set in and the room spun like a top until I came crashing down again. Understanding that getting to the bathroom was not an option, I lunged for a nearby trash can just as the explosion occurred. I vomited for what seemed like an eternity, hugging the trash can like my life depended on it. Again and again and again . . .

After the dry heaves subsided, I rested my sweaty, still-spinning head on the top of the trash can to catch my breath and take stock of what had just happened. If I hadn't been pinned between the trash can and bedroom wall, I would have completely collapsed and melted onto the floor. When I passed out from exhaustion, the horrendous odor worked like smelling salts and rudely summoned me back to consciousness. I had to get this out of my room! I cinched up the drawstring on the trash bag and once again attempted to stand up. Everything was still spinning; upright was not an option. I channeled all my focus toward getting the source of that smell as far away from me as possible. While on my hands and knees, I grabbed the bag and army-crawled out of my bedroom through the quiet, dark living room of our three-bedroom apartment. Dragging my foul-smelling baggage with me, I ventured out the front door as far as I could go without jeopardizing my chances of making it back. I pushed the bag—surely full of everything I'd eaten since the third grade—outside and started the strenuous trek back to my bedroom. Once there, I grabbed the cordless phone from its base on my nearby desk and then struggled back into bed.

Physically exhausted from the vomiting and crawling expedition across the apartment, my body sank into the mattress, but my mind didn't succumb as easily as I tried to process what was happening. Okay, it looks like this is more than just a cold. I feel like I have vertigo or something...I'm never eating boxed potatoes again!

I glanced at the cordless phone and saw it was 4:26 a.m., too early to call my parents. Looking at the light coming from the phone's small LCD screen felt like I was staring directly at the sun. Whoa! I'd better just close my eyes and rest. I bundled up under the covers and hoped my body would stop shaking soon.

After I'd cycled in and out of restless sleep several times, the clock finally registered a few minutes past 6 a.m. I made the call to the mothership. I told my parents I was sick but didn't go into the details about dizziness and weakness because I wasn't sure it was necessary, or because I was trying to be a tough teenage boy, or maybe because I was simply so exhausted that all I could manage to report was the minimum amount of detail. After all, it was flu season, and both of my parents had been ill with the flu just a week earlier. My parents told me to take something to settle my stomach and get some rest. Their magic potion was Alka-Seltzer. I told them I would take some, and they promised to check on me later in the day. Although my pantry had enough gourmet boxed potatoes to feed a fraternity house, there was no Alka-Seltzer in sight.

Once again, I tried to sit up, but the overwhelming spinning sensation forced me back down. I slid out of bed, back onto the floor, and army-crawled out of my bedroom to Kevin's bedroom door. I knocked and knocked while calling his name. Eventually, Kevin opened the door and was surprised to find me lying on the floor. After briefly telling him what had happened, I asked if he would go to the nearby convenience store for me. He agreed and quickly went on his way. About fifteen minutes later, he returned, delivered the supplies and a cup of water to my bedroom, and shuffled back to his room to sleep.

Plop, plop. Fizz, fizz…I chugged the Alka-Seltzer and sat for just a moment to feel the tingly bubble party make its way into my stomach. I had one more call to make to my political science professor. I left a voicemail at her office to say I was sick and wouldn't be in class to take the test that day but would be in touch next week to make the necessary arrangements. I tossed the phone down next to me and once again collapsed in bed.

That call was my last memory before it all went dark.

FADING OUT OF THE PICTURE

Though I have no recollection of it, Kevin and Ryan report that later in the day, as they were going to and from class, I was up and walking around the apartment. While it was clear that I was sick, it didn't appear to be anything out of the norm for something like the flu. Apparently, I strongly advised them to stay far away from me and the apartment. I told them that spending the night elsewhere would be a good idea because they wouldn't want to catch whatever I had. Soon thereafter, Kevin and Ryan left and got an early start on the weekend.

At the end of her workday, Mom called to check on me. She said I told her that things seemed to be stabilizing, but I was still weak and not feeling well. My plan was to take it easy and rest. She reminded me to keep drinking plenty of liquids and encouraged me to visit the campus health clinic if I wasn't feeling better by tomorrow. The campus health clinic, affectionately referred to by students as the Quack Shack, didn't exactly have a reputation for stellar medical care, but at the time, it was really my only option for something minor like this. (Urgent care facilities were not yet a thing.) Mom told me that she would check in again with me the next morning.

As evening began to settle in, my girlfriend of a few weeks, Jenn, also called to check on me. She was a sorority sister of Kevin and Ryan's girlfriends, so it didn't take long for the news to travel. According to Jenn, I didn't go into a lot of detail but surmised that I must have the flu. I also encouraged her to keep her distance because whatever I had was terrible. I didn't need anything—I was just going to take it easy tonight. I was bummed because it was Friday and we had a big weekend planned, but I definitely wasn't going out that night. I told her she should go on without me and have fun.

That evening, my friends got into the normal Friday rhythm. Three hundred miles away in Plano, my parents did the same. Every Friday, they joined Mom's sixth-grade teaching partner, Eileen Rogers, and her husband, Al, for dinner at the same quaint Italian restaurant to share a bottle of wine, unwind, and swap crazy school stories. The four of them had become very close friends over the years. At dinner, Mom casually told Eileen she thought I was down with the flu, the kind of passing comment you make without much thought.

Back in Lubbock, I was all alone in my apartment. Unbeknownst to anyone, with each passing moment the stakes grew higher, the window of opportunity for intervention narrowing by the minute. It reminds me of a scene from *Back to the Future*, where the main character, Marty McFly, has traveled back in time and is playing guitar onstage at his future parents' high school dance. He watches his likeness slowly disappear from a future family photo because it seems his teenage parents will never get together at the dance, marry soon afterward, and bring Marty into being.

I was slipping toward disappearance, fading out of existence like Marty. After telling everyone I was okay and pushing them away, I needed someone to take action because I could do nothing to save myself.

Saturday morning, before heading out to run errands, Mom made several calls to my apartment with no answer. This was not unusual, especially on a Saturday morning. Mom left a message saying, "You're either at the campus medical center for treatment or hopefully feeling better and able to get out and run around. Call me back." Not long after, she and Dad left to enjoy brunch and a jaunt to an antique mall before taking the scenic route to the grocery store just to feel a sense of adventure—simple things parents do with kid-free time on the weekends.

Sometime early that morning, apparently between calls from my mom, Kevin returned to the apartment to grab something quickly. Noticing my bedroom door was closed, he decided not to check on me, a decision that has haunted him ever since.

A few hours later, my fraternity "big brother," Brad Smith, arrived at my apartment. Earlier in the week, we had arranged to meet before lunch on Saturday to get the necessary provisions for the fraternity party that evening. We'd met during Fall 1996 Rush, about twenty months earlier, when I was deciding which fraternity to join. We hit it off immediately. When I joined Delta Tau Delta, Brad was a natural fit as my big brother. A couple of years older than me, Brad definitely knew how to have a good time but was levelheaded and more responsible than most. He would act as a great guide into fraternity life for the wild-eyed eighteen-year-old freshman who'd just been unleashed on the world.

When Brad rolled up at my apartment around 11 a.m. that Saturday, he parked next to my teal green 1994 Honda Accord and made his way up to our second-floor apartment to get me. He knocked on the front door a couple of times before trying to open the door himself. Miraculously, he found the door unlocked and entered an unusually silent and seemingly empty apartment.

There was no sound or trace of me, my two roommates, or anyone else known to hang out there. Entering the apartment, Brad investigated further, calling our names to find out if anyone was home. He slowly opened my bedroom door to find the room apparently empty—but then he caught a whiff of a foul odor.

He called my name again and got no response, but heard a noise from the other side of my bed, out of his line of sight from the doorway. He entered the room to examine and found me unresponsive, face down on the carpeted floor, with soiled gray sweatpants and lying in a pool of vomit.

Shocked, he picked up the cordless phone from my bed and called 911, reporting that he thought I was having a seizure.

Within three minutes, an ambulance arrived. Paramedics placed me on a stretcher and got me into the ambulance as quickly as possible. All the while, they unloaded a barrage of questions on Brad, for which he had few answers.

Coincidentally, one of the paramedics who arrived with the ambulance was from Plano and assumed my condition was due to a heroin overdose. At the time, there was endemic heroin use among teenagers in Plano, an upper-middle-class suburb north of Dallas. Just a few months prior, MTV spotlighted my high school, Plano Senior High, in a news segment about the alarming rise of heroin use. Although I knew some of the kids on the MTV segment, I'd never seen heroin during my time at Plano Senior High. A class as large as mine, with nearly 1,300 students, had many cliques, and I never interacted with those kids. Even so, on the paramedic's suspicion, the team quickly scoured my room for evidence but found none.

THE RACE IS ON

Within minutes, the ambulance headed to University Medical Center just two miles down the road. Kevin returned to the apartment as Brad was pulling away in his vehicle, and they both followed the ambulance to the hospital.

Upon arrival, the frantic quest for a diagnosis began. Kevin started calling those closest to us at school. Meanwhile, hospital personnel and Brad Smith attempted to reach my mom and dad. The only number they had was our home telephone number—no one was there to answer. But a newly recorded voicemail greeting provided my younger brother Brad's pager number.

My brother Brad, a high school junior, had gone to work that morning at the Dallas Galleria shopping mall with the family cell phone and his trusty pager. He'd acquired that brand-new pager just a week earlier and, after a couple of days of pleading, had convinced my parents that the pager number should be added to our home phone's answering machine greeting so important people (his friends) could reach him. Many high schoolers in Plano at the time had pagers; it was that mystical time in the '90s just before cell phones became ubiquitous and just after drug dealers and doctors were no longer the only ones lucky enough to receive round-the-clock notifications that drove them to rush to the nearest phone and respond to the "emergency."

While Brad was at work that Saturday sometime around noon, the buzzwords "important people" and "emergency" that he'd used to sell my parents on the pager turned real and surreal all at once. The hospital paged Brad with the all-too-familiar 911 "postscript" that would read something like this on a pager screen: 8061234567 911 (a phone number + 911). Pager screens could display numbers only, no letters, so 911 meant urgent, or, in this case, literally, an emergency.

Brad's pager buzzed in his pocket. He told his manager he needed to make a phone call because he'd received a page with 911 from the 806 (Lubbock) area code, where his brother went to school. From the break room, he called the number from his pager on the family cell phone. The hospital would not give him specifics, though, because he was not my parent or guardian. They did tell him I was found unconscious in my apartment and rushed to them in serious condition. This truly was an emergency, and the doctor needed to talk to my parents immediately.

Handling the news with maturity, Brad remained calm, cool, and collected amid the confusion and instantly left the mall. On his thirty-minute drive home, he called the Elders (our neighbors two doors down and my best friend Chris's parents) and the Rogerses to explain the situation and see if they knew where Mom and Dad were. No one knew definitively, but they all started making calls and checking known places.

David and Bobbie Elder came over to the house to help Brad make phone calls and search for Mom and Dad. David, the Special Agent in

Charge for the FBI in Dallas, placed a direct call to the Plano police chief, whom he knew both personally and professionally. The police chief ordered a "Lookout" (the noncriminal equivalent of an All-Points Bulletin, or APB) for Doug and Betsy Grimes. Now hundreds of Plano police officers were searching for my parents, too.

My brother made several airline reservations for Mom and Dad. Southwest Airlines, based in Dallas, had a flight from Dallas to Lubbock almost every hour on most days. Al and Eileen Rogers arrived at our home and began packing bags for my parents to leave quickly.

In the meantime, back in Lubbock, hospital staff frantically tried to diagnose my condition. They were confused by my unconscious arrival and the "burns" on the face and hands of an otherwise healthy-looking teenager. The staff continually peppered my friends about a possible drug overdose. The "burns," however, were not burns at all but rather road-rash-like abrasions to my skin from lying face down in vomit and moving my head from side to side as though convulsing on the carpet.

Brad Smith explained that even though he had only known me for about a year and a half, he had never seen or known me to use any substances other than alcohol. He and Kevin assured the staff that my dire condition had not been caused by drugs, but the hospital team still seemed to think Brad and Kevin were covering for me.

Miraculously—or luckily, or at least very astutely—the ER doctor was finally convinced by my friends and moved on to consider other possibilities. He began to suspect the condition was bacterial meningitis and ordered a lumbar puncture (also known as a spinal tap) to confirm or rule out meningitis.

Minutes later, a powerful intravenous antibiotic treatment was initiated to counteract the suspected bacterial meningitis. Just before my diagnosis began to crystallize in Lubbock, another critical event unfolded, one that would deliver my parents to my side with shocking urgency.

Meandering on their casual, carefree Saturday, in ignorant bliss of what was transpiring hundreds of miles away, Mom and Dad stopped at a traffic light at the intersection of Ohio Drive and Spring Creek Parkway in Plano. Headed north on Ohio Drive, their Suburban was the first vehicle in line. With a front-row seat, they watched as the eastbound and westbound traffic flowed in front of them on Spring Creek Parkway. The driver of a vehicle headed west on the parkway misread the oncoming traffic, turned left, and was T-boned by an eastbound vehicle. The impact sent one of the vehicles spinning out of control until it slammed into the front of my parents' idle Suburban. Although their vehicle was damaged and disabled, my parents were not injured. Others were not so fortunate.

Plano police and paramedics arrived on the scene within minutes and began the standard crash investigation. The paramedics immediately started treating the injured, and the police asked my parents to move away from the scene. After what seemed like an eternity to my parents, an officer approached them and asked for their license, registration, and insurance details. Upon examining my parents' licenses, the officer solemnly said, "Mr. and Mrs. Grimes, we've been looking for you two. Your son, John, is in critical condition in a hospital in Lubbock. The hospital needs you immediately." The officer called my parents' house, which had been converted into Mission Control and had just completed its first task of locating my parents. Al was immediately dispatched to the accident location. Within fifteen minutes, Al arrived in his truck, scooped up Mom and Dad, and raced home, leaving their Suburban at the scene.

When Mom and Dad arrived at home amid a flurry of activity, they found my brother, Eileen, and the Elders gathered there, anxious to help and to know more. In short order, my parents spoke with the hospital by phone. They were briefed on my dire condition, which had not yet been diagnosed, and given urgent direction to get to Lubbock before it was too late. My parents grabbed their already-packed bags and once again jumped in Al's truck, this time for the forty-minute sprint down the Dallas North Tollway to Love Field Airport. Like a whirlwind, my parents blew through the airport and reached the gate just in time to board the fifty-minute flight from Dallas to Lubbock. Southwest Airlines was known for its "good time in the sky" environment. But my parents, with minds and hearts racing, were in no mood to have fun on board.

QUARANTINED

After the antibiotic treatment began, I was moved from the emergency room to a quarantined section of the ICU and placed in a medically induced coma to protect my brain and other organs, halt the severe bacterial infection, and give my body a chance to heal.

When my parents' plane touched down in Lubbock, Kevin picked them up at the airport and rushed them to the hospital. Evening was setting in just after 6 p.m. on a cold winter day on the South Plains of West Texas when they arrived at the hospital, where staff immediately escorted Mom and Dad into a consultation room. You know, that small, cramped room with a cheap desk and chairs, a ficus plant, and soft, dim lighting. Generally, when you're ushered into that room, no good announcements are forthcoming…but prior to their arrival at the hospital, my parents didn't know I had bacterial meningitis.

Fighting off a slight sense of foreboding, Mom remembered thinking, "I hope this is just a really bad case of the flu." (They had no idea how grave the situation was.)

In truth, they were taken into the consultation room straightaway because the health care team would not let my parents see me before preparing them for what they would encounter. I had been on a strong acne medication that had made my facial skin very delicate. As a result, it looked like I had third-degree burns on my face from the bile and rubbing my face on the floor. The tip of my nose took the brunt of the abuse. I had rubbed off all the skin down to the cartilage. At this point, the gnarly skin and blood made it look like a grenade had exploded in my face.

A couple of doctors briefed Mom and Dad on my dire situation. They concluded that my age, symptom set, the rapid progression, and initial spinal tap results were consistent with meningococcal meningitis, a bacterial meningitis. The condition, invasive meningococcal disease, is rare but real and carries potentially severe outcomes. Although they had started treatment, it might not have been soon enough. The doctors gave me long odds to make it through the night. When asked if I was an organ donor, Mom and Dad truly understood the gravity of the situation. Stunned, they asked the doctor, "Bacterial what?"

Only after this wrenching discussion were my parents allowed to see me for the first time. IVs, wires, tubes, ventilator... Their son lying motionless with a mangled and bloody face.

Speechless, they took in the sight they'd later describe as "horrific." Mom remembers almost hyperventilating because she was so shocked at the sight of me connected to life-sustaining devices after speaking with me just twenty-four hours earlier.

Down the hall, through a set of double doors, there was a waiting room where my friends were holding vigil. They had stashed some pillows and blankets they'd gone home and collected so that my parents might sleep.

In the eerie silence of the hospital, my parents sat in shock, trying to grasp the surreal situation. As the night wore on, their thoughts were a maelstrom of fear and helplessness, their minds racing to understand how the common flu had rapidly morphed into this life-threatening ordeal. Each tick of the clock felt like a countdown to an uncertain fate, the faint beeps of hospital machines echoing the precarious rhythm of my existence. They were told to prepare for the worst, but could they really be ready for what was to come?

For my parents, this night was a battle against time, the darkness filled with desperate prayers and fragile hope. As the first light of dawn approached, the question loomed large: Would I survive to see another day, or would the dawn bring a heartbreak that would change our lives forever?

—SECTION II—
While You Were Sleeping

THE STILLNESS
AFTER THE STORM

Morning light slowly spilled over the West Texas winter horizon, each ray a warming whisper of hope in the aftermath of the prior day's trauma. Contrary to the experts' prognostications, I survived the first night! A stark contrast to the mayhem of Saturday, day two in the hospital began with nothing. No change in my charts, no change in my appearance. No changes anywhere—nothing. The chaos of my collapse had passed. But as I lay still in that hospital bed, time didn't completely stop; it started dragging its feet.

The only one who had slept overnight was me. That's not saying much, though. With the adrenaline still pumping through their veins, my parents were on high alert and held in suspense by doctors who continued to be anything but optimistic about my chances. So far, they had been proven wrong—a theme that would repeat itself again and again.

Just before 7 a.m., my brother Brad's flight touched down at the Lubbock airport. He'd made the same trek our parents had made less than twelve hours earlier. One of only a handful of passengers on the early flight from Dallas, Brad couldn't sit still. His mind was still racing; he'd also had a restless night.

Back home in Plano, the phone rang countless times through the night with calls from the hospital. It was Dad, providing updates, working out logistical details, and adding items to the list of things Brad was to bring with him on the flight. As he stared at the ceiling in his upstairs bedroom, Eileen answered the calls downstairs in the living room. Eileen and Al had spent the night with Brad to help support him and do their best to stabilize things at home. Every time the phone rang, Brad's body tensed; he feared the worst. Although he couldn't understand Eileen's words from upstairs, by lying still and focusing on her voice, he could easily decipher her brief and matter-of-fact tone.

His thoughts raced with the swirling events of the turbulent day. He couldn't stop thinking about how he had almost lost his parents in a car wreck and his brother to some freak medical condition. He had been so close to losing his whole family in a matter of just a few hours.

Still reeling from it all, Brad tried to maintain his brave face. Dad picked him up in my Accord, which Kevin and Ryan had brought to the hospital for my parents to use. On the twenty-minute ride from the airport to the hospital, Brad sat in stunned disbelief as our dad—forever the ultimate positive thinker—put a positive spin on what had transpired over the last twelve hours while warning him about the tenuous situation at the hospital and my ghastly appearance.

Dad and Brad wound through the maze of hallways, doors, and

elevators to reach my ICU room. Through the final set of double doors, they encountered another long hallway lined with a dozen of my friends camped out along the walls. Under the circumstances, the nurses broke protocol and permitted my family and friends to be gathered there overnight. At the end of the hallway and nearest to my room was Mom. She greeted Brad, her chin trembling uncontrollably, with a long, tight squeeze. With tears streaming down her face, she led him to my room.

From the hallway, Brad got his first look at me. Eyes squinted, he peered through the small tempered-glass window in the door and thick sheets of clear plastic draped from the ceiling that created a sterile perimeter around my bed. I lay motionless, enveloped in a cocoon of medical equipment. Tubes and wires snaked from my body to machines and monitors displaying vital signs in real time. A large ventilator tube strapped to my mangled face provided life-sustaining breaths. My serene, unconscious state contrasted starkly with the intense, invisible battle being waged within my body against the relentless and highly infectious bacterial meningitis.

During the first forty-eight hours in the quarantined section of the ICU, anyone entering my room was required to wear isolation gowns, gloves, and masks to be fully protected. After suiting up, Brad timidly entered my room with Mom and Dad. Once inside, Brad encountered the harmonized, quiet symphony of sounds: the soft, rhythmic sighs of the ventilator and the steady beep of the heart monitor that punctuated the air, joined by occasional hisses and clicks from infusion pumps that delivered vital medications.

From the side of my bed, Mom grabbed my hand and encouraged Brad to grab my other. Brad reached down and held my limp hand, staring at the shell of what used to be his big brother.

Dad interrupted the mechanical symphony with an announcement. "Hey, Champ, Brother Brad is here to see you."

Still overcome by the sobering scene, Brad fumbled for words and could only muster a choked and impotent "Hey, John."

Brad recalls the excruciating awkwardness of this solemn meeting that took place at the urging of the doctors and nurses. By all accounts, this could have been the last time my family would ever speak to me, and it was doubtful that I could even hear them. Despite the onslaught of emotions sparked by seeing me in this state, compounding the upheaval of the last twenty-four hours, Brad's words utterly failed him. What hope could he express? What words could comfort Mom and Dad, not to mention himself? What could anyone say in this situation? While Brad was rendered speechless in the ICU, my dad found himself doing the opposite—talking. A lot. Because someone had to.

Still in shock, Mom was incapable of talking with others about my condition, so Dad was tasked with communicating with the outside world. At that point, less than a full day in, things still did not look good. Dad made several phone calls, starting with our extended family in Chillicothe, Ohio—his parents and my mom's parents and sister, Aunt Judy, whom Brad and I long considered our second mom. He also updated the Elder and Rogers families and a friend in my parents' Sunday school class back in Plano. Dad delivered the latest status about my grave condition, asked them to disseminate the details to others, and requested prayers.

After Mom's parents, Kenny and Sharma Trusler, received the disturbing details of my condition, they hastily packed for an indeterminate stay and fueled up their car to make the familiar 1,000-mile, eighteen-hour drive from Chillicothe to Plano. Their mission was to hold down the fort at home with Brad while my mom and dad were in Lubbock attending to me. After we relocated from Ohio to Texas six years prior, both we and the Truslers had made this journey dozens of times and no longer needed to follow a map. It would take two days, with a stop halfway in Memphis, Tennessee, for an overnight stay with Kenny's brother Jack and his wife, Martha.

As word back home began to spread among those closest to me, Bobbie Elder phoned her son Chris, my best friend. She told him about the events of the past day and what she knew about my fragile condition in the hospital. Chris was a student at the University of Texas in Austin, about 250 miles south of Plano and 375 miles southeast of Lubbock. Disturbed by the news, Chris asked his mom what he should do. His first instinct was to get in his car and make the journey across Texas to the hospital. She strongly advised against going to Lubbock, telling him he would just be in the way, and insisted he stay put and wait for more details before doing anything.

Chris was the first person I met after our family relocated to Plano during the middle of my eighth-grade school year. On the day we moved into our home, Brad and I were excitedly exploring our new surroundings. That afternoon, a school bus stopped nearby and several kids filed out. Chris was in a group of boys who passed along the sidewalk right in front of our new home. Brad and I ran out front to inquire what was going on. Just like that, a friendship began that has spanned more than thirty years and counting.

Back in Lubbock, something intriguing started to stir: hope. Not loud or dramatic, but quiet. Steady. The kind that tiptoes in when no one's looking. Generations of both my mother's and father's families were raised in the United Methodist Church. As staunch Christian believers, my parents always anchored themselves in faith in times like this. Although they couldn't attend their physical church that day, they had already met with the hospital minister and spent a great deal of time praying for God's mercy.

Over the years, my parents had accrued countless friends from church. Many of them rallied quickly to help Mom and Dad after learning the news at Sunday school. One of them, Marsha Sparks, had a best friend whose parents, Wayne and Emily Finnell, lived in Lubbock. After leaving church that day, Marsha immediately called and told the Finnells about me, my situation, and my parents.

In the middle of the afternoon, in walked Wayne and Emily. They were a super-sweet couple, the same age as my grandparents, and still dressed in their Sunday best. My dad, recounting his first interaction with them, described Emily as having an angelic presence about her. After introducing herself, she grabbed my dad's hand with both of hers, squeezed, looked him straight in the eyes, and professed, "Your son is going to be okay. He's going to make it."

My dad could feel a jolt of positive energy move through his body. Up to this point, all interactions at the hospital had been sterile and pessimistic, very data driven, with low odds of survival being the unavoidable conclusion. Wayne and Emily had arrived out of the blue, bringing some welcome fresh air; they proffered not only optimism but a contrary guarantee that this would not end like the "experts" were predicting.

The Finnells were not the only unexpected visitors to infuse some hope and lift the heaviness that day. After appeasing his mother on the phone about staying in Austin, Chris hung up and immediately stuffed essentials in a bag before hitting the road. Back in the 1900s—before GPS and online maps—Chris relied on paper maps he kept stored in his glove box to make the unfamiliar expedition from Central to West Texas. He knew that time was critical and that I was in grave condition. Not necessarily adhering to the posted speed limits, Chris made the journey in just under six hours and arrived late in the afternoon.

Once he entered Lubbock, Chris didn't know exactly where I was. A town with a population of over 200,000, Lubbock had several medical facilities. He stopped at a pay phone, grabbed a handful of quarters from his car, opened the phone book, and started calling hospitals until he found the right one.

At the hospital, Chris quickly found his way to my ICU room and spotted the familiar faces of my parents, brother, and some of our mutual friends. My parents weren't their normal selves, and he could tell they were under a great deal of stress. From the hallway, Chris peered into the room through the window in the door. Despite being warned, Chris was shocked by my appearance—my torn-up nose from the vomit-covered carpeted floor, the road rash on my face, plus the feeding tube taped to my nose. After he suited up, my parents escorted him into my room.

Unlike my brother's acute awareness of the equipment's hushed, rhythmic industriousness, what struck Chris was the familiar slow melody of "Sex and Candy" by the '90s band Marcy Playground coming from a small boom box on the floor. Earlier in the day, at my parents' request, my friends had retrieved a few things from my apartment, the most important of which was my music collection. A huge lover of music, I had an enormous CD collection that spanned decades and genres, neatly curated in a 256-disc Case Logic binder. The idea was for the music to lift my spirits or make me feel more comfortable by bringing the familiar into an unfamiliar environment. And maybe it did, ultimately, but when Chris entered the room, the "Sex and Candy" selection playing on repeat struck an odd dissonance with the heavy ICU scene.

Dad announced the new arrival in the room. "Hey, Champ, Chris is here to see you."

Without prompting, Chris instinctively grabbed my hand, squeezed, and said, "Hang in there, buddy. You're going to make it." He stayed for several minutes, mostly in stunned silence, keeping me company the only way he could, by just being there. At one point, he even started quietly humming along to that ridiculous song we both knew so well.

After he left, the nurses noted something interesting: my vital signs—heart rate and brain activity—had spiked while Chris was in the room and returned to normal once he was gone. Maybe it was a coincidence, or maybe, deep in that coma, I still recognized the voice of my best friend … or the questionable lyrics of a '90s one-hit wonder playing on loop.

Either way, it was the first real sign that I wasn't entirely gone. That somewhere inside, something was still responding. Still listening. Still fighting.

THE FACE SHE
TRIED TO SAVE

While my body showed slivers of life, my face told a different story. If bacterial meningitis didn't seem terrifying enough, my face looked like I had gone ten rounds with a cheese grater—and lost.

No one knows how long I lay face down on that vomit-soaked carpet before Brad Smith found me. However many hours it was, it was long enough to do serious damage. One of the first things people mention from those early hospital days isn't the coma or the machines. It's my face. "It was all scabbed up," "like you got mauled by a bear," "like your face was ripped off," or, my personal favorite, "you looked like one big scab."

Mom was especially concerned. But while the doctors were

busy trying to keep me alive, my face didn't even crack the top ten on their list of priorities. That didn't stop her. Every chance she got, she asked the nurses for creams or lotions. She'd gently apply them to my scabbed skin like she was tending a garden. It gave her something to do. Something she could control. And maybe, in her own quiet way, something she believed might bring me back.

She wasn't wrong to care. I'd always been self-conscious about my skin—teenage acne, magnified by a teenage ego. What felt like the end of the world back then was probably mild to moderate at worst, but I'd tried everything short of voodoo to clear it up. Creams, scrubs, even toothpaste in a pinch.

Eventually, Mom and I went to see a dermatologist, and we talked about a stronger solution—a prescription medication that might finally clear things up. But there was a catch. It was a powerful treatment, one that required regular checkups to monitor side effects. And because I was living away at school, making it back to Plano for frequent visits wasn't an option.

The Plano dermatologist suggested I find a doctor in Lubbock to administer the treatment. I quickly saw a local dermatologist, got the prescription, and hoped I'd finally have a clear face. It was just one more thing I could fix. Or so I thought.

Mom had already contacted my Lubbock dermatologist. Since the doctor didn't have hospital privileges at UMC, she quickly sent a nurse to check on me. Based on what the nurse saw, the dermatologist recommended some over-the-counter treatments. That was all Mom needed. Armed with a few drugstore bottles, she went to work.

But it wasn't just my face she watched. Between applying lotion and whispering quiet prayers, she kept an eye on the monitors, tracing every blip, every beep, trying to decode what they meant. If my heart rate changed, she'd glance at Dad, who was already calculating what it could mean. They were learning to read the room the way generals read a battlefield.

When evening came, the nurses returned to strict ICU visitation rules. Everyone—friends, family, even my parents—had to clear out. Wayne and Emily graciously insisted that my parents stay with them, but they politely declined. As kind as the offer was, they didn't want to be a burden. Instead, they checked into a nearby Holiday Inn, where Brad joined them. For the foreseeable future, that hotel would be their base—rotating visitors, fitful sleep, and morning trips back to the hospital.

Early Monday morning, when they returned, the same unspoken question hung in the air: Would this be the day things got better? Or would this be the day everything fell apart? There was still a massive battle being waged in my body. The meningitis was being neutralized, but had the treatment started soon enough to save me?

The doctors weren't optimistic. With every passing hour that I remained unchanged, their predictions seemed to darken. Death was still a very real possibility. But if I didn't die, I'd most likely end up in a permanent vegetative state: my body alive, but my mind gone. Every nurse's visit, every doctor's grim assessment only seemed to hammer this home. They spoke clinically, cautiously, and always with the same bottom line: nothing was improving.

If this limbo stretched on, the impossible choice would fall to my parents—how long to keep my body alive knowing my mind might never return.

Within a couple of days, my parents began to adapt to the discomforting rhetoric and sterile rhythms of the ICU. The daily rounds. The language of clipped updates and cautious pessimism. The lead doctor on my case was a master of that language, brutally literal and emotionally tone-deaf. Not only was this an awful combination for a professional tasked with delivering life-or-death news, but it also made him the exact opposite of my parents, especially Dad.

Dad was the ultimate optimist, the guy who could find a silver lining in a tornado. Even when reality weighed heavy, he stubbornly insisted on finding a thread of hope. In that clinical, unforgiving ICU, his staunch optimism was being put to the test. Although he refused to believe them, he was painfully aware of the odds the doctors kept reciting.

Because UMC was a teaching hospital, the doctor always showed up with a small crowd of medical students in tow, each clutching a clipboard like a shield. After a few minutes inside my room, they'd exit and huddle up just outside the door. My parents couldn't hear what was being said, but they watched the body language and expressions like detectives trying to crack the code.

Brad noticed how calm Dad seemed: stoic, composed, and, of course, optimistic, but Brad suspected it was mostly a show. He assumed that when Dad wasn't standing beside me, looking for the faintest sign of improvement, he was probably falling apart. There was one moment, though, when Dad's mask slipped. The organ-harvesting team had begun circling the ICU just outside my room, waiting for a likely "code blue." A normal part of hospital protocol, but to Dad, it felt like vultures taking early flight.

WAITING ROOM
PURGATORY

As I continued to lie still in that hospital bed, time just kept dragging its feet. Mercilessly, in the ICU, the minutes seemed like hours. For my parents, for my friends, and for the steady stream of visitors, it felt like a bad dream that refused to end.

With each passing day, the hospital became less like a place of healing and more like a holding cell—a place where faces changed, but the story stayed the same. My parents settled into the routine: morning visits marked by hopeful tension, afternoons defined by crowded waiting rooms, and evenings blurring together in a quiet, exhausted silence.

Every morning began the same way. The doctor made his rounds, always flanked by his silent, clipboard-wielding students. He'd step inside my room, check my chart, glance at the monitors, and deliver his verdict in the same dull tone: "No significant change." His voice was flat, mechanical, as though reading off a grocery list. The students scribbled notes, nodded seriously, and, after their hallway huddle, moved on to the next patient. My parents sat there, unsatisfied with his answers to their questions, watching him leave, hope shrinking just a little each time.

My dad later nicknamed him "Dr. Downer." The man was as dependable as the sunrise, arriving on schedule with his entourage, offering nothing but a steady stream of guarded pessimism. He never cracked a smile, never spoke beyond the basics. Even the nurses seemed to brace themselves for his arrival.

But the waiting room was a different world. It was a revolving door of familiar faces—my core crew of friends who came and went, trying to keep each other's spirits up. My roommates, our girlfriends, fraternity brothers, and sorority sisters were regulars. My parents watched as they tried to laugh, joke, and pretend things weren't as serious as they were. But between the small talk, their eyes always drifted toward the hallway leading to my room.

Brad flew back to Plano and met our grandparents, who had arrived from Chillicothe. Chris returned to Austin, but the stream of visitors didn't stop. Jasmine and MacKenzie arrived from Austin, as did Micah from Dallas, close friends from high school. Even my youth minister from church made the trip, sitting quietly with my parents and offering soft words of prayer. A couple of senior administrators from Texas Tech—and many strangers—also came by to check on me, a surreal reminder that I had become a campus headline.

And just a hallway over, a different kind of crowd was gathering. Public health officials had turned part of the hospital into a makeshift distribution center for Cipro—the so-called "horse pill," thanks to its size—meant to prevent an outbreak of meningitis. But it wasn't just my immediate circle that lined up; it was my classmates, my intramural basketball foes, fraternity brothers, sorority friends, neighbors from my apartment complex, and people I had never met. Anyone within two degrees of contact with me over the past several days was contacted and encouraged to take the antibiotic. Some came in quietly, anxious but polite. Others whispered nervously, asking questions about meningitis and swapping rumors they had heard.

Meanwhile, our apartment was treated like a biohazard site. A hazmat team arrived to clean and disinfect, scrubbing every surface and bagging anything that might be contaminated. My roommates evacuated as strangers in full protective gear swept through, turning our familiar home into something out of a disaster movie. It was hard to believe that the same carpet I had collapsed on was now being sterilized like a crime scene.

Back at the hospital, the waiting room became its own ecosystem of awkward tension. Most of my friends weren't sure what to say. Some clung to hope, trying to stay upbeat. Others just sat in silence, staring at the daytime TV lineup: Ricki Lake airing worst fears, Jerry Springer tossing chairs, and *The Price Is Right* blaring its cheerful jingle while lives hung in the balance. It felt like a cruel punch line no one could laugh at.

Still on the ventilator, I remained motionless in the ICU, alive... or was I? My face was a patchwork of scabs, but the real damage was somewhere deeper, somewhere the monitors and doctors couldn't fully explain.

And time continued to drag on. More friends came to see me and more shuffled out, leaving behind the awkward tension of hugs that felt like goodbye forever. The waiting room TV played another round of mindless daytime shows. Just down the hall, you could just about hear the announcer's booming voice: "Come on down, you're the next contestant on *The Price Is Right!*" The nurses continued their rotations, checking my vitals with the same muted professionalism. My mom's hand never left mine for long, and my dad kept tallying the faintest signs of hope as if clinging to an invisible thread.

Dr. Downer made his usual appearance on Tuesday morning. He walked in, gave me a quick, almost obligatory glance—just enough to verify I still existed—then let his gaze drift back to the monitors, his students in tow and a row of anxious onlookers.

"No significant change," he murmured almost automatically. He paused, then glanced at my parents reluctantly. "We just have to keep waiting and let the medicine run its course." His voice was as flat as ever, but his posture seemed to say something else, something my parents had learned to read as a silent warning: Don't get your hopes up.

And then he left. Another day with no change and nothing but more praying and hopeful waiting.

THE HAND THAT SQUEEZED BACK

That night, as the hospital settled into its uneasy quiet, my parents reluctantly left my room and began their now-familiar trek through the winding hallways toward the elevators. It was a routine they knew by heart—past the hushed nurses' station, through the dimly lit corridors, tracing the cold, tiled path beneath their feet. Familiar exhaustion clung to their shoulders, and a heavy knot of helplessness tightened in their chests.

Dad hit the down-arrow button and, while waiting, whispered a prayer, one he'd said so many times it was almost muscle memory. "Thank you, God, for another day with John. Please, give us a sign that he will pull through. Give us strength to face another day."

The doors slid open to an empty elevator. My parents stepped inside, and Mom pressed the ground-level button. Silence settled between them as their thoughts raced, emotions almost tangible in the air, pressing against the cold, brushed-metal walls.

Just as the doors began to close, a hand reached in, stopping them. A stranger stepped in—a man neither of them had seen before. Middle-aged, with a serene, quiet presence. He nodded politely, and they nodded back.

As the elevator began its slow descent, Dad's eyes met the stranger's, just for a second. A brief, almost accidental lock. But in that instant, a warmth washed over him, a calm so profound it nearly brought tears to his eyes. The crushing weight in his chest seemed to lift; his breathing grew easier.

Still caught in that euphoric, floating calm, when the elevator bumped to a stop at the ground floor, Dad didn't even feel it. The doors slid open and the man stepped out, disappearing down the hallway without a word.

Dad followed Mom out of the elevator, then gently grabbed her arm, stopping her.

"Did you feel that? When that guy was in the elevator with us? Did you see his eyes? Who was that?" Dad whispered, his voice a mix of wonder and disbelief.

Mom's wide eyes met his, her voice barely a whisper. "Yes…I felt it. Like a weight just lifted. Like…somehow, everything is going to be okay."

Within seconds, they turned to look for the mysterious man, but he was gone. He'd vanished down the long hallway as if he had never been there.

That night, for the first time since arriving in Lubbock, Mom and Dad slept deeply, their hearts lighter with a renewed spirit of confidence.

Wednesday morning, they returned to the hospital with a fresh spark of determination. My doctor arrived at the usual midmorning time, flanked by his understudies. He checked the charts, consulted with the nurses, and gave me a quick visual examination. His report was the same: no change.

But this time, my parents pressed harder for more details, desperate for any insight or alternate plan. "Is there something else we can do? Or something else we can try?" they pleaded.

The doctor, however, seemed indifferent and quickly shut down their inquiries. "We've done everything we can. We just need to wait for the medicine to run its course."

His words and demeanor sucked all the oxygen out of the room, threatening to extinguish the hope the elevator encounter had ignited.

As if on cue, the Finnells arrived for their daily visit, stepping in just as the doctor's grim shadow faded from the room. After being updated on my status, they suggested a change of scenery and took my parents to lunch. With a dozen of my friends still holding vigil just down the hall, I was in good hands.

Over lunch, my parents shared the incredible story of the divine encounter they had in the elevator the night before. Emily listened, her eyes sparkling, and without hesitation, she reached across the table, placed her hand on my dad's hand, squeezed, and once again spoke with unwavering certainty.

"Your son is going to be okay. He's going to make it."

And with those words, the memory of the angel's calming presence returned—a beacon of light, a reminder that sometimes, in our most desperate hours, miracles can happen.

Still riding the wave of confidence, Dad returned to the hospital with a renewed sense of purpose. He strode straight to my bedside and grasped my right hand firmly. With focused intensity, he leaned in.

"John, if you can hear me, squeeze my hand."

Bam! I squeezed his hand.

Dad's eyes widened. He looked at Mom, who sat up straight, her eyes fixed on our hands.

"John, if you can hear me, squeeze my hand twice."

Bam! Bam! I squeezed it twice.

Shocked, Dad leaned closer. "John, if you can hear me, squeeze my hand three times."

BAM! BAM! BAM! I squeezed his hand three times.

Elated, Dad bolted from the room, found a group of nurses, and breathlessly recounted what had happened. They seemed excited, promising to pass the news on to the doctor. But Dad wasn't willing to wait. He tracked down the doctor and his flock of clipboard-wielding students, delivering an Oscar-worthy rendition of the hand-squeezing miracle.

The doctor barely reacted. "It's likely just a reflex. Muscle spasms are common in cases like this."

Dad's expression hardened. "Reflex? Three separate commands, three perfect responses. That's not reflex."

The doctor offered a mechanical nod, his students scribbling notes without even looking up.

Flabbergasted, Dad returned to my room. He told Mom about the exchange, and this time, my parents huddled up. They'd had enough. Something had to change.

Dad found my nurse and demanded to speak with a senior hospital administrator—immediately.

In a matter of minutes, he found himself delivering a passionate account of the hand-squeezing episode to the ICU medical director. He didn't hold back, describing how the assigned doctor's pessimism seemed to drain all hope from the room, how his detached demeanor was unacceptable. My parents weren't asking for false hope; they were asking for a doctor with a heart. Someone who saw more than a coma patient; someone who believed I was still in there.

The ICU medical director listened intently, nodded, and promised to take a closer look at my case.

Something had shifted. My parents could feel it. They didn't know how or why, but they believed this was a turning point.

Their prayers were answered. First thing Thursday morning, a new doctor stepped into my room, one who didn't just see my condition but saw a possibility. After consulting with the nurses, reviewing my charts, and examining me, he visited with my parents. He didn't literally tell them that everything was going to be all right, but his interpretation of my condition, despite the same data that had been used to suggest I would likely remain in a vegetative state, was refreshingly optimistic. He saw subtle signs of increased brain activity, a revelation that directly challenged the grim predictions my parents had heard for days. He also had a favorable interpretation of the hand-squeezing occurrence. He made no promises but delivered a bedside manner that my parents were excited about.

There was an unmistakable shift, an electric hum of hope that had been missing. A review process was initiated, and several other physicians were convened. A newfound buzz of activity stoked the fire of hope that had been slowly suffocated under the old regime.

Over the next thirty-six hours, the ICU transitioned into a battleground where I wasn't just existing, I was being fought for. A team of physicians scrutinized every aspect of my condition, while my parents stood by my side, their hearts gripped with a mix of hope and fear. Nearby, my friends gathered, their faces etched with anxiety and anticipation, all of them waiting for the moment when I might finally wake up.

The doctors knew the stakes. They weren't just fighting an infection; they were racing the clock. The meningitis had to be eliminated, the swelling in my brain reduced, and my body had to be ready to wake up. They kept a constant watch on my intracranial pressure, knowing that if it didn't stabilize, brain damage was almost certain. Every vital sign—heart rate, blood pressure, oxygen levels—became a signal flare, a whisper of hope or a warning of disaster. Stability meant there was a chance. Instability meant the abyss.

I needed to breathe on my own or at least with minimal support, a basic but crucial test of whether I was ready to rejoin the living. But even as they monitored the machines, they were watching for the invisible enemies: complications that could turn fragile progress into a free fall.

The decision to lift me from the coma wasn't made lightly. It was a calculated risk, the product of tense discussions among a team of specialists. They debated, they weighed the odds, and finally, they agreed; it was time to see if I was still in there.

LOVE IN THE
WAITING ROOM

By midmorning on Friday the 13th—because of course, it had to be—everything came to a head. The ventilator was coming out.

As the process began, the atmosphere in the room was electric with anticipation. My parents clung to each other, their emotions a tumultuous blend of fear and hope. The sedatives that had kept me under were gradually tapered off, the veil of unconsciousness slowly lifting. Every second was critical; I was closely monitored for signs of distress, changes in vital signs, or neurological responses. It was a delicate, nerve-racking process, like pulling someone back from the edge of a precipice.

As the sedation slowly lifted, there was a palpable sense of suspense. Would I respond? Would I wake up? And if I did, would I be the John everyone remembered? My parents watched every twitch, every eyelid flutter, their breath held in anxious silence. My friends, too, stood on the threshold of the unknown, their faces reflecting the gravity of the moment. It was a scene fraught with emotion, where each breath or flicker of response carried the weight of a thousand prayers.

But for those who weren't superstitious, it was like destiny had hired a Hollywood screenwriter because Saturday was Valentine's Day. A day for sweethearts and whispered promises, a day designed for grand gestures and quiet romance. But in the ICU, it felt more like a cruel parody of everything love was supposed to be.

This year, love wasn't roses and chocolates. It was a choice to stay.

Earlier in the week, my mom conspired with Kevin's girlfriend, Mindy, to get Jenn a gift. In any other context, this would have been a classic Mom move—to make sure her teenage son was being a proper boyfriend and maintaining decorum. But this wasn't any other context. I was in a coma, and my fate was very much hanging in the balance. This was my mom's way of staying active and positive, of preserving a semblance of normalcy.

Just a few days earlier, the gift could have been a sad memento of what could have been. But by Valentine's Day, the tide had shifted. It could now be seen as a galvanizing symbol of hope and love to come. Honestly, I don't think my mom was thinking about anything that deep. The gift, a heart-shaped pendant from James Avery, was her way of filling in the gaps, of showing Jenn that even in the midst of all the mess, there was room for small, tender gestures.

When my mom handed the gift to Jenn, she said, "John wanted you to have this." A simple statement, but one that carried the weight of a relationship being defined and redefined in real time. We had been dating for only six weeks, still in the early stages where everything was light and low stakes. And yet, here she was, being thrust into a situation neither of us could have anticipated.

But Jenn didn't hesitate. She went all in, choosing to be there for me despite the newness of our relationship. That's just the kind of person she was: unwaveringly supportive, even in the face of something as overwhelming as this. While most people would have taken a step back, unsure of how to navigate such an intense situation, Jenn stepped forward.

Suddenly, the normal progression of our relationship was thrown out the window. What had been a casual, budding relationship was now vaulted into the kind of seriousness usually reserved for years down the line. In the eyes of my family and friends, Jenn was no longer just the girl I was dating; she was someone who decided to stand by me through one of the hardest moments of my life. It was as if our relationship had been fast-tracked, skipping over all the intermediate steps and landing straight into a scenario that resembled a marriage engagement.

For Jenn, it must have been surreal. One minute, we were just a couple of college kids enjoying each other's company, and the next, she was navigating a situation that even seasoned couples would struggle with. The gift, intended as a sweet gesture, now symbolized a commitment neither of us had anticipated making so soon.

As for me, I was blissfully unaware of all of this at the time. I didn't know that my mom had taken it upon herself to play Cupid in my absence. I didn't know that Jenn was grappling with the intensity of a situation neither of us had asked for. All of this was happening around me while I was lying there, oblivious to the turmoil and the decisions being made on my behalf.

In a strange way, my coma acted as a catalyst for our relationship, forcing us to confront questions and emotions that most couples don't face until much later, if ever. We skipped over the early, exciting stages of dating and were suddenly catapulted into the deep end. And somehow, in the midst of all the uncertainty and fear, Jenn stayed by my side.

Those days left an indelible mark on both of us, a reminder that life can change in an instant and how a casual relationship can, without warning, become something far more serious and profound. Love doesn't always arrive with grand gestures. Sometimes, it's a quiet presence, a steady hand, a whispered promise. Our story was only beginning. Where that left us in the end...well, that's a story for another chapter. Because even if I woke up, who would I be when I did?

—SECTION III—
Life, Re-Entered

WAKING UP IN
DARKNESS

I didn't burst back to life with a dramatic gasp or a miraculous jolt of clarity. There was no cinematic moment of awakening. My return was slower, murkier, more like surfacing through a heavy, endless abyss. The coma was a place without time, without thought. Just nothing. Not even dreams or memories, because even those require something to hold onto. This was absence. Void.

Then, the first signal reached me. Faint, almost imperceptible, I began to hear sounds. Beeps. Murmurs. An ever-present hum. The sounds were warped like they were underwater. But they were there, distant signals that didn't belong in the abyss. They pulled at me, calling me upward. I couldn't move, couldn't think clearly. But I could hear.

As I began to drift toward consciousness, the first thing I saw was darkness—disorienting, impenetrable darkness. It wasn't just the absence of light; it was an all-encompassing black hole. Confusion swept over me, dense and suffocating. My body felt heavy, and the sounds began to dissolve again, slipping away like echoes swallowed by distance.

The darkness was overpowering. Even when I managed to briefly poke through to the surface, it remained. But I could still hear. Like a beacon, the distorted signals slowly returned—the beeps and hums growing louder, the murmurs closer, almost like voices. And suddenly, just as quickly, they slipped away again...

Through the darkness, familiar tones finally reached me—my parents. They were calling my name, desperately trying to pull me back.

Before being dismissed from my case, Dr. Downer had warned that even if I did pull through, much of who I had been would likely never return—physically or mentally. I might still be there, but I wouldn't be me. Unwilling to accept those grim predictions, my parents found themselves riding waves of excitement and terror as I wandered in and out of consciousness.

Their voices were laced with hope and fear, a battle playing out just above my awareness. I felt my hands being squeezed, a touch anchoring me to reality. "Hey, Champ, Mom and I are right here." Dad used the nickname he'd always called me, a comforting reminder of better days.

I tried to respond, but nothing came out. My voice was missing. My throat felt sore and tight. Something was lodged uncomfortably in my nose. My muscles were strangers, unresponsive and weak, and my lips wouldn't move. I tried to nod my head, but lifting it felt monumental, as if gravity had doubled its pull. I couldn't see, I couldn't move, and speaking was beyond my grasp. Everything faded out again…My parents persisted, calling to me, their voices a lifeline. "Johnny, it's Mom. You're in the hospital in Lubbock. We're all here for you. Dad and I and dozens of your friends, we're all here. You got sick and needed help. It's been over a week, and we're so happy that you're awake. You're doing a great job of getting better."

Reality began to sharpen, but I was still trying to understand it all. Why are the lights off? Why is everyone here in the dark? What is in my nose? Why are my parents so close to me? This is weird. I've never had a dream like this. Is someone squeezing my legs? It feels like something is in my throat. My mouth is dry. I am thirsty. Wow, I am thirsty!

Looking back, I'm surprised I wasn't freaking out. I'd like to say I was calm and collected, taking things in stride, but in truth, I was too disoriented to operate in the real world. I kept bouncing in and out of consciousness.

My parents' voices were the thread that finally became strong enough to pull me out of the void and back into myself.

And then came the questions. Everyone wanted to know if I could beat the odds again by being the John they remembered rather than the unrecognizable version of me the doctors had predicted.

"John, can you see me?"

"John, how many fingers am I holding up?"

"John, do you know who I am?"

From the outside, everything about my right eye appeared normal. Open, alert, no cause for alarm. To my dad, who stood there talking to me, it must have seemed like I was looking straight at him. But I couldn't see him. I couldn't see anything. I was still trapped in the darkness and just assumed the room was strangely pitch-dark.

My left eye was a different story. It was also giving me darkness, but that was because my eyelid wouldn't open. Unbeknownst to me, the muscles on the left side of my face were frozen in place, including the one that controlled my eyelid. Still trying to make sense of anything, I had no reason to suspect that I couldn't see. Neither did anyone else.

Recognizing my confusion, Dad moved to the other side of my bed and cautiously pried open my eyelid. And just like that, darkness lost its grip—light rushed in. My so-called vision was almost more disorienting than the total blackness, but it did offer one piece of comfort. What I could vaguely see was my dad, standing by my hospital bed. I knew, without a doubt, that he was there with me, even if he didn't quite look like himself. He appeared to be miles away despite being right next to me.

"Hey, Champ, what color is my shirt?" Dad asked again. It took a minute to make sense of the space through my newly narrowed and distorted field of vision. Finally, I found it—the blur that had to be his shirt. All I could manage was a whisper-faint word that sounded something like "blue."

"Tremendous! That's right. My shirt is blue!" Dad responded with excitement.

That simple, almost mundane exchange—just one word—was anything but ordinary to my parents. After the longest eight days of their lives, my answer hit like a lightning bolt of hope. It wasn't just that I could see color; it was proof that I was still in there. There was still a long road ahead, but in that fragile syllable, they found something they hadn't dared to feel in a while: relief.

After a few more rounds of my new least-favorite game ("Hey, John, what can you see?"), we discovered that I was sightless in my right eye. The news should have been devastating, but it barely registered. I had just resurfaced from the depths of the abyss; my brain was still coming online, and there wasn't room yet for grief or fear.

With so much happening all at once, it was impossible to grasp the weight of any single issue; I was still taking inventory. My left eyelid and facial muscles wouldn't move. My throat was raw. I was thirsty, whatever was jammed in my nose was unbearable, and I couldn't sit up. What was with the constant stream of people coming and going? The questions, the beeping and humming, the strange pressure on my legs; it was all too much. I was irritated, exhausted, and completely confused.

Did I mention that I was thirsty?

SURVIVAL'S LITTLE SURPRISES

Almost nothing about me was normal at that point. Even the simplest movements, like lifting my head off the pillow, shifting an arm, or wiggling a toe, demanded herculean strength. My body was weighty, each limb a stubborn artifact from a life I barely recognized. And yet, of all the discomforts that plagued me, one demanded my full attention: thirst.

But thirsty didn't even begin to describe it. My mouth was a desert. After more than a week without a sip, it felt as if my tongue had become a wad of dry cotton, a scorching canyon cutting through the roof of my mouth. Sure, I'd been hydrated by a steady drip of liquids through an IV during the coma, but my mouth craved something cold, something wet—an ice-cold drink of water.

The nurse explained that the firehose I was convinced had been rammed up my nostril was, in reality, something much smaller: a nasogastric tube, mercifully shortened to NG tube. A new entry in my medical vocabulary I never asked for. Everyone just called it a feeding tube, which sounded friendlier but felt more like a medieval torture device. Up one nostril and down the back of my throat, it was like having a spaghetti noodle stuck in reverse. This, she informed me, was the most effective way to deliver nutrition while I was in the coma, and the doctors were worried I might have trouble swallowing (a common issue after being intubated), so the tube had to stay put for the time being. But when I pleaded for something—anything—to drink, she eventually offered a compromise.

"We can give you some water through the tube," she suggested.

"Great! Let's do it!" I practically cheered.

What happened next is a sensation I will never forget: the unbelievable relief as cool water flowed through the feeding tube. It was an unconventional route, up my nose, but a tidal wave of refreshing coolness all the way down to my stomach. The feeling was incredible. Let's do that again. And again. The only problem was this magical, nose-fed water did nothing for the desert in my mouth. I was still parched.

"Can't I just drink water like a normal person?" I asked, bewildered.

"No," the nurse explained with a calm, practiced patience. "You could aspirate." (Another new term for my suddenly growing medical vocabulary.)

I didn't know what aspirating meant, but I didn't care. I knew how to drink! I'd been doing it for almost twenty years without issue. Come on…For crying out loud, I was in a fraternity. Drinking was practically an elective. But the answer remained a firm no. Instead, she offered me ice chips.

"Yes, let's do that. I'm ready," I agreed, grateful for anything.

A microscopic piece of ice was dropped into my mouth and it melted instantly, flooding the dry canyon with a sensation so incredible it was euphoric. I reveled in it, savoring the cold wetness that washed over my dry tongue. "More, please." Rounds two and three were just as glorious. The ice chips vanished, sucked dry by my desperate mouth. The nurse warned me that was enough for now. We needed to pace ourselves. She'd keep the cup of ice nearby.

I soon understood why we needed to "pace ourselves." All the nasal water infusions and ice chips caught up with me.

In the dead of night, alone in the room, I was hit with a new, uncomfortable feeling. I needed to go. Badly. But how? I couldn't sit up—couldn't even lift my head without a struggle—so how was I supposed to get to the bathroom? Panic buzzed around the edges of my mind. I opened my mouth to call for the nurse, but my voice was weak, a raspy whisper that wouldn't carry. I fumbled around the bed, anxiously searching for the call button. Earlier, the nurse had explained how to use it and my mom made sure I knew what each button did since I couldn't see the labels. Found it! I pressed the button and collapsed back onto the pillow.

When she finally arrived, I explained my predicament. She responded with the calm, casual tone of someone who did this every day.

"Just go. You've got a condom catheter on. It'll go straight into the bag on the side of your bed."

"A what?" I thought. Was that even a real thing? It sounded like a gag gift you might get at a bachelor party, but I tried to stay focused.

"Wow, that sounds easy. Okay, thanks."

She left, and I prepared myself for the familiar sweet relief. Just relax and go. Simple. I've done this a million times. I took a deep breath and waited for that rush of relief. But...nothing happened.

I tried again. Nothing. I concentrated harder, like I was taking the SAT. Still nothing. It was ridiculous. I called the nurse back, embarrassed. "I can't go," I admitted, like a kid confessing to breaking a toy.

She sighed, checked the setup, and said, "Hmm…looks like it's come loose. Hold on." Moments later, she returned with a plastic urinal bottle and placed it in my hand. "Try this," she said, rolling me slightly to one side and adjusting the sheets.

Attempting to go while flat on my back was awkward enough. Now I was on my side, one hand gripping a plastic bottle, the other trying to aim blindly—literally. I couldn't see a thing unless I pried my eyelid open, which, unfortunately, required a third hand I didn't have. It was a logistical nightmare.

I gave it a shot. Nothing.

I tried again. Nothing. I began to sweat. My bladder felt like it was about to explode. I could feel the pressure building, but there was no release.

"Just relax," the nurse advised, as though that was possible. "Take a few deep breaths," she said, trying to comfort me by stroking my back.

I tried one more time, but it was useless. The pressure built to unbearable levels. Frustration turned to anger, and then anger turned to fear. I was genuinely scared. What happens if I can't go? Will I pop? The thought wasn't as ridiculous as it should have been.

"Okay, I have another idea," she said, and left again.

She returned, rolling me back onto my back, and I heard the rustle of plastic, the snap of gloves. Was that a motor starting? A pumping machine being wheeled into place? Umm . . . My mind nervously raced. Was this some kind of peeing machine? Had technology advanced that far?

And then, suddenly, she pulled back the sheets and, with a steady hand, grabbed what my high school coach might've called "the equipment." My body tensed and my brain screamed, *What is happening down there?!* But before I could even begin to process the shock, a new sensation took over—an overwhelming, blissful relief. My bladder finally surrendered.

The sound of urine rushing into a container was music to my ears. My body finally relaxed. It was like the Austin Powers "Evacuation Complete" scene, only I'd been in a coma rather than cryogenically frozen. But the relief was just as groovy. "Yeah, baby!"

I was convinced that I'd just encountered the best invention in human history, the "peeing machine." It was simply amazing!

Except, of course, there was no machine. What I'd imagined as some advanced urine-extraction technology was, in fact, my introduction to the humble yet life-changing intermittent catheter. Turns out, meningitis had damaged the nerve connection to my bladder. "Neurogenic bladder," they called it. Another new term for my collection. And that little tube? That was something I'd be using for the rest of my life. No buttons to push, no motors to start—just me, a simple tube, and a new reality.

MOVING UP, MOVING ON

Day nine in the hospital was graduation day. Not the kind with a cap and gown but the kind where you get wheeled out of the ICU and into a recovery room. Just thirty-six hours after my foggy reentry into consciousness, the machines that had kept me alive were gone, leaving just a few lingering sensors and an IV—barely a blip on my radar. But that wretched feeding tube crammed up my nose remained a constant nagging reminder that I wasn't out of the woods yet.

The world around me was still a blur (quite literally) since I could only partially see through one uncooperative, pried-open eyelid. Time had lost all meaning, day and night blending together like a twenty-four-hour Vegas casino without clocks. My bed doubled as my chariot as I was wheeled out of the ICU, and it wasn't a straight shot. No, this was more like an odyssey.

Double doors opened, then closed. We turned left again. Or was right? My sense of direction was in a tailspin. Elevators hummed. Were we entering another dimension? I clearly remember asking if we were going up or down, only to be baffled when I thought we'd somehow ended up outside on a tree-lined path. Spoiler alert: we hadn't.

At some point during the fantastic voyage, a nurse materialized beside me, clipboard in hand, firing off get-to-know-you questions like I was on some sort of twisted game show. Most were easy, but then she got into some awkward social-behavioral questions that made me a bit nervous to answer in front of my mom, including one about my "extracurricular activities" with friends before casually moving on to alcohol consumption.

At nineteen, I wasn't a saint and Mom wasn't naïve, but I'd never had to put my personal social habits on public display, especially not with her right there. Noticing my discomfort and my still-clouded brain stumbling for an appropriate answer, the nurse jumped in to save me, dubbing me a "weekend warrior," a title I wasn't exactly in a position to argue with.

But in the grand scheme of things, these awkward confessions were small potatoes. The real miracle was that I was there at all: alive, squirming, and still able to embarrass myself in front of my mom. She was just happy to have me back, revelations and all.

As my chariot rolled to a stop in my new recovery room, I assumed the worst of the journey was behind me, but it was just beginning

What followed was nothing short of a full-body audit. A procession of physicians and therapists paraded in and out of my room, each on a mission to see what was left of me—physical, cognitive, occupational, neurological, visual—and a few specialists who seemed to be making up their disciplines on the spot. It was like a reality show competition where the prize was figuring out if I could still function.

They assumed that after nearly a week and a half in a coma, I'd be a shell of my former self. And maybe I was. But I didn't have time to dwell on that. I was too busy relearning the basics—swallowing without choking, opening my eyelid on command, trying to make sense of a body that felt like it had been swapped out for a broken model.

I wish I could say I was overwhelmed with gratitude for simply being alive, but I was too busy being overwhelmed by everything else. I didn't even know what meningitis was. At that point, I could infer it was the reason I was in this predicament, as it was a term I kept hearing tossed around. But it meant nothing to me beyond a confusing new chapter of existence. Seemingly, just the day before, I'd gone to bed in my apartment with the flu, a young, invincible, independent college kid on his own. Now I was trapped in a dark hospital room with a body that was like a rebooted system with none of the original settings.

One of my first battles in recovery? Simply sitting up. Sounds trivial, right? Wrong. Sitting up from even a half-reclined position felt like trying to push a boulder uphill with a spoon. Up, up, up…nope, back down. Retry, retry, retry—finally! You'd think I'd just scaled Everest. But before I could celebrate, my backside launched a protest. My gluteus maximus had atrophied so much from lying around that even the weight of my own body was too much for it to handle. Great. Add "butt strength" to the list of things I needed to rebuild.

Then came the facial-muscle therapist. If you've never had someone hook a finger in the corner of your mouth and demand you pull back with all your might, you're missing out on a unique kind of torture. We worked on my lips, eyelids, cheeks, jaw, and tongue until my still-healing face felt like it might detach and crawl off on its own.

By the end of that first exhausting day, I figured sleep would come easily, but I was wrong. That hospital was the worst place to get shut-eye. The blood-pressure cuff revved up every two hours like a tiny freight train trying to cut off my circulation, and my newfound "pee machine" schedule meant short naps instead of real rest.

The feeding tube, a special kind of torment, was still stuck up my nose. I made it clear to anyone within earshot that I wanted it gone, but each time I was reminded it was still necessary and had to remain. So, in one of my brief, frustrated catnaps, I took matters into my own hands. I yanked that sucker out. Apparently, I'd also done this while still in the coma, which required the nurses to restrain my arms and reinsert it. I don't remember pulling the tube out, but I do remember the tremendous relief of an unobstructed nose and throat. Ah, freedom.

Of course, that freedom was short-lived. Within an hour, a nurse discovered my rebellion. "John, you pulled your feeding tube out. You can't do that. We've got to put it back in."

Cue the horror: a thirty-inch tube, slathered in lubrication, shoved up my nostril, scraping the back of my throat, and then force-fed down my esophagus while I was told to "try to relax and just keep swallowing." It was a delicate dance of choking and obedience under protest. And despite the torturous experience, I still managed to pull that detestable tube out one more time in my sleep. It seemed my subconscious was even more stubborn than I was.

Then came the cognitive therapist. "What day is it? Where are you? Who is the president?" Once I'd progressed from the basics, we moved on to simple math, number sequences, and multiple-choice questions. When I cleared those, she started reading passages and asking me to identify the main character, the main idea, and a plot point. I felt like I was in fourth grade again. I'd rather have taken another feeding tube than go through any more of her quizzes.

The occupational therapist wasn't any better. She seemed to

specialize in pessimism, always pointing out what I couldn't do and predicting bleak outcomes. She must have been related to Dr. Downer. Sure, some of what she said was a necessary reality check, but most of it just felt like she was auditioning for a role in a tragedy I hadn't signed up for.

Yet, despite all of this, I refused to give in. Keep getting up, keep moving forward, keep on keeping on. It became a mantra. Every grueling session, every humiliating exercise, every doubt-ridden night I treated as battles to be won.

Survival had been a miracle, but learning to live again? That was war. And I wasn't about to surrender.

LIQUID COURAGE, WOBBLY LEGS

T herapy had become a daily ordeal, an endless spectacle of poking, prodding, and prying that I tolerated mostly because I had little choice. But not all therapies were created equal. Two stood apart: swallowing and physical therapy. These weren't just more routines to endure; they were my tickets to freedom.

After days of being tethered to that miserable feeding tube, I learned another new term: dysphagia, a fancy way of saying that swallowing, something I'd always done without a second thought, had become an Olympic event.

Unlike the mundane sessions of cognitive therapy, this was one I looked forward to. I wanted nothing more than to get rid of the feeding tube. The muscles that once made drinking a glass of water effortless were now on strike. Even saliva seemed to rebel. I'd try to swallow, only to be met with a sudden, sharp cough, a desperate gasp, or the uncomfortable sensation of something going down the wrong way.

The therapist had all kinds of techniques and tools at her disposal, but the best exercise was the simplest: just swallow, over and over. It was a cruel irony—something I'd done instinctively my whole life now demanded laser focus. Chin tucked to my chest, I'd force down saliva and tiny sips of liquid, each one a gamble. Sometimes it went down smoothly; many times, it triggered a coughing fit.

The early sessions were rough. I choked a lot. I coughed even more. But the therapist assured me this was normal, a necessary part of the process. And she was right. After a few days of intense practice—swallowing, choking, coughing, and trying again—I made noticeable progress. I was far from cured, but I was improving.

To escape the feeding tube's nasal tyranny, I had to pass a series of barium swallow tests—basically drinking liquids of various consistencies laced with a chalky substance while clinicians watched an X-ray screen like a suspense thriller. Every swallow lit up on the monitor like a neon sign, and they scrutinized the path it took. If even a drop of barium snuck into my airway instead of my esophagus, the tube's tyrannical reign held firm. And wouldn't you know it, thin liquids proved to be my mortal enemy.

When it was clear I couldn't handle anything close to water, I was introduced to Thick-It—the magic powder that could convert even the thinnest of liquids into something resembling pudding, because nothing says hydration like drinking dessert. This powder could alter any drink into a range of consistencies, from a smooth nectar to a slow-pouring honey and even a thick, spoonable sludge. It was an acquired taste, one I wasn't eager to acquire. But it was better than that nose-spaghetti tube, so I forced it down.

Even if my drinks moved at a snail's pace, they carried me forward, one heavy swallow at a time. I was making progress. I quickly went from pudding-thick to honey-thick liquids. A victory? Sure. But it also meant Thick-It would be around for a while, a powdered reminder that normalcy was still out of reach.

Just before discharge, I advanced to the exalted status of nectar-thick liquids, basically a gourmet smoothie texture. The feeding tube, that constant, agitating reminder of my loss of independence, was finally behind me. My nurse pulled it out, and I remember the magnificent feeling of the tube sliding free, leaving me with the sweet sensation of an unobstructed nose and throat. It felt like being released from a straitjacket—suddenly lighter, freer, more human.

Thickened grape juice was a bizarre twist on refreshment, but it was nothing compared to what came next: the fight to reclaim my legs. I didn't just look forward to physical therapy; I craved it. I wanted out of that bed. I wanted to move. After weeks of helplessly sinking into the mattress, I was ready to climb my way back to life.

Mom, recognizing my determination and wanting me to look good, went out and bought me a new wardrobe of "athletic" gear: warm-ups, T-shirts, shorts, fresh socks, and shoes. With my new gear, I certainly looked like an athlete, but that's where the comparison stopped. It was a convincing disguise...right up until I tried to stand without toppling over.

The first time I tried to stand was like a bad slapstick routine. My legs felt like wet noodles, my sense of balance was still on backorder, and the whole room seemed to tilt. "Drop foot," they called it—a condition where the muscles in my lower legs were too weak to keep my feet from flopping down. So each time I tried to stand, my feet just hung there like broken hinges.

The nurse introduced me to a gait belt, a thick nylon strap they wrapped around my waist. "What's a gait belt?" I asked, joking that it must be some kind of stylish accessory. Not quite. It was a handle, something for the therapists, my parents, or my friends to grab hold of and keep me upright while I wobbled through my first steps.

Jenn was often there for these walks, sharing the duty with my parents and friends. I'd shimmy to the edge of the bed, clutch the sides, and then—with the help of two steady hands—launch myself forward into a wheelchair. She would roll me down the hall to an open area where I could practice walking. Well, not walking; more like a jerky, stumbling march. I felt like a toddler trying to conquer my first steps, only this time the stakes were higher and the fear of falling was all too real.

The process was both humiliating and humbling. With every shaky step, I could feel the atrophied muscles in my legs screaming for mercy. I'd try to move one foot in front of the other, but it was like trying to dance with two left feet, only someone had swapped them for bricks.

But I was tenacious. Even in the early days when I could barely manage two or three steps before collapsing back into the wheelchair, I kept at it. The alternative was a life stuck in that bed, and that wasn't an option. Keep getting up, keep moving forward, keep on keeping on. The world outside the hospital wasn't waiting for me; I needed to catch up.

Progress was slow, but it was progress. With each session, I could stand for a little longer, shuffle a little farther, and lean a little less on my handler gripping the gait belt. One wobbly step at a time, I was inching my way back toward something resembling independence. These weren't just physical battles—they were battles of will. And I was determined to win.

FIELD TRIP TO REALITY

After becoming something of a thickened fruit juice connoisseur and slowly regaining a little mobility, I finally got my first taste of freedom since the coma. Freedom, of course, was a relative term. I was being wheeled out of the hospital and into a van, but it might as well have been a limousine. It was my first time outside in two weeks, and the sharp February air was a shock to my senses. I shivered, but it was the kind of shiver that makes you feel alive.

The destination? The nearby Quack Shack, the campus health clinic, a nickname that undoubtedly inspired confidence in a medical facility. But that day, it was my gateway to adventure. The sunlight pierced through the clouds in brief, hesitant bursts, just warm enough to graze my face, a reminder of what the world outside felt like. The wind whipped around me, crisp and biting, carrying the distant hum of life: cars whooshing by, muffled voices, and the rustle of leafless trees. The air smelled fresh and alive, a sharp contrast to the sterile, antiseptic scent of the hospital. The world hadn't stopped while I was stuck in there; it had just gone on without me. But I was catching up.

The journey to the clinic wasn't far—just across campus—but it felt momentous. Every bump, every creak and groan of the van's suspension was a reminder that I wasn't confined to a bed anymore. The low rumble of the engine beneath me was comforting, a steady vibration that told me I was moving, even if I couldn't see where. When the door slid open with a forceful *thunk* and I was lowered down the ramp, I felt an odd surge of excitement. I didn't care where we were going. I was out. I was moving.

Inside, reality hit harder than the winter wind. The usual tests began, and I recognized them from high school when I learned I was mildly nearsighted. Back then, I wore glasses only when I felt like looking studious. Now, I couldn't even see the giant E on the chart across the room. Not blurry—not fuzzy—just gone. I knew it was supposed to be there, but I couldn't find it.

"Let's try the handheld chart," the doctor suggested, but that didn't go much better. I had to bring it so close to my face that it practically grazed my still-healing nose before I could decipher anything. My sight wasn't just bad; it was devastated. The world had become a hazy puzzle I couldn't piece together. But I still didn't fully understand. I was naïve, sure that this was just another hurdle to clear. I mean, I had already regained full functionality of my eyelid and facial muscles. And I was relearning to walk and swallow. Why wouldn't my vision bounce back?

I'm sure there's a therapist for this too, I thought.

Then came the gut punch when the doctor examined my optic nerves. Both of them were damaged. Yet another new term for my rapidly expanding vocabulary: "optic neuropathy." My right optic nerve was completely shot, which explained why I saw nothing but darkness out of that eye. My left one wasn't much better: scarred but still hanging on. "Damage to the optic nerves," she explained, "is not something glasses, therapy, or surgery can fix. It's not going to improve."

Her words hit my parents like a sledgehammer, but I barely felt them. Nineteen-year-old me simply didn't process them. After all, everything else was coming back. Why would my eyes be any different? I wasn't just hopeful; I was convinced. I could beat this.

We also learned something else, that my field of vision was a narrow, distorted sliver. I wasn't just nearsighted; I was taking in the world through a keyhole. I instinctively discovered that I had to move my head instead of just my eyes to see things. But there was another trick too: sound. I had already been relying on it, unconsciously using the direction of sounds to help triangulate where things were. It wasn't some complicated concept; it was survival. I was beginning to learn how much I needed sound to navigate a world I could barely see.

By the time the examination ended, I was ready to move on to the next adventure. My parents asked questions (questions I didn't hear) while pamphlets were handed to us that I couldn't see to read. But it didn't matter; I had already mentally checked out. I was too busy trying to explore my new surroundings. As we wheeled out into the cold, I was once again exhilarated by the wind. The sharp gusts pressed against my face, carrying the scent of diesel exhaust. Back in the van, the engine's low growl rumbled beneath me, soothing in its steady, predictable vibration.

Rather than processing the weight of the news, I was more interested in trying to recognize campus buildings through my distorted vision: landmarks, dorms, anything familiar. I leaned forward, squinting, trying to identify the hazy shapes. Based on my memory of the campus layout, I was pretty sure I recognized the rec center, the place I'd spent countless hours playing basketball, soccer, and racquetball, socializing with friends and fellow students. My mind drifted to those memories, a warm comfort against the cold reality of my new limitations.

With hindsight, I now realize what my parents were thinking in that van. They heard the doctor's words about the damage to my optic nerves loud and clear. Unlike me, they were already grappling with the reality that this wasn't something I could train my way out of. While I was busy trying to spot campus landmarks, they were preparing themselves for a different reality—one I was just beginning to stumble toward. I was leaning forward, trying to recognize my old life; they were leaning back, trying to recognize a new one.

CONNECTION IS A LIFELINE

I've always needed to feel connected to people. It's just how I'm wired. I thrive on conversation. As far back as I can remember, I was fascinated by the telephone, thrilled by the idea that, within seconds, I could be talking to someone far away. And I wasn't picky; if you were on the other end of the line, I was all in.

My grandparents felt this most acutely. Though they lived in the same city and I saw them plenty, that simply wasn't enough. I called them constantly. I guess they enjoyed it enough that they went so far as to install a phone in their bedroom just for my calls. This was the 1980s, mind you, when "modern" phones meant wrestling with a tangled twenty-foot cord and experiencing the technological marvel of transitioning from rotary dials to push buttons. I kept pace with every innovation: call waiting, three-way calling, cordless handsets. It was like living in *The Jetsons*.

And back then, I didn't need a contact list. I had numbers committed to memory. Friends, family, the local pizza place. If you were important, you were already stored in the best directory around: my brain. I could dial faster than a speed typist and talk for hours, even when I had nothing to say. If there was a phone, I was in business.

So, when I could reliably talk again in the hospital, it was a no-brainer. I picked up right where I'd left off. After all, a coma was just a brief interlude in my ongoing mission to keep the lines of communication open. My parents set things up so I could chat with family and friends back in Plano and Chillicothe. This was the '90s, long before unlimited talk time, so every minute on the phone came with a price tag. They covered the still-hefty price of long-distance calls with a calling card, but I needed their help to dial those numbers. Local calls, though, were fair game, and I'd use that hospital phone anytime I could.

Disoriented by my blindness and the odd timelessness of the hospital, I had no real sense of day or night. Without natural light or the ability to see a clock, time became an abstract concept. I couldn't tell if it was morning or midnight, which led to some questionable decisions.

One night, early in my recovery, in a half-hallucinated haze, I decided it was the perfect time to dial up a professor. I called the campus operator, as I'd done many times before, and confidently requested my professor's office phone number. I must have sounded groggy or just plain out of it because after providing the number, the operator added, "You know it's 3:00 in the morning, right?"

That sudden clarity was like a splash of cold water. I snapped back to reality, realizing the absurdity of what I was about to do. A 3:00 a.m. call to a professor? Maybe not the best way to secure an A.

That operator saved me from leaving a half-asleep, likely incoherent voicemail that might've lived in campus infamy.

But the impulse to connect didn't stop there. It was the lifeline that kept me tethered to the world beyond the hospital's sterile walls. And I wasn't just relying on the phone. I had a constant stream of real, live visitors, my own personal support squad cycling in and out like clockwork.

Aunt Judy flew in from Chillicothe and stayed for several days, alternating with my mom to take care of me. If they both weren't at my bedside, the other was running errands, like cleaning my apartment, getting food, buying clothes, and doing whatever they could to create a sense of normalcy. Mom never left Lubbock. It wasn't even a question. She stayed, period. My dad was there as much as he could be, splitting his time between the hospital and his responsibilities at work and back home in Plano.

Dad's parents, Don and DeDe Grimes, drove in from Chillicothe and stayed for several days. Don brought me an electric razor, which I thought was super cool, probably because I'd always seen him use one. Everyone else seemed pleased, too, as I'd apparently grown a bit scraggly.

And then there was Jenn. She was all in with me, always by my side. Even her mom got in on the action. Jenn's mom became well acquainted with my mom, and suddenly the two of them were a support team of their own. It was like some kind of parental alliance, ensuring I was never left alone.

My friends weren't just visitors; they were active participants in my recovery. My roommates, friends, fraternity brothers, and countless others didn't just stop by for a quick "get well soon." They hung out, they talked, and they filled my hospital room with the familiar soundtrack of college life. Updates on campus drama, gossip, and what I was missing in my classes were delivered like news bulletins. It felt like I was still part of it all, just reporting in from a remote outpost. They didn't stop at moral support, either. They were there for the grueling physical therapy sessions, grabbing hold of the gait belt and helping me stand, walk, or at least not face-plant.

Through all of this, the Finnells, our new family friends who were miraculously placed in our lives, were there, too, providing meals, taking care of my caregivers, and making sure the burden on my parents wasn't unbearable. Their unwavering confidence in my recovery, fueled by a bold and visible Christian faith, brought a layer of hope we so desperately needed. Over time, they became well acquainted with my ever-rotating support squad, sharing in the mission to see me through.

Retrospectively, I remember those two weeks in recovery with a strange sense of fondness. For all the chaos, discomfort, and uncertainty, they were also marked by a deep sense of connection and camaraderie. Friends and family didn't just come to visit. They came to stay, to talk, to laugh, and to walk with me, quite literally, as I fought to rebuild.

For a kid who'd always loved to talk, who found comfort in the familiar crackle of a phone line, those voices—both through the receiver and at my bedside—were the real medicine. And I didn't just survive on those connections; I thrived.

CLEARED FOR TAKEOFF

As the wheelchair rolled through the airport, a mix of excitement and apprehension bubbled inside me. My mom's presence was a steady warmth beside me, her hand resting lightly on my shoulder. While she and I boarded the flight from Lubbock back to Dallas, my dad drove my Accord home—a small, silent reminder that life was moving forward even if I wasn't quite ready for it yet. The flight marked more than just a change of scenery; it was a leap into a future that felt both thrilling and terrifying. I was weak on my feet but resolute in my spirit, determined to reclaim my life, one small step at a time.

Leaving the insulated world of hospital care behind felt like shedding a heavy winter coat. Nearly a month of IV lines, feeding tubes, beeping monitors, and the relentless carousel of physicians and therapists had become my normal. Now, I was swapping that chaos for something even more uncertain: home. But as I sat in the airport, a tide of confusion swirled in my mind. The past three weeks had been a collision of moments, a whirlwind of survival, recovery, and resilience. And now? Now I was expected to just step back into the world.

But I wasn't the same. I was coming back to Plano with Thick-It, catheters, and a wheelchair—not exactly the souvenirs I had in mind. The thought of it all loomed over me like a dark cloud, triggering a flurry of questions I didn't have answers to. How would I manage this? How would I tackle that? Would I even recognize my life? Would it still be mine? I felt terrified and lost, grappling with the weight of those uncertainties. Beneath that fear, a flicker of determination refused to die out. I had come a long way in those three weeks, and I wasn't about to stop now.

As we boarded the plane, I took a deep breath, trying to drown out the anxious chatter in my mind. My mom helped me settle into the window seat, her calm presence a lifeline. The engines grew louder. I leaned back, closed my eyes, and felt the plane surge forward, wheels leaving the ground. A slight jolt, a moment of weightlessness, and we were airborne; my world was once again in transition.

The view through the window was a shifting kaleidoscope: bright blue sky, streaks of clouds, and fading patches of the brown West Texas earth sliding out of view. I could feel the upward pull, that subtle pressure pressing me against the seat. I thought of my dad driving alone down the highway, my car making the same journey we were taking above. Everything felt surreal. This wasn't just a flight home; it was a bridge between what I'd been through and whatever came next.

I tried to focus on the positives. I wasn't alone. My parents, my family, and even my friends were a support system, an unbreakable safety net. My Christian faith, bolstered by the Finnells, remained a quiet, steadfast presence, an anchor I could hold onto when everything else felt like a free fall. I didn't have a clear picture of what the future would look like—my vision literally wouldn't allow it—but I knew I wasn't facing it alone.

It was February 28, spring was just around the corner, and with it came the promise of new beginnings. I was ready to embrace whatever came next, even if I had to stumble and fumble my way through it. I wasn't just leaving the hospital; I was leaving the first chapter of my survival story behind. I was stepping into something new, something unknown, but something I was willing to fight for.

—SECTION IV—

The Space Between

ROUGH LANDING

The bounce of the airplane as its wheels collided with the runway at Love Field was more than a landing; it was a metaphorical wake-up call. Time to get to work. Moments earlier, I had felt the lift of takeoff, the hope of forward momentum, the fresh-start optimism that only spring—and an actual flight—could bring. But landings have a way of reminding you that gravity gets the last word.

My mom helped me from my seat into the wheelchair, and a gate attendant rolled me into the terminal. Waiting for us were my brother, Brad, and my grandpa, Kenny.

Brad had seen me in the hospital, so my appearance wasn't shocking. If anything, I looked better than the last time he saw me. My grandpa, on the other hand, hadn't seen me since before meningitis. I couldn't imagine what it was like for him to see me so thin, so weak, so far from the person I used to be. He hugged my mom tightly, then turned to me, his eyes softening. Instead of an awkward hug with me in the wheelchair, he greeted me with a playful punch to my shoulder and said, "Well, hello, John!"

It was a small gesture, but one that carried the weight of normalcy, as if nothing had changed. But everything had.

Although my balance and walking were improving, I wasn't anywhere near ready for the kind of distance and bustle that came with an airport. The wheelchair wasn't a fallback; it was a necessity.

We gathered our bags and made our way to the parking garage, where we loaded into my parents' Suburban—the same battle-tested Suburban from the "lucky crash" that had alerted my parents to my critical condition in Lubbock. It had been repaired and was back in action. I loved that vehicle. Everything about it was oversized: big tires, big windows, big seats. The perfect Texas ride. Suburbans were known as the "Texas Cadillac." Ours was no exception, with a TV, a VCR, a stellar sound system, and "limo lights" inside.

Creature comforts aside, I was uneasy during the ride home. What should have felt familiar—cruising down the same Dallas roads I'd driven so many times—felt distant, almost foreign.

When we arrived, my grandma Sharma and my friend Bethany were waiting. For weeks, Kenny and Sharma had been holding things together at home, helping Brad while my parents stayed with me in Lubbock. Bethany had flown in from Kentucky the day before. Also a sophomore in college, she and I had been close friends since preschool back in Chillicothe. Our moms had both been teachers in our city schools, and our families were well acquainted. Over the years, a special bond had formed between us. After my family moved to Texas in the middle of our eighth-grade school year, we remained tight through frequent phone calls and visits.

Bethany had timed her trip with my return home. I could tell it was tough for her. Seeing me in such a weakened state, barely able to care for myself, wasn't easy. I was more than a little embarrassed and reluctant to admit it. I spent most of her two-day visit lying in bed, drained physically and emotionally. I longed for our old days together, when we'd just hang out or go find silly things to do. But this time was different; there was no escaping the reality of what had happened to me. Still, her presence lifted me, even if our time together wasn't much fun for either of us.

We talked optimistically about her next visit—but that seemed like a lifetime away. There was a long hug and then an unspoken feeling that said she didn't know what to say, and neither did I. The goodbye was a little awkward, heavier than either of us had expected. When the door closed behind her, the silence hit hard. But the silence didn't last long. My parents had a plan.

With all the medical challenges facing me, I now needed an entire support team: a primary care physician, a urologist, an ophthalmologist, and a physical therapist, just to name a few. Before meningitis, my health care had been simple and within the purview of my pediatrician. Now I was thrust into the world of adult medicine, a place I never expected to be that soon. It felt like I had aged a few decades overnight.

Mom sprang into action and arranged an appointment with her and my dad's family physician. I remember the visit well. The day was bitterly cold, and the wheelchair ride from the parking lot seemed to stretch on forever, each bump reminding me how fragile I had become. Inside the doctor's office, I sat there, mostly silent, while my parents explained my situation. Only weeks before, my medical history had been remarkably mundane. Now I came with a laundry list of complications. The doctor looked at me—a pale, broken kid in a wheelchair—and seemed palpably uncomfortable. For reasons I still don't fully understand, he told us he couldn't handle my case; I was too much for him.

The news landed like a punch to the gut. For my parents, this was more than rejection; it was a harsh reminder that leaving the hospital wasn't the finish line but the beginning of an uphill battle. Despite the setback, we quickly found a glimmer of hope. The doctor referred us to a nearby internal medicine specialist who, thankfully, was eager to help. The next day, we met with him, and it felt like we were back on track.

My parents weren't about to let me sit around and wallow. They insisted I get out of the house, no matter how tired or weak I felt. And I was weak; really weak. I had lost so much weight and muscle mass that I barely recognized myself. Every step was exhausting, but I knew they were right. I had to keep moving, even when my body didn't want to. To help fuel that movement, we needed to increase my caloric intake. My parents and I hopped on that assignment immediately.

After meeting with my new doctor, we stopped for a milkshake, a seemingly perfect solution: calorie-dense, far more palatable than hospital food, and compatible with my swallowing restrictions. I ordered a mint chocolate chip milkshake, one of my favorites. But my body had other plans. Weeks of antibiotics and medication had wreaked havoc on my digestive system, and the milkshake triggered something in my gut that I couldn't control. I made it home just in time to spend the rest of the afternoon locked in the bathroom, undone by something as harmless as a milkshake.

The next day, Grandma tried to make me feel better by cooking one of my all-time favorite meals: baked steak, a hearty family recipe passed down through generations of our Ohio roots. The aroma of steak and potatoes wafted through the house, but instead of bringing comfort, it brought a wave of nausea so strong I had to bundle up in blankets and escape to the back porch while they aired out the house. It felt like another loss in a week filled with too many.

As if that weren't enough, I capped off the week with my first urinary tract infection. Using a catheter was now part of my life, thanks to my neurogenic bladder. At discharge, I was sent home with a set of reusable catheters and some vague instructions on how to sterilize them. Dad had gotten a crash course from the nurses, but it was clear neither of us was prepared for the real deal. After a few days of trying to manage, I woke up feeling feverish and nauseated. We rushed back to my new doctor, where tests confirmed I had a UTI.

The infection hit me like a ton of bricks. My body, already weak, struggled with every wave of nausea, and vomiting was an energy-zapping task. I remember lying in bed, too tired to move, feeling utterly defeated by my body and my circumstances. I had survived meningitis, but the aftermath felt unbearable. "I'm sick of being sick," I told my dad, my face buried in a pillow, my voice barely above a whisper. It wasn't just a complaint. It was a quiet confession of everything I'd been holding in. And in that moment, it felt like I had finally told the truth out loud.

WHEN SPRING BREAK CAME HOME

With the start of a new week, the first priority was clear: I needed to get my catheter situation under control. After the trauma of a UTI, we couldn't afford another setback. We had to make sure things were right this time.

Dad and I headed to my new urologist's office, located in the same hospital as my new internal medicine doctor, not far from home. As Dad wheeled me through the parking lot, the cool midmorning air felt markedly warmer than the biting cold of recent trips to the hospital, a refreshing sign that spring was near.

Once inside, the sterile hospital smell brought back memories of my recent stay, which I'd been trying to forget. The urologist's office had the same sharp, clean scent, and the familiar sounds of clattering heels and distant voices echoed through the hallways. As we checked in and waited, the reality of where I was—and what we were about to discuss—settled over me heavily.

When we were called back, it didn't take long for the appointment to get uncomfortable. There I was, still trying to come to terms with what my body had been through, while sitting in a room talking about catheters, bladder function, and urethras. *What's a urethra?* I wondered as the doctor droned on. The whole process of catheterizing had been awkward enough at home, but now I had to discuss it in clinical detail with a doctor, a nurse, and my dad right there beside me as I lay pantsless on an exam table. I was nineteen but felt like a child all over again.

The urologist was professional, explaining everything carefully, but I couldn't help feeling the weight of the situation. At one point, they conducted an ultrasound on my bladder and kidneys. The cool gel felt strange against my skin, and the machine's low hum filled the room as the doctor traced the device over my abdomen. Everything looked as it should, which was a relief, but it came with the reminder that I had to work to keep things that way.

Thankfully, I was given a prescription for individually packaged disposable catheters, which meant we were done with the reusable ones that required a witchcraft-like boiling ritual between uses. These were sterile, ready to use, and would be discarded after one use. The doctor emphasized the importance of maintaining my bladder health by keeping track of my urine output and preserving a steady routine in a sterile environment to avoid future infections. He recommended some additional accessories and handed us a week's supply of catheters and a measuring bottle, explaining the details with clinical precision, but to me it all felt overwhelming. It had never occurred to me that I'd need an instruction manual for my own plumbing.

I hadn't realized how unique my situation had become until we tried to fill the prescription at our neighborhood pharmacy only to be told they didn't stock catheters, another reminder that my life was now full of unexpected complications. Sitting in the wheelchair, frustrated with this news, I couldn't help but wonder. *Why don't you stock catheters? Why didn't the doctor warn us of this? Why do I even need a prescription for catheters anyway?* As I sat there stewing, I couldn't think of a single person I knew who used a catheter. Am I the only one?

The pharmacist directed us to a specialty pharmacy across town that had the catheters I needed, and lots of them. They also had the gloves, lubrication, and antiseptic wipes I'd need to make the process more manageable while maintaining a sterile and safe environment.

At home, it was clear I wasn't yet capable of handling the catheter process on my own. I was still weak, my body struggling to regain coordination, and most of the time I couldn't even see what I was doing or where I was aiming (yikes). I was still lying on my back in bed for the whole routine, emptying into a repurposed gallon milk jug, which was then carefully measured and poured into the toilet. Who knew "going number one" could feel like training for the Olympic trials?

I couldn't manage it without help. Dad was my best—and only— option for this very personal procedure. We developed a routine, going through the process four or five times a day. It was tedious, uncomfortable, and humbling, but there was no denying the necessity. I quickly realized this was just another part of my new reality. There was no way around it.

That became our daily rhythm, until, almost without warning, spring break was suddenly upon us.

While my friends were packing swimsuits and gearing up for beach vacations or bar crawls, I was still perfecting the art of peeing in a milk jug. Not exactly the postcard version of spring break. But despite my less-than-exotic plans, something had shifted. I was beginning to feel stronger. My coordination was improving. I was even getting more confident moving around the house.

Since coming home from the hospital, my parents had set me up in the downstairs guest bedroom (my new HQ) so I didn't have to face the Everest that was our staircase. I was getting pretty good at shuffling around the first floor, but the second floor and my old bedroom remained uncharted territory.

Even though our house wasn't a spring-break destination hotspot, it saw a steady stream of visitors, friends home from Texas Tech, neighborhood buddies, and high school pals I hadn't seen in a while. For many of them, this was their first time seeing me since everything had happened. And while they seemed the same, it was clear I was drastically different. Still, having them around felt like a mini-reunion, full of laughter and memories of high school antics. Reliving those days was exactly what I needed.

Jenn was home for the week, too. Her family lived in a nearby Dallas suburb. She knew a couple of my high school friends but mostly just hung back, listening as we retold our ridiculous stories. I imagine it must have been dull for her at times, being on the outside of all those memories, but she didn't let it show. She hung in there with us, even though there was probably a lot she didn't fully understand. At the end of each day, she stayed late, helping me move around the house and eating dinner with me and my family. We talked about a lot, but not everything. I wasn't ready to share all the details of my recovery with her—or with anyone, for that matter.

She'd been there, witnessing my day-to-day life at home, so she already knew plenty, but there were some topics I still wasn't eager to broach, like the whole catheter situation. My incontinence issues mortified me. She didn't press; she just knew to give me privacy when

I needed it. But beneath the surface, things between Jenn and me were starting to change. She could sense it, too.

As the week went on, I started getting more adventurous. The warmer weather made me eager to get outside, so we took short walks up and down the street: me, my gait belt, and at least one friend holding onto me like I was a walking retirement home commercial. I was improving, but I still moved with the grace of an old man.

Chris, always on the move, suggested we take it up a notch and hit Country Burger, an old favorite from our high school days. The idea was both thrilling and terrifying. I hadn't left the house without my parents, a wheelchair, or Thick-It, and I certainly had not left spontaneously. But something inside me said, *Why not? Let's go for it!* So, after a pit stop in my bedroom with Dad and a disposable catheter, I headed out with Chris, Jenn, and a couple of other friends.

As we pulled into the parking lot that perfect early spring day, I was hit with an incredible sense of nostalgia. Country Burger was still a hot spot for the high school crowd. Just like old times, it was buzzing. What I hadn't considered, though, was how tricky it would be to navigate the place. Tables crammed close together, kids everywhere. And, oh yeah, stairs. Four massive, intimidating stairs stood between me and my all-time favorite, the chicken tender sandwich. But with Chris and Jenn on either side of me, we made it up. Shuffling inside, I put my arms around them as we maneuvered through the chaos of high schoolers in the dining room to find an open table.

As Chris made his way to the counter to order, a kid who'd witnessed my *Weekend at Bernie's*–style entrance stopped him and asked, "Hey, man, is that dude drunk?" Chris, not missing a beat, shot back, "No, he's blind!" The kid turned beet red and hurried away, and while the whole exchange was quick, it was another reminder of how different I had become. More importantly, it made me appreciate the fierce loyalty of my friends.

Despite the awkward entrance and likely stares I fortunately couldn't see, the lunch went great. The food was as greasy and satisfying as I remembered, and I felt a real sense of normalcy for the first time in a long while. It was a far cry from the hospital bed I had been confined to not long ago. Leaving Country Burger that day felt like a victory. Not just because I'd made it through without a bathroom or choking crisis, but because I'd reconnected with old friends, rediscovered a sense of independence, and realized how far I'd come.

Spring break 1998 might not have been wild, but for me, it was a turning point. I felt hopeful, recharged, and ready to tackle whatever came next. As bittersweet as it was to say goodbye to my friends at the end of the week, that taste of the good old days gave me the energy I needed to keep pushing forward.

REHAB, RIDES, AND REALLY BAD AIM

While my friends were keeping me entertained and feeling just a little more like myself, my parents were quietly making moves behind the scenes, plotting my next mission: outpatient physical rehabilitation.

After conferring with my new medical team, they landed on a facility across town, where I'd be spending two hours every weekday for at least the next six weeks. It was my next job, essentially. But we needed to figure out the logistics of getting me there because I wasn't commuting alone.

With my grandparents wrapping up their mission—keeping things steady for Brad while my parents focused on my care—they were preparing to return to Chillicothe. It had been nearly a month and a half, and they'd earned the break. Their rock-solid support kept us all afloat, but it was time for them to regroup and plan a return in a couple of months.

Both of my parents were going back to work, so Mom orchestrated a smooth ride-share system that rivaled Uber long before its time. The rotation included my dad, some of my parents' neighborhood friends, and a few of my buddies who were still in town. Before I officially began, we made a visit to the rehab center so I could get the lay of the land and meet the therapists. At nineteen, I was practically a rehab rock star—at least two or three decades younger than any of the other patients.

Day one, Dad was my chauffeur. It was mostly orientation: getting the schedule, learning the exercises, and doing some light stretching. I was still wearing the gait belt, but the wheelchair stayed behind. Big win. We started with walking drills and time on the stationary bike. As someone who loved biking, this was my jam. I pushed harder than they expected and ended up completely wiped by that afternoon, but it was the kind of exhaustion that felt earned. A small, triumphant ache.

By the second day, I was getting stronger but needed the gait belt for guidance. I still bumped into walls, tables, and the occasional elderly patient like I was learning to walk for the first time.

Then came day three, which threw a wrench in our well-oiled machine. Dad had a last-minute work conflict, and that meant only one person was available to handle my midday catheter procedure.

Mom.

Cue the horror music.

I knew this moment was coming, but that didn't make it any easier. I went into full protest mode, drinking the bare minimum in a half-hearted attempt to delay the inevitable. But the inevitable showed up anyway . . . on her lunch break. It was the most traumatic fifteen minutes of my life. I don't think she enjoyed it either. And neither of us have spoken of it since.

That mortifying experience was the catalyst I needed to finally take matters into my own hands. From that day forward, I ditched the lying-in-bed approach and made my way to the bathroom for the procedure. Dad supervised the first few times to ensure I didn't tip over, but I was determined. With my balance still shaky and my vision practically nonexistent, my aim was predictably terrible. The workaround? The walk-in shower. After a few laughably bad attempts, I eventually figured it out. Chalk up another victory on the road to independence.

Meanwhile, Mom had somehow managed to get my political science class transferred to a home-study setup. I didn't exactly volunteer for it, but she wasn't taking no for an answer. Since I'd withdrawn from my other classes, this meant I would remain enrolled at Texas Tech. And, more importantly, it established another routine and kept my brain active.

Twice a week, we'd sit outside with Mom reading from my textbook while I recorded my answers into a handheld cassette recorder. I didn't realize it then, but she was helping me retrain my brain to learn audibly, a skill I'd rely on for the rest of my life. Mom, with the heart of a teacher, always had a way of staying one step ahead.

A couple of weeks in, I was flying on the stationary bike and walking independently indoors. I was feeling like a champ until the therapists surprised me with a new challenge: walking on grass.

I couldn't help but wonder why. I'm here to rehabilitate, not walk in the park.

But sure, I gave it a shot. Two steps in, face-plant.

Confidence: gone. Two lessons quickly learned: life is not a walk in the park, and I literally cannot walk in a park.

Turns out it wasn't a strength issue; it was balance. Grass, with all its tiny variations, was like a field of land mines for someone relearning how to walk with limited sight and a tenuous grip on equilibrium. I fell. A lot. But I also got back up. A lot.

At home, rehab continued. Dad and I took walks around the block. Initially, I kept my eyes on the ground, trying to avoid uneven pavement and any lurking curb demons. He taught me how to look up and ahead, how to start trusting my instincts. I began counting steps to orient myself. Twelve to the curb. Twenty-six to the low tree branch that smacked me in the head the first time. Eighteen up to the second floor of the house.

I was making progress on the stairs, too. We tackled them one cautious step at a time, but I wasn't quite ready to move back up there permanently. My progress echoed one of Dad's favorite metaphors: two steps forward, one step back. Anytime I'd get discouraged, he'd rattle off the setbacks I'd already overcome: the UTI, the failed park walk, the milkshake incident. Then he'd remind me that every time, I got back up stronger. Taking stock of the path I'd traveled, I realized just how far I'd come.

And with my birthday around the corner, I found myself reflecting even more. I wasn't a teenager any longer, and after everything I'd survived, I wasn't the same person either. Turning twenty should've felt like a launchpad into adulthood. Instead, it felt like a pit stop in a slow-motion reboot. But I'd survived the unimaginable and hit my rehab milestones ahead of schedule. So, yeah. This birthday had a certain heroic energy.

True to form, Mom threw a full-scale party at the house. Balloons, cake, all the usual things. It was sweet, but the vibe was more "eight-year-old's birthday" than "independent young adult college student." The only thing missing was a clown making balloon animals. Nonetheless, I was grateful. Just maybe a little embarrassed, too.

Aunt Judy and her life-partner, Wilbur, flew in for the occasion. Judy had been there in Lubbock during the beginning stages of recovery, and her presence now felt like a full-circle moment. Judy wasn't just family, she was our "bonus mom," the one who spoiled us and always made our time together unforgettable.

Micah, one of my closest high school friends, also showed up. He had last seen me in Lubbock, still in the coma, and was stunned at how much I'd improved. He'd been coordinating with my parents behind the scenes to help with my next steps, literally.

Anne came too. She'd become part of the weekly rehab ride rotation and had been a longtime music buddy. We used to swap CDs, dissect albums, and treat lyrics like they were the most profound poetry that ever existed.

I'll never forget a moment in high school when we were lying on the floor in her room listening to "The Score" by the Fugees. Out of nowhere, she asked, "If you had to choose, would you rather lose your sight or your hearing?" We were just teenagers tossing around ridiculous hypotheticals, but I thought about it seriously.

Lying there, eyes closed, letting the music take over, I chose sight. I couldn't imagine a life without sound, especially music. The thought of being blind was unsettling, but living in silence? That felt like losing the part of life that made it dance. I mean, Stevie Wonder couldn't see a thing and still made the world listen; he saw the soul in everything.

Fun fact: "The Score" dropped on February 13, 1996, exactly two years before I woke up from a coma blind. Life has a twisted sense of humor sometimes.

Riding around town with Anne was among the few times I felt independent again. With her and my friends, the music was loud, the conversation light, and the vibe familiar. Riding with my parents or their friends? Not quite the same. It was during those rides that I started to realize something deeply troubling: I was a passenger now. No longer a driver, I had lost control: of the route to the destination, of the music I would hear on the way, of the little freedoms I used to take for granted. That shift hit much harder than I expected, especially when the soundtrack of my day was no longer mine to choose.

Soon after the birthday bash, I outgrew what the rehab center could offer. It was time to level up. Micah connected me with Jay, a trainer at a local gym who didn't flinch when he heard the words "blind" and "post-coma."

Jay was a pro. Not only did he agree to make me stronger than I'd ever been, but he would also help me navigate a space that was essentially a maze of machines, sweaty bodies, and weights with potentially dire consequences.

We developed a system: I'd walk behind him, right hand on his right shoulder. He guided me from machine to machine, adjusting each setup so I didn't trip or accidentally bump into someone midsquat or take out a row of free weights.

With Jay's help, I wasn't just rebuilding strength; I was building something better than before. Something more intentional. Something defiant.

I WILL SURVIVE

Training with Jay was no joke. I'd started putting on serious muscle, my appetite was back to normal, and best of all, no more Thick-It. I was finally downing water and real food again without that dreaded thickened consistency. As my physical health improved, it was time to move the focus to something less visible but far more daunting: my sight loss. I needed answers, which meant another specialist, another waiting room, and another shot at clarity. This time, it was an ophthalmologist at UT Southwestern Medical Center in Dallas, recommended by my medical team.

The doctor was kind and thorough, guiding me through a lineup of tests. What stands out most from the appointment wasn't the tests; it was the weight of what came next. After reviewing the results, the doctor wheeled his stool closer and spoke with a calm finality that made the air feel heavier. My optic nerves had been permanently damaged by meningitis. Because optic nerves are part of the central nervous system, they don't regenerate. There was no treatment, no surgery, no training plan that could bring my sight back.

We'd heard a version of this back in Lubbock, but come on, that was the Quack Shack. My parents processed it, but I wasn't ready. Whether I couldn't or wouldn't hear it, the truth never quite landed. This time, though, it hit with the force of a slamming door: loud, final, and impossible to ignore. There was no ambiguity, no wiggle room, just the certainty of a future I hadn't asked for.

He explained the term "legally blind." I wasn't totally blind, but I was close: no vision in my right eye and 20/300 in my left. The blindness in my right eye made sense—that was the pitch-black I woke up to coming out of the coma. But "legal" blindness was a distinction that took more to understand. It wasn't just a medical label; it came with real-world implications. Under the law, it meant I could no longer do certain things—like drive a car—and that I now qualified for government services and support reserved for people with severe vision loss. And in more practical, everyday terms, he broke it down like this: while someone with normal vision could read a sign from 300 feet away, I'd need to be within twenty feet. For context, that's an American football field, a full field of distance between what others could see and what I couldn't.

He also advised wearing sunglasses anytime I was outside, not just to protect my remaining sight but to avoid physical harm, since I'd already managed to walk into tree branches and other hazards. They'd also help my one good eye adjust more gently to shifting light. Coming in from the bright Texas sun often felt like standing at the edge of a cliff into pitch black—each time, I'd freeze in place, waiting for my internal dimmer switch to catch up and expose whatever innocent bystander, wall, or coffee table I was about to crash into.

I was twenty years old. My driving stint had lasted less than four years. Thanks to meningitis, it was over. I wasn't about to argue with the doctor (I wasn't getting behind the wheel), but the finality of it still hit like a sucker punch. Driving wasn't just a convenience. It was independence. It was spontaneity. It was freedom. This wasn't something I could outwork, out-train, or rehab my way through. It was permanent.

My parents, in classic form, transitioned straight into problem-solving mode. While I was reeling, they were researching. First step: contact the Texas Commission for the Blind. We hadn't known it existed, but it would soon become a lifeline. The doctor said they offered services I'd need and stressed how essential technology would be. It wasn't just about surviving with sight loss—it was about adapting and learning to forge a new kind of independence.

The next blow came not in a medical office but in our own driveway: selling my car. It made perfect sense. A car I couldn't drive was just a monument to what used to be. But that didn't make it much easier.

To distract from the trip to the dealership, I took control where I could, by curating the tunes for our final journey. Dad and I shared a love for music, and I knew exactly what to play. I pulled out my Case Logic CD binder, found *Fashion Nugget* by Cake, and handed it over. "Track seven," I said. "Trust me."

It was a cover of "I Will Survive," a song from Dad's disco era, redone by one of my favorite '90s alt-rock bands. The irony wasn't lost on me. Gloria Gaynor's classic, now laced with Cake's signature detachment, hit differently that day. It was part tribute, part anthem, and 100 percent on the nose.

As we pulled into the dealership, the lyrics hit full stride. "At first I was afraid, I was petrified…" The words filled the car as I sat in the passenger seat, staring out the window and tapping along to the beat. That track was the last song to play in my teal-green Honda Accord.

We had made it through high school, college road trips, and late-night drives. And that was the end of the road. Literally.

I didn't cry. But I felt it. I felt the goodbye: to the car, to my freedom, and to the version of myself who'd lived behind that wheel.

Letting go of the car felt like losing the last symbol of who I had been. If I couldn't control that, I had to find something I could control. And that meant learning how to live in this new body, in this new reality. It was time to lean into adaptation, which meant heading to the Texas Commission for the Blind to meet with a counselor named Sherry.

That visit was . . . eye-opening (I couldn't resist the sarcasm). Other than the DMV, I'd never been inside a state agency office. The place was buzzing with people, most of them visually impaired. I didn't know how to interact, especially with Sherry, who was totally blind. She met me with grace and patience and extended her hand to shake mine, which I missed until Mom nudged me. "John, she wants to shake your hand." I fumbled. "Oh! Sorry. Hi, Sherry."

There was a guide dog curled at Sherry's feet, unmoved by our arrival. Naturally, we asked questions. She kindly answered, then gently explained that he was working and shouldn't be distracted. She was used to fielding questions like these from the blissfully sighted. We were just getting started.

I'd brought documentation from my doctor verifying my vision loss, which made everything official. Sherry walked us through services available to me, the orientation and mobility training, vocational programs, school accommodations, and assistive technology. I listened as Sherry took notes on her computer, which talked to her in a robotic voice. It was quiet and fast. I could barely understand it, but she typed effortlessly.

I asked her about her setup, and she explained she used software called JAWS, a screen reader designed for people with no vision at all. It read everything on the screen out loud using keyboard commands; no mouse required. Because I still had some usable vision, she recommended different software, ZoomText. It included a screen reader like JAWS but also offered magnification, allowing users like me to enlarge and focus in on portions of the screen. Same mission, different tools.

I'd always been a whiz with computers, better than most kids my age, maybe even some of the teachers. In fact, I was one of the best in my high school class. But back then, I relied on my eyes. Now I was starting from scratch. Sherry ordered ZoomText for me and lined up training so I could learn it, along with proper touch typing. My "hunt-and-peck" strategy wasn't going to cut it anymore. Without sight, my hunting days were over.

The training took place at the Dallas Infomart, a futuristic glass building that felt like a tech utopia. The elevators even spoke the floor numbers aloud; a pleasant surprise and my first real introduction to the concept of accessibility. Over the next few weeks, my computer instincts kicked in. I learned to type without looking, mastered ZoomText, and started feeling like I had a little control again.

The Commission provided the software and the training, but I needed to get a computer on my own. So, we ordered a new Gateway PC with Windows 98, a giant twenty-one-inch monitor that looked like it belonged in a NASA control room, and speakers that could shake the walls. The boxes arrived covered in black and white cow spots, like a dairy farm had joined the tech industry. Short of mooing, they had it all. I loaded ZoomText and got to work.

This was the beginning of a whole new world. One with robotic voices, blown-up screens, and lots of explaining. But also one with tools, support, and, bit by bit, hope.

I wasn't cured. I wasn't whole. But I wasn't broken either. My body was growing stronger, my spirit getting scrappier. I was picking up adaptations, figuring out how to get along, how to live with sight loss instead of against it. My driving days were over, sure, but that didn't mean I couldn't still steer. With Cake's vibraslap still reverberating in my head, I slid into the driver's seat of my computer and hit the gas. I've got all my life to live. I will survive. Yeah, yeah!

FRIENDS, FUMBLES, AND FAMILIAR PLACES

Between workouts and regular trips to the Infomart, I kept a pretty full schedule as summer rolled in. Part of that included reconnecting with nearby friends, another step in reclaiming a sense of normal. I had decided I wanted to return to school as soon as possible. By design, this busy routine was all part of gearing me up for a return to Lubbock. Each time I ventured out, my confidence with mobility and adapting to new surroundings grew.

Dad had a meeting in Austin. It would be a quick overnight trip, and he suggested I tag along for a change of scenery. I jumped at the idea, coordinating with Chris for a chance to hang out while Dad handled business. In short order, we were southbound on I-35. Three hours later, Dad dropped me off at Chris's place with plans to pick me up the next morning.

Chris was living at his fraternity house in a typical setup: beer posters on the walls, that worn-in couch nobody questioned, and a faint smell of something that definitely wasn't Febreze. I'd been there before; in fact, only nine months earlier, my roommates Ryan, Kevin, and I had piled into my Honda and made the drive for a big game weekend. That road trip had been rowdy and unforgettable. This time, it couldn't have been more different. Most of the brothers had cleared out for summer break, and the quiet suited me just fine.

This was more than a visit; it was a trial run of independence. Chris and I kept it low-key, mostly hanging around the house. We grabbed some tacos for dinner and took them back to eat. Between navigating unfamiliar spaces and keeping up with my catheter routine, I was learning what freedom looked like now—messy, imperfect, but mine. It felt good to be in a friend's space, to hold a conversation, to laugh about the good old days, and to try to believe new ones were coming.

Back home, Bethany came in for another visit. This time, I was in much better shape—able to get out and about, which was a stark contrast from her stay three months prior. We worked out with Jay, ran errands, shopped, and even relaxed by my parents' pool. With Bethany in town, I could finally move around without my parents in tow, and it felt amazing—like reclaiming a piece of my old life with someone who'd known me at my best and seen me through the worst.

As it happened, Jenn was also in town that weekend. We hadn't seen each other since spring break, and our calls had dwindled. The drift between us was undeniable, but we planned to meet up for lunch. With Bethany around, I could finally meet Jenn somewhere without my parents chaperoning. A win in itself. We picked the Dallas Galleria: a midpoint that was lively and full of good places to eat.

Sensing potential awkwardness, Bethany offered to drop me off and give us space. "Oh no, don't worry, it'll be fine," I told her. Everyone was cordial, although I think I was the only one who felt truly comfortable. I chatted away while chomping on a Monte Cristo, blissfully unaware of how odd this setup might look to Jenn. She was probably still trying to figure out whether Bethany was just a friend or the writing on the wall.

In hindsight, the optics weren't great. After everything Jenn and I had been through, with our relationship on the rocks, I showed up to lunch with another close female friend—one who could easily be mistaken for my replacement plan. At the time, I didn't think twice. Bethany being there was just coincidence, a moment of borrowed freedom in a life still under repair. But I know now how Jenn must've seen it: a lunch date doubling as her unofficial dismissal.

Soon after, it was time to start preparing for my return to school. With my low-vision accommodations squared away, Sherry transferred my case to the Texas Commission for the Blind's campus office at Texas Tech. I'd be working with a new counselor named Margaret, and she was eager to help smooth my path back into school life.

Meanwhile, in Lubbock, summer meant it was time for the classic college roommate shuffle. Ryan was moving out to be closer to his girlfriend, Kelly, leaving Kevin and me in need of a new place. Fortunately, Brad Smith was also looking and had found a three-bedroom house. It sounded good to me, so Kevin and Brad took charge of moving my things from our old apartment to the new spot.

That gave Mom and me two solid reasons to make a quick trip to Lubbock: to get settled in the new house and lay some groundwork for my full return that fall. We loaded up the Suburban and hit the road for the familiar three-hundred-mile trip out west. I'd made that journey countless times before, sometimes as the driver, sometimes as the passenger, but this time felt foreign. Scenery that should've been familiar slipped past in a blur. I could pick out large landmarks now and then, but without reading the road signs or mile markers, my internal map was useless. I kept asking, "Where are we now?" as if the answer would somehow reset my bearings.

About halfway there, my bladder chimed in. This was my first long drive with the catheter, and it dawned on me I hadn't thought this through. A roadside gas station wasn't exactly a sterile environment, and let's just say I wasn't eager to test my luck in a bug-filled rest stop bathroom. So, I held it.

By the time we pulled up to the new house, I was in agony. I raced to the bathroom, no chance for the catheter routine. I just sat down, forced it, hunched over, gave a push, and . . . voilà! Success! Not a textbook approach, but effective. I mentally thanked my abdominal muscles and swore my urologist to secrecy, without telling him, of course.

Mom headed to her hotel that night, and I stayed behind to catch up with Kevin and Brad. Setting up my room, talking late into the evening . . . it felt familiar, almost easy. It wasn't perfect, but it was something close to real.

The next morning, Mom picked me up early and we went out for breakfast at our favorite West Texas diner, where the coffee's strong and the cowboy hats speak volumes. It felt good to be back.

Then it was time to meet Margaret on campus. I was pleasantly surprised that the Commission for the Blind had an office tucked inside the library, a building I'd been in countless times without noticing. Margaret's office was on the third floor, but the elevator setup was nothing like the Infomart's: old, painfully slow, and totally inaccessible for me. Mom could tell the buttons would be hard for me to find. "We're taking the stairs," she declared. It would be easier, faster, and give us a little exercise.

Margaret, like Sherry, was totally blind but used a white cane for mobility. She was the only counselor on-site, assisted by a fully sighted staffer. They welcomed us warmly, and after the usual awkward moment when I missed Margaret's attempt to shake my hand, we settled in. She introduced me to even more resources I hadn't thought about—volunteers to record textbooks onto cassette tapes, a testing center where I could dictate exams, and early access to registration through my advisor. Even better, the Commission would cover tuition and course materials—my first glimpse at an advantage hidden within a disadvantage.

Afterward, we met with my advisor in the business college to map out my marketing degree plan. My previous semester's withdrawals had set me back a bit, but with their help, I could sketch out a new path. I decided to ease in with three classes. We registered on the spot. Just like that, I was officially enrolled for the fall semester.

By the end of the day, Mom and I were wiped, but it was the kind of tired that came with progress, not just exhaustion. For the first time in months, I wasn't reacting to what had happened to me; I was moving forward, one step at a time. There were still plenty of unknowns ahead, but I had a plan, a schedule, and even a few unexpected silver linings. It felt good to be back on campus, retracing old steps and starting to refamiliarize myself with a place that once felt like home.

I was back in Lubbock. And this time, I wasn't just surviving; I was showing up with purpose.

BREAKUP CALL

When I got back to the house, Kevin let me know that Jenn had heard I was back in town, but not from me. Word had made its way to her through the grapevine, her friends, the ones still dating my friends. And just like that, the clock on my avoidance ran out. I hadn't called, hadn't reached out, hadn't even hinted that I was coming. She was understandably upset. The truth was, I'd been putting it off because I knew what needed to happen, and I wasn't ready for how hard it would be. But now there was no more stalling. I had to face it: it was time to move on.

I took a deep breath, grabbed the phone, and went into my room, closing the door behind me. My heart was pounding, not because I was having second thoughts, but because I had no idea how to say what needed to be said. I liked Jenn, and I respected her even more. But how do you thank someone for standing by you during a medical crisis and then explain that the relationship no longer feels right? I needed a way to be honest without sounding heartless or ungrateful, but it felt like there was no way out of this without hurting her.

Normally, I could navigate breakups with clarity and care, ending things in a way that left both people feeling okay, usually even staying friends. I'd always been good at explaining myself. But this? This was a mess I didn't know how to clean up. There was no version where I didn't come off as the bad guy.

From where I stood (or, more accurately, where I had lain, in my hospital bed), the relationship had taken a significant story arc in the style of *While You Were Sleeping*. In that sweet and funny '90s rom-com, a misunderstanding leads a family to believe Sandra Bullock's character is engaged to their comatose son, but things quickly turn awkward when he wakes up. Jenn and I weren't in a whirlwind romance like that, but the situation felt eerily familiar: while I was out cold, our relationship had intensified without my knowledge or involvement. By the time I came to, it was as if we'd fast-forwarded through months of connection. It's not often that a relationship actually improves while you're in a coma.

By all accounts, we'd only been dating a handful of weeks when I landed in the hospital. But by the time I woke up, it was like I'd been signed up for something way beyond our still-developing casual relationship. My parents, friends, and even Jenn's mom rallied around us as if we were some epic couple. Over those chaotic days, I unknowingly became her "boyfriend in crisis." She visited. She supported. She endured. It was a lot, and she did it all without complaint. Everyone had the best intentions, like the Valentine's Day necklace I'd supposedly wanted Jenn to have. My mom and hers even became friends. I slept through all of it.

Jenn was kind, generous, and steady through everything. She was truly remarkable. Breaking up made zero sense on paper. But here's the thing: I felt bound by a role that had somehow been assigned to me. It felt like life had painted me into this relationship. I was barely beginning to understand my new reality, and while I could have leaned into the relationship, it just didn't feel right. Furthermore, it felt like I didn't have a choice.

So I did what I had to do. I dialed her number, even though I hated that it had to be a phone call. It felt cold, impersonal. But this was my new reality. I couldn't just spontaneously drive across town anymore when something needed to be done. The phone, which had always been my favorite tool for connecting with people, would now become the tool I used to disconnect.

I fumbled my way through the conversation. I was not as eloquent as I wish I could have been. I told her that it wasn't her fault, that I appreciated everything she'd done, that this wasn't what I wanted for either of us, and that it felt like our relationship had been put into a time machine—catapulted years ahead of where we actually were. None of it sounded right, I'm sure.

Because of our lack of communication and the botched lunch "double date" a few weeks earlier, she knew the end was coming. But she was still upset. She said very little, her end of the line heavy with unspoken anger, disbelief, and hurt I couldn't begin to name. She didn't yell or cry. She just took it in, steadied herself, and held it together.

We said goodbye with finality, and I knew I'd made the right choice for us both. But that didn't make it any easier. At the time, I told myself that sometimes the only thing you can do is walk away—even if it means hurting someone you still care about—to close a chapter you never meant to start. Because no one wants to wake up in the middle of a story that isn't theirs.

After hanging up, I didn't feel relief immediately. I felt... hollow. Like I'd broken something I hadn't meant to. Part of me wanted to rewind time, to before meningitis, before the hospital, before everything got so incredibly complicated. But grief doesn't play by those rules. It doesn't just show up for the obvious losses. I didn't realize it at the time, but I was grieving the control I once had and the version of myself I thought I still was.

The next morning, Mom came to pick me up for the return drive to Plano. As we cruised down the highway, I told her that Jenn and I had broken up. She didn't press for details. She didn't share what she must have been thinking, but I hoped she understood.

We rode in silence for a while, the hum of the tires filling the space between us. I looked out the window, not seeing much but sensing everything. The sky was wide, the road stretched long, and in the quiet of that drive, I let the grief settle in. I hadn't just ended a relationship; I'd stepped further into my new life.

And with the benefit of hindsight, I can now admit something I couldn't back then: I was scared. Scared of my new limitations. Scared of who I was becoming. And scared of the unknowns that came with all of it. But at twenty years old, my ego didn't leave much room for fear. I made decisions like I was in control when, deep down, I felt anything but. Some of those decisions would serve me well. Some would not. But ending things with Jenn—even clumsily—was still the right call. I didn't want to be in the relationship. And the longer I delayed the ending, the worse it would have been for her. I didn't handle it perfectly, but I knew it had to be done. The pressure, the tension, the disappointment; it was all too much. We had to move on. Both of us.

Looking back, that goodbye wasn't just the end of a relationship; it was the beginning of learning who I was without all the noise, without the roles others had assigned me. A painful step, yes, but a necessary one. Because before I could move forward, I had to let go of who I thought I had to be.

THE SUMMER OF JOHN...REWRITTEN

After our consultation in Dallas, we were still chasing clarity. The ophthalmologist there had given us the facts, but we couldn't shake the question: was there really nothing else to try? My parents, eternal optimists and ever-dedicated, did what parents do: they found a backup plan—the Mayo Clinic in Scottsdale, Arizona.

It was a long shot, but if there was even a slim chance for better answers or some glimmer of new research, they wanted to take it. The appointment was scheduled for early July, right before I'd be heading back to Lubbock. So Dad and I packed our bags and boarded a flight west, chasing the faint promise of answers waiting in the desert.

Arizona in the summer felt like standing inside a hair dryer, but even with limited sight, I could make out the low, jagged mountains and the wild sprawl of cacti dotting the horizon. Desert heat hit differently, but I liked it.

At the Mayo Clinic, we navigated a maze of pristine hallways before finally landing in the ophthalmology wing. The doctor we saw was top tier: thoughtful, kind, and thorough. After a battery of exhausting tests, he sat down with us and laid it out plainly: the optic nerve damage was permanent. No cure, no surgery, no miracle drug. He explained that millions of delicate fibers transmit visual signals to the brain, and once these are lost, they're gone for good. Despite promising research, current treatments focused only on preventing further damage, not restoring what had already been lost. My case wasn't rare or groundbreaking enough to qualify for a trial. There was nothing to do but preserve what vision I had and move on. I wouldn't wait for a cure; I would adapt.

On the flight back to Dallas, I couldn't stop thinking about what that meant. The pragmatist in me knew this was the same answer we got in both Dallas and Lubbock. But something about hearing it from this guy, after flying across the country, after holding out hope, made it feel more final. It didn't crush me. It clarified things. This wasn't the beginning of some long fight to get my sight back. That path was closed. And with that closed door came a new kind of freedom. Now I could focus on the life I could build, not the one I thought I'd get back.

We landed just in time to catch the end of the World Cup quarterfinal game, a shootout. The airport terminal had TVs showing the match, and crowds were gathered around like it was a concert. I was pulling for Italy, but without sound, I couldn't follow what was happening. Dad, knowing I was eager to keep up, tried his best to narrate, giving me a play-by-play of each shot. I knew most of the players' names by heart, while Dad didn't know any, and when he did try to provide a name, it was usually hilariously off. Part of adapting, I was learning, meant I wouldn't always get the information I needed, at least not exactly as I wanted. In this case, though, I understood enough: France took the win.

Back home, some things had improved. I'd returned to sleeping upstairs in my old bedroom—a quiet milestone that felt oddly triumphant. My body, thanks to Jay's relentless workouts and a renewed appetite, was stronger than it had been in years. The pool became my escape, and visits from old friends brought welcome normalcy.

It was a far cry from just a year earlier, what I'd jokingly dubbed "The Summer of John." Back then, I was a carefree college freshman, working easy shifts at the dry cleaners for fun money, bouncing between house parties, and soaking up the freedom of summer. The highlight: Rockfest at the brand-new Texas Motor Speedway, where nearly 400,000 people packed in to see Bush, No Doubt, Counting Crows, Jewel, Collective Soul, and more. That summer felt like a rite of passage. This one felt like a reckoning. But in its own way, it marked progress, because even though everything had changed, I was starting to adapt.

Still, other things—the less visible ones—were off. My balance was unpredictable, and simple trips to the kitchen could turn into unintended obstacle courses. I'd lost the visual cues I never knew I relied on. It's been said that humans get about 85 percent of our information visually. My senses of hearing, smell, taste, and touch were scrambling to pick up the slack, but the adjustment wasn't instant. Sound quickly became my strongest ally.

Thankfully, two new album drops gave me something to look forward to. My favorite Dallas station, 94.5 The Edge, had been hyping *Hello Nasty* by Beastie Boys and *Stunt* by Barenaked Ladies for months. I couldn't wait to get my hands on them.

When I finally made it to Virgin Records to grab *Hello Nasty*, I handed it to the cashier like it was a golden ticket. Eager to get home and fire up the CD, I rushed out, only to walk full stride into a clear plexiglass security post. WHAM. Nearly knocked the thing over. Nothing like a head-on collision to humble your hype. My ribs were fine, but my ego limped out of there. Still, I didn't let it stop me from going back the next week for *Stunt*. I thought to myself, I'm the kind of guy who laughs at a sensor. You can bet I paid close attention to those security posts on that return visit.

That summer also brought a trip to see the Texas Rangers. I should've been excited. Ballpark hot dogs, time with Dad, the whole experience. But once we got to our seats, anxiety kicked in. I couldn't track the ball, couldn't follow the game. And worse, I started imagining a screaming line-drive foul ball flying right at my defenseless head. I sat there, stiff and silent, until I couldn't take it anymore.

Sensing my unease, Dad moved us to a remote upper section where danger wasn't on the menu. The view was worse, the sound much less clear, and the connection I usually felt at a game just wasn't there. I tried to follow the action through crowd reactions and the distant *thwack* of the bat. But for the first time, it hit me: I was physically present but felt completely removed. That feeling—being surrounded yet separate—was becoming all too familiar.

This was the new reality. And it wasn't dramatic or tragic; it was subtle, frustrating, sometimes even funny. But it was also deeply real. I wasn't chasing cures anymore. I was adapting, adjusting, and occasionally walking into things. I was searching for a new way to see the world, even if I had to do it mostly by sound.

WHEN SUMMER BREAKS YOU

Something more sensitive—and somehow even more personal—than my catheter use had surfaced, and it was something I couldn't ignore. I discovered that I had no sensation in the area that defines manhood that, to a twenty-year-old, felt like a life sentence. It wasn't apparent immediately. I first noticed odd patches of numbness running from my belly button to my knees. I brushed it off as a side effect, something temporary, like everything else was supposed to be. But that theory didn't hold up.

The first real confirmation came during a brief, quiet moment with Jenn back in March. We were alone, and things started to feel... familiar. Comfortable. Romantic, even. It was one of those moments when time slows down, the room gets quiet, and you're pretty sure a romantic comedy would cue the soft lighting. Then—nothing. No response. It was like flipping a switch in a dark room and realizing the bulb was missing. I didn't say anything to her at the time—I just pretended to be tired or distracted—but the truth unsettled me. At that age, most guys could find a breeze stimulating enough to get a reaction. This wasn't true for me anymore, and it was every teenage boy's nightmare brought to life. I figured that with some therapy or the right medication, it would just be a matter of time before this was corrected.

But months later, it wasn't. And my optimism was starting to run thin. During a regular checkup, I finally mustered the nerve to blurt it out to my urologist: "I can't…well …get things to work." He calmly explained that it wasn't uncommon after spinal or nerve trauma, and he had solutions.

His first attempt? A pellet. Designed to dissolve "upstream," so to speak. Knowing my catheter history, I had a sinking suspicion of what "pellet" and "dissolve internally" meant. I was right. And it was weird.

Next came the little blue pill, hyped in commercials as the miracle men had been waiting for. He handed me a discreet sample pack and told me to give it a go at home. I tried. Several times. The breeze test? Failed. My body's once-reliable chemistry now felt like a broken vending machine. I'd press the button, wai…and nothing dropped.

After I updated him by phone, the urologist referred me to a specialist in Dallas. Dad drove me, but we both knew what this was about. There was no pretending this time. When we checked in, the intake paperwork was so personal, so anatomically specific, that Dad took one look and quietly suggested the doctor skip the middleman on that one. This was one lane he didn't want to merge into. I didn't question it. That wasn't a road I wanted to go down with him either; that territory was best navigated one-on-one with the doctor.

Inside the exam room, the doctor came off like a confident magician pulling tricks from a drawer. Another pellet. A topical cream.

A second round of the little blue pill. He handed me the pill and told me it needed a little time to "kick in," then, with complete seriousness, offered me a stack of magazines to help "get things going." That's when the full absurdity hit me: here I was, mostly blind, expected to make the most of some reading material that made *Reader's Digest* look racy. *Glamour* might've worked for George Costanza, but it wasn't even close to cutting it for me. The whole experience felt awkward and gross, like being told to start a fire with wet matches and a gentle sense of shame.

Nothing worked. Not even a flicker. That's when he brought out the final act: a sleek blue box with a tiny syringe tucked inside. He explained that this last-ditch treatment involved an injection at the base of my situation. I don't know what shocked me more, the idea of a needle there or the casual way he said, "You might want someone to help you with this."

I nodded like I was fine, but I was numb all over again, and not just physically. I couldn't see well enough to administer a shot, let alone there. And the idea that intimacy now required medical equipment? It crushed me. I stared at that box, wondering how this could possibly be my new normal. My body had already betrayed me in so many ways. Was this really the final punchline?

That summer had started out with so much promise—strength returning, friends visiting, glimmers of independence—but each little victory was met with an invisible weight. I was trying so hard to will my life forward that I hadn't stopped to process what had actually been lost. And now, staring down at that tiny syringe, it finally caught up with me. My future wasn't waiting around the corner. It was here, already changed. And some parts of me weren't coming back.

A couple of days later, MacKenzie was in town and came to pick me up for dinner. She had this bold, electric energy, the kind that made you feel like anything was possible. My dad lovingly referred to her as "a party waiting to happen," and that may have been an understatement. She carried this fearless optimism that made you believe things could still turn out okay. And even when they couldn't, she was the kind of friend who'd sit with you in the wreckage and hand you a joke.

As we cruised around town, windows down, the summer heat swirling in the car, I told her what I had been up to the past few months. I gave her the highlights: how far I'd come, the strength I'd rebuilt, the milestones I quietly celebrated. Then emotion took over, and my tone darkened. I described how those wins were starting to feel buried under a growing stack of frustrations. Before I knew it, the floodgates opened, and everything I'd been holding back came rushing out.

I told her how I felt stuck, trapped between progress and grief. I'd lost control of so many pieces of my life. No more driving. No independence. Constantly adapting. The awkward encounters and the invisible ache of social disconnection. And now, the looming return to Lubbock, to school, to a version of life I no longer fit into. I didn't feel ready to go back into the world as this new version of me. I didn't even know who that version was yet.

And then there was the most vulnerable part: the urologist visits, the failed "treatments," and the needle I was supposed to use on myself. I told her how it wasn't just about sight or bladder control anymore. I was mourning something deeper—something tied to identity and confidence and connection. I felt like I'd lost the parts of myself I never imagined I'd have to question.

She pulled the car into an empty parking lot near my parents' house and just let me cry. Really cry. I hadn't done that—truly sobbed—since I was a kid. It was all hitting me now: the weight I'd carried all summer, the pressure to get better, to be okay, to pretend I was fine. I wasn't.

After I let it all out, MacKenzie stayed calm, like my unraveling didn't faze her one bit. She looked me square in the eye and said, "You've been to the brink of death and come back. You've got this, John. This stuff doesn't stand a chance against you."

It was exactly what I needed. Not a solution. Not a fix. Just a reminder of who I still was. Her presence that day helped glue together the pieces I thought I'd lost. I wasn't whole—but I wasn't broken beyond repair, either.

The truth is, I didn't come out of that summer cured. I came out cracked open. But sometimes, that's what healing looks like: wreckage that eventually lets the light in. I still didn't know exactly how I was going to face the fall semester, but thanks to MacKenzie, I knew I could.

THE ROAD BACK

With my emotional rock bottom behind me and my confidence on the mend, it was time to head back to Lubbock. I was far from the same John who had left just six months ago; that John wouldn't recognize me now. But there I was, in the Suburban, flanked by my parents and my grandparents, Kenny and Sharma, who had come back to see me off. Once again, the Suburban was loaded to the brim with college essentials, although this time "essentials" had a different meaning. My new computer, my lifeline to classes and my digital world, was carefully stowed, along with my stacks of CD binders, catheters, and tubes of lubrication.

Somewhere between Fort Worth and Abilene, it hit me: I'd made this same trek just two years earlier, riding shotgun with Mom and Dad in this exact Suburban, a wide-eyed freshman brimming with possibility. I had no idea what college would hold, but I couldn't wait to find out. Now, I sat in the same seat, on the same stretch of highway, but the person riding out west this time was different. I don't mean that in a heavy, melodramatic way. Just honest. Life had changed. I had changed. But deep down, I still had that same hunger to figure out what came next. I just had to do it differently now. Slower, maybe. More cautiously. And yes, sometimes with a travel bag full of catheters.

The ride out to Lubbock felt different this time. Often, I found myself silent, just staring out the window, lost in thought. It was one thing to go through recovery with family around, knowing Mom and Dad were just in the other room if I needed help, and quite another to be three hundred miles away, figuring it all out on my own. From the driver's seat, Dad noticed I'd grown quiet and checked in on me. "You good over there, JB?" I nodded and gave a thumbs-up to let him know I was okay, even if a part of me wasn't totally sure.

Kenny and Sharma were in the back seat, quietly supportive, watching the West Texas landscape roll by as we made our way west. This was their first trip to Lubbock, and Dad pointed out places of interest: giant stockyards, miles of open pasture, the occasional roadside oddity that only made sense in Texas.

After taking a quick drive through campus, we made our way to the new house I was sharing with Brad and Kevin. The neighborhood was a quiet one, with streets lined with ranch-style houses, all single-story and stretched flat beneath the unmistakably big, clear blue West Texas sky. I could already feel the familiar dryness of Lubbock in the air, the kind that clings to your throat and reminds you that you're on the South Plains. We pulled up to the house, and the sight of it filled me with both a sense of relief and a prickle of unease. This was my "new normal," which I found both exciting and terrifying.

Mom and Dad helped me haul everything into my room. As they unpacked my boxes, Sharma wandered around the house, immediately noticing all the little spots that needed cleaning in a boys' college rental. She found plenty to keep her busy while Dad, with his usual efficiency, helped me set up my computer station. Eventually, we all stood around in my new bedroom, looking at each other, trying to figure out what to say. There wasn't really anything left, just that awkward, unavoidable pause before goodbye.

Dad broke the silence first. "All right, Champ," he said, clapping me on the shoulder with an optimistic grin. "Remember, you know where we are. You're going to be tremendous out here!"

Mom hugged me tightly, probably a little longer than she intended, her usual way of saying everything she couldn't find the words for. Sharma was next, pulling me into one of her warm, comforting hugs, squeezing me like only she could. Kenny gave me his customary playful punch on the shoulder and said, "Give 'em both barrels, John!"

Once they drove off, the quiet in the house felt louder than anything. I dropped onto my bed, looking around, half expecting someone to pop back in to remind me I'd forgotten something or offer one last piece of advice. But no one came. I was on my own again; really on my own, in a way that felt at once thrilling and unsteady. It was time to pick up where I'd left off. Only now, everything had changed.

I reminded myself that while I was on my own, I really wasn't alone. Over the past six months, my friends had rallied around me, showing me they'd be there no matter what I faced. I had a network that went deeper than I'd realized, people willing to step in and help me, not out of obligation but because they truly wanted to see me succeed.

Sitting there, I took a deep breath, letting the quiet settle around me. I thought back to that first drop-off two years ago. Then, it was a dorm, and I couldn't wait to be on my own. Now, it was a rental house, and I was still eager, but much more aware of what "on my own" actually meant. I thought about that boy I used to be. He was still with me, but meningitis had changed everything. And yet, something inside me was still pushing forward. I began to understand that resilience isn't about returning to the life you had; it's about building a meaningful one with the life you have now.

It was time for that boy to become a man and find new meaning in familiar territory. Tomorrow, a whole new chapter would begin. I knew that from where I was, anything was possible. And while I couldn't see what lay ahead, maybe that was just part of the thrill.

—SECTION V—
Finding Myself in the Dark

NO SYLLABUS FOR THIS

I t was early—first full day back—and I was the only one awake. The house was quiet, but my mind wasn't. I sat alone in the stillness, the kind of silence you can only get just before sunrise, and let it all wash over me. I was back in a familiar place that suddenly felt foreign. I knew the streets. I knew the campus. I knew the people. But I wasn't sure I knew myself, or at least how I would fit back in.

Sure, I'd done the hard work: the rehab, the planning, the relentless effort to prepare for life back on campus. And yet I couldn't shake the feeling that I was a stranger here, orbiting a world I used to belong to. Over the past six months, I'd built back some confidence, regaining little pieces of my independence along the way, but that early morning, it was clear this wasn't going to be as simple as just picking up where I left off. Grandpa Grimes used to say, usually with a chuckle when he couldn't find something or needed a hand, "I'm a lost ball in tall weeds." Now, I finally knew what that meant. The ball's in there somewhere, but no one, not even the ball itself, has a clue where to start looking. I was still trying to find the humor in it all, but that morning, it felt more like a riddle than a punchline.

Surviving meningitis was the easy part—I did it in my sleep. The real challenge was learning to live after. That felt daunting. Was this the beginning of life after me? Did the person I'd become, with the limitations I now had, stand a chance of finishing college or building a meaningful life?

I'd spent years building friendships and making social connections effortlessly. But now, I felt like a one-man exhibit, someone no one could relate to. I didn't have any blind friends. I didn't know anyone else who used a catheter. How would I fit into the world I used to belong to? Would people see me as a burden? Or worse, pity me?

Somewhere down the hall, I heard the creak of a door and the sound of footsteps—one of my roommates starting to stir. It broke the silence, and with it, the spell.

Time to get moving. No more pondering; now came the proving.

We started with prep runs to campus. Kevin, Brad, and I matched up our schedules and built a weekly routine. We mapped out classrooms and walked campus routes, but being there—really being there—felt off. It reminded me of the disconnect I felt at that summer baseball game with my dad, sitting in the stands while everyone around me cheered. Before, I would've been part of the moment. Back on campus, the same thing: familiar noises, familiar buildings, but I couldn't shake the feeling that the scene had moved on without me.

Navigating campus felt like an extreme sport. I knew the layout, but each step still felt uncertain. The curbs, stairs, buses, bikes zipping by, every movement a potential hazard. My ears were doing overtime trying to compensate for what my eyes no longer could. Even the basics were frustrating. I'd instinctively glance at my wrist to check the time, only to remember I couldn't actually read the watch anymore. It was a nice one, a high school graduation gift from my parents. Still looked sharp on my wrist, but it just didn't do much in the functionality department. The time? Always the same: time to get a talking watch.

To make things trickier, I didn't look blind. No cane, no guide dog, no shirt that said, "Hey, I can't see you." So when I passed someone without acknowledging them, they probably assumed I was rude or ignoring them. The truth? Most of the time, I had no clue who I was walking past. I couldn't recognize faces—just vague outlines and movement. My go-to strategy was a confident "Hey, man!" and a prayer that it sounded natural. If they called me by name, I'd start frantically scanning their voice for clues. If they pressed for more . . . well, that's when things got awkward.

I was reliant on a small but solid network of friends for rides and other day-to-day logistics. And while I trusted them completely, I hated how much I needed them. It was less about pride and more about control. I'd always been the guy who called his own shots, figured things out on the fly. Now, even something as basic as getting to class or finding a seat felt like a multistep plan that required coordination and favors. I appreciated every bit of help, but that didn't stop the nagging frustration of knowing I couldn't do it all on my own.

But even with all the uncertainty, something inside me still sparked a stubborn belief that I could pull this off. I didn't know how, but I was determined to find a way. If I had to fake it to make it, so be it. This wasn't necessarily the comeback story I had planned, but it was the one I was living.

After a week of preparations, trial runs, and easing myself back into the paces of college life, it was finally time to launch. I'd been part of countless first days of school, but this one felt like a whole different universe. Moving from Ohio to Texas in the middle of eighth grade had been nerve-wracking and socially awkward, but that paled in comparison to the headwind I felt walking into this first day.

One benefit I did have was a handicap parking tag. It reminded me of something Dad and I talked about during my recovery: taking advantage of a disadvantage. That parking tag was a perfect example. Because of my visual impairment, I was granted front-row access on campus. That meant whoever was driving me essentially got the VIP parking experience. My friends didn't need an incentive to help, but let's just say that perk didn't hurt.

Brad pulled right up in front of the English building. "You good?" he asked. We'd rehearsed this route more than once, and even though my nerves were buzzing, I told him yes. "You go on, and I'll meet you outside the Student Union after class."

I wanted to arrive early to get settled before the room filled up. We were running just a few minutes behind, so while I wasn't late, I wasn't early either. I made my way across the busy sidewalks, moving cautiously through clusters of students, then carefully climbed the stairs and pushed through the doors.

I knew the direction, but when I got to the hallway, my nerves kicked in. Third door or fourth? All of a sudden, I couldn't remember. And I couldn't get close to the room number sign on the wall because there were students gathered around it. I needed to be only inches away to read the number, so I circled a couple of times before sneaking close enough to confirm. Fourth door on the right. Got it.

Inside, the professor—at least I assumed it was the professor—greeted a few of us as we entered and said to sit anywhere. Finding an empty seat in a half-full room felt like playing pin the tail on the donkey. Thankfully, I didn't end up in someone's lap. I slid into an open seat somewhere in the middle, not exactly where I wanted to be, but good enough. At least I was in the right room.

I hadn't introduced myself to the professor yet, so I planned to hang back afterward and explain my situation and set up a time during office hours to talk accommodations. Class began with the usual overview: syllabus, grading, expectations. Then came the reading list. That's when things started to spiral.

The books were massive. And they kept coming. My mind spun. "How am I going to read all of this?" I thought. "What have I done? Why did I choose literature as my comeback course?" I pulled my hat a little lower and kept my head down, hoping not to draw attention as anxiety pulsed through me.

When class ended, I waited for the crowd to thin, shoved the handouts into my bag, and slipped out. The professor already had a line of students waiting, so I decided I'd come back later. I just wanted to escape, regroup, and reset.

Brad was waiting on the bench outside the Student Union. We grabbed lunch and found a few friends. Luckily, that was my only class for the day.

CTRL + ALT + RETREAT

With all the noise in my head—socially, on campus, and everywhere in between—everything seemed to quiet down when I sat in front of my computer. My anxieties vanished, so diving deeper felt like the most natural thing to do. And with the early internet just taking off, there was a lot to explore. Between connecting with friends across the country and completing some of my school assignments, the computer was my way of communicating with the world in a way that respected my reality.

In 1998, getting online required patience and a dial-up modem. Nothing said "futuristic" like hearing the symphony of screeches, beeps, and staticky wails as the modem connected. Ah, the sounds of progress and the thrill of watching the little "connected" icon light up.

One of my online connections was Nathan, another preschool buddy who was then a cadet at West Point Military Academy in New York. In his spare time, he had designed a website on GeoCities, one of the first big web-hosting services that let people create and host their own sites for free. I was intrigued.

GeoCities was organized into "neighborhoods" based on themes, and our neighborhood, College Park, was a digital playground for college students. Our web pages were like dorm rooms—messy but full of personality, with guestbooks, hit counters, and auto-playing MIDI tunes you couldn't turn off (even if you wanted to). It was the height of internet cool to throw together a page with spinning graphics and a soundtrack. I was all in, and with Nathan's help, I was learning a new language, HTML.

While I spent hours in front of my enormous twenty-one-inch monitor, I needed music in my bedroom to set the vibe. I started by tuning into the college radio station, KTXT, which was… interesting. They played some great music and some stuff that could only be called "experimental." I couldn't always tell what was coming next, and half the time, I wasn't sure I even wanted to know. Still, it sparked something in me. I wondered what it takes to get behind that mic and share some interesting songs of my own.

Ultimately, I landed on KCRM, "The Cream of Classic Rock." I was hooked. My CDs were mostly current '90s artists, but now I was delving into my dad's era, the '60s and '70s: the Beatles, Eric Clapton, Joe Cocker, CSN&Y, Fleetwood Mac, Jimi Hendrix, Led Zeppelin, Van Morrison, the Rolling Stones, and even Buddy Holly.

I'd heard of Buddy Holly, but he was just a historical figure to me. I loved Weezer's song "Buddy Holly" and had seen the video with the '50s outfits and horn-rimmed glasses, but that was about it. I learned that Buddy was born and raised in Lubbock, Texas, right where I was. So I went down the Buddy Holly rabbit hole. I loved that raw and rhythmic rockabilly sound and, as a music collector, had to get some of his albums, along with those of the classic rock bands I was getting into.

Luckily, BMG Music Club was still at the height of its glory. With a huge online catalog of music, they had all the classics, and their "12 CDs for the price of one" deal was legendary. There were just a few strings attached, but if you knew the trick, you could land those 12 CDs for about $48, or roughly $4 each. Five weeks, twelve CDs. Rinse and repeat. I was a man on a mission.

As the CDs arrived in droves, I popped them into my computer. My computer's sound system rivaled anything in our house, and Windows Media Player even showed album and track details as each CD played. I could see the track number, track name, duration, and other details that were on the album insert that I hadn't been able to read since my sight loss. Discovering that my computer could give me all this information was a game changer.

Bit by bit, I was zoomed in on my digital world, dialed up to connect, and tuned in to the classic rock that made every hour in front of the screen feel a little more like home. This digital transformation was becoming an alternate existence, one I'd need to learn to pair with my real-world life in ways I was just beginning to understand.

The more time I spent behind the screen, the less time I spent outside of it—and my friends noticed.

They went from nudging to demanding that I rejoin the real world. On some level, I understood and even agreed with their concerns. I wanted to get back out there, back into the routines of my old college lifestyle. But that was easier said than done. Life was different for me now. Normally, we'd make loose plans and let the night take us wherever. By the end, we'd sometimes split up, and getting home wasn't a given. And, of course, drinking was almost always involved.

This mix of spontaneity and alcohol was a recipe for disaster in my world.

In addition to the obvious dangers, for me, drinking was a risk, one with the potential for a bathroom catastrophe. I mean, it was pretty much the worst possible hobby for someone with bladder issues. And I needed near-hospital-level sanitation to avoid another UTI, which was impossible if I couldn't control the night's agenda. Plus, with limited sight, new environments felt like obstacle courses, and my extreme anxiety around meeting girls only made things worse.

And then there was the issue of feeling emotionally and physically castrated, terrified someone would discover that my manhood didn't exactly work as expected. I wanted nothing to do with a serious physical relationship; it just wasn't an option for me. Still, suppressing the instinct for connection and intimacy was brutal. I was a single, twenty-year-old, red-blooded male on a college campus. The wiring was all there, even if the system had shorted out.

In short, going out had become a challenge I wasn't thrilled about. But I knew I'd need to start having some experiences if I was going to build up confidence again, so finally, I gave in.

I decided early on that I wouldn't take catheters with me. There was no way to bring them along and even pretend to feel like my old self. That decision was my own way of trying to appear "normal." I was just not willing to admit how different I really was; an almost lethal combination of pride, embarrassment, and pure stubbornness wouldn't let me.

On my trial run to Lubbock over the summer, I discovered that I could "force" my bladder empty, but it required a sit-down restroom, which wasn't always an option. So, when it wasn't, my strategy was to just hold it all night. Uncomfortable, yes, but less uncomfortable than carrying catheters, lube, and gloves everywhere.

For many good reasons, I had to pace myself on drinks, with certain games and traditions now off-limits. That didn't make socializing any easier. I was even uncomfortable around groups I knew because I couldn't recognize who was there.

Back in the day, I'd float around a room like a social butterfly. Now, the anxiety around seeing—or rather, not seeing—people still lingered. Sure, I had jokes ready about why I couldn't tell who people were to ease the awkwardness, but that routine wore thin pretty fast. It wasn't that I was trying to hide my blindness; I just didn't have the energy to explain things to everyone.

Being dependent on others for rides complicated things. With no car or taxis available, I was captive to other people's schedules. I didn't like the feeling and was constantly asking, "When are we leaving?" or "Where to next?" I could never fully relax and just be in the moment. This wasn't the carefree, spontaneous college lifestyle I'd once known. It was like that for everyone else—but not for me.

Eventually, I started easing back into fraternity life: parties, weekly meetings, the works. I got comfortable with the discomfort, rebuilding some social connections. But I had to learn to limit myself. Drinking less wasn't popular with my friends, but I couldn't really explain it to them. I operated on a "bend but don't break" premise; don't break my bladder, that is. It worked for a while but wasn't something I could sustain. So socializing and going out became something I waded back into carefully, on my own terms when possible, but it didn't always work out that way.

SOUNDS LIKE LEARNING

At some point, I did find a beat of my own that first semester back. I dropped the literature class and doubled down on the other two. Adjusting to a new style of learning, on top of everything else, was a serious challenge, but day by day, things started to feel a little more manageable. I got to know my professors and their TAs, and they turned out to be more than just instructors. They genuinely wanted to help me succeed. They made time for me and provided options, even when I couldn't see much of what was happening around me. It was up to me to figure out how to absorb the material, and that meant listening ...closely.

Truth is, I'd always been tuned in to sound more than most. Even as a kid, I could recognize specific sounds and attach meaning to them. My mom's keys, for example. Those weren't just anyone's keys jingling. To me, they had a distinct signature, a kind of audio handshake, an announcement of her presence. From the time I was little, all the way through high school, Mom would shake her keys to let me know she was nearby. I remember being on the soccer field, focused on the game, when I'd hear that familiar jingle. Mom didn't need to wave or shout. Just a subtle shake of the keys on their way into or out of her purse and I'd know she was there without looking.

Turns out I'd been training for this style of learning long before meningitis rewired my life. Now, those same ears had become my best tool. In class, I wasn't just hearing, I was processing, mapping, interpreting, surviving. What used to be a background skill had become the main act. But even as I adapted, an increasing unease lingered. I was acutely aware of how different I had become, and that awareness often simmered just beneath the surface.

One of the biggest changes was physical—literally. I sat in the front row. Pre-meningitis John wasn't a front-row guy. That wasn't my crowd. But now, it was the only place I had a shot at catching even a blur of what was on the board. It also let the professors see me better, which helped with communication. Still, I couldn't shake the feeling that I was on display, an increasing and persistent worry about whether people noticed my struggle or were judging me for it.

Socially, things were more problematic. I knew there were familiar faces around me; I just couldn't see them. That frustrated me greatly. There was no class roster I could scan, no easy way to match voices to names unless someone spoke directly to me. So even in the front row, I often felt like I was on an island. Close enough to hear the current of college life flowing around me, but just far enough to never fully connect with it.

During that fall, I spent a lot of time in the library waiting around between rides. My friends' schedules didn't always match mine, so I had hours to kill. That's where I really got to know Margaret, my counselor at the Texas Commission for the Blind. She was kind, insightful, and became an invaluable guide to my new life with sight loss. When I confided in her about the anxiety that had begun to cloud my days and make even sitting in class feel unbearable, she gently suggested I try counseling. I wasn't sure I was ready, but I told her I'd consider it.

Somehow, I made it through. I passed both classes and managed to sprinkle in a few social moments with my fraternity. Heading home for the break felt like crossing a finish line. And this time, I wasn't limping across; I walked across under my own power. It was far from perfect, but it was progress. I'd earned something that semester: the belief that I might actually be able to do this. Still, I worried. If two classes felt like a marathon, how would I ever handle more? Was I going to be in college forever?

Christmas break gave me a chance to regroup. I had time to reflect—on what worked, what didn't, and how to tweak the formula. I wasn't optimized yet, but I was getting closer. I also visited my doctor for a checkup. He'd mentioned the possibility of anxiety medication earlier that year, and now seemed like the time. I didn't love the idea, but I hated the creeping feeling that was starting to take over—like something was gaining on me and I couldn't quite outrun it. So I figured I'd try a low dose, just half a pill to start.

When classes resumed in January, I began counseling sessions. Let's just say it wasn't a match. The office was in a weird part of town, and the therapist wasn't exactly what I'd call engaging. She wasn't unkind, just . . . flat. The kind of flat that made you want to keep your emotional boxes sealed tight. I went through the motions, but I never really opened up. Unpacking the heavy stuff? That would have to wait.

February 7 marked one year since my battle with meningitis. It passed quietly. No ceremony, no fanfare. Just me in my room, reflecting on the day my life changed forever. A full year since everything I thought I knew about myself and my future was upended. I needed that moment; I needed the stillness, the solitude, the space to remember how far I'd come. Maybe counseling wasn't working, but sitting with the weight of it on my own, I realized I was capable of carrying it. It wasn't easy, but I'd made it this far. So the next day, I folded it back up, packed it away, and got back to work.

Academically, things improved. I was taking three classes and had managed to align my schedule with friends. Kevin and Brad were in the business school with me, and having them in class made a big difference. They didn't just offer rides and moral support; they shared notes, helped me study, and kept me looped in. With all the office hours I logged, professors sometimes gave me test tips that I passed along to my friends. Another advantage of a disadvantage.

Even better, Kevin's girlfriend, Mindy, who was brilliant, had already taken most of the classes I was in. Through the Texas Commission for the Blind, I could pay her to tutor me. She was a lifesaver in stats and accounting. I probably wouldn't have passed without her. She might've helped anyway, but this setup made things easier for both of us.

Socially, things loosened up too. I'd stopped using a catheter entirely, which gave me a lot more freedom. My new system of hold and push was certainly not medically recommended but highly effective for me. By the end of the semester, my bladder must have doubled in size. If there'd been a contest for that, I'd have medaled in the bladder Olympics. Gold, obviously.

The semester ran more smoothly. I started feeling better about school, about my routines, about myself. In pretty short order, I stopped going to counseling and quit taking the medication—I was convinced it was a sugar pill anyway. Everything seemed to be trending in the right direction. I didn't need a perfect plan; I just needed proof I could move forward. And that spring, I started to believe I could.

A FLAMING RITE OF PASSAGE

As the semester wound down and my confidence ticked up, a new milestone approached: my twenty-first birthday.

The year before, Mom had thrown me a full-blown birthday bash at home. It was sweet and I was grateful, but the vibe leaned more "Chuck E. Cheese matinee" than "college guy coming into his own." Fast-forward a year and it was time for a different kind of party, one with fire, friends, and a rite of passage that didn't include party hats.

Among my fraternity brothers and friends, turning twenty-one came with certain expectations—mainly, the kind that involved consuming heroic (and often questionable) amounts of alcohol in one night. I'd seen plenty of guys celebrate with style, and others with... less grace. With my situation—limited sight, bladder issues, and a newfound appreciation for not waking up in a hospital bed—I knew I'd need to handle things differently. I wasn't out to prove anything or win the night. I just wanted to mark the milestone in a way that felt right for me. So instead of taking a rain check or bracing for the traditional booze gauntlet, I opted for something more intentional, a controlled burn, if you will.

I decided to head to Austin to celebrate with Chris. The city had a reputation. Sixth Street, in particular, was basically Bourbon Street's Texas cousin, and I was ready to meet it in a way I could own. Chris had turned twenty-one a few months earlier, and he wasn't the type to push rituals. It felt like the right move.

Once again, I found myself boarding a flight, this time from Lubbock to Austin. It was my first solo flight since meningitis, and that alone made it feel like a personal victory lap.

Chris scooped me up at the airport the day before my birthday, but he had to work that evening, so I made plans with MacKenzie. She and I caught an outdoor Cypress Hill concert just outside of town. It was appropriately *insane in the membrane*. By the time we met back up with Chris on Sixth Street, midnight was approaching.

Just in time for my first legal drink.

I'll never forget it: a Flaming Dr Pepper.

The bartender set the scene like a pyromaniac magician, lining up a beer and a shot of amaretto capped with a giant splash of 151 rum. He poured a trail of rum down the bar like it was a runway, then flicked his lighter. WHOOSH—flames raced toward the shot glass in a blaze of glory.

"You ready?" he asked with a maniacal tone. I nodded, mesmerized by the spectacle.

He dropped the flaming shot into the beer. The fire vanished in a fizz, and I threw it back. It tasted just like Dr Pepper but with a whole lot more kick. If last year's birthday had the innocence of juice boxes and streamers, this one was full-grown Texas chaos with a fiery twist. It was part initiation, part chemistry experiment, and wholly unforgettable.

After MacKenzie headed home, Chris and I kept the night rolling. We bar-hopped our way down Sixth Street, soaking in the sights, sounds, and sticky floors of Austin nightlife. I had enough drinks to satisfy tradition—and then some—but I was still upright, coherent, and shockingly proud of my bladder control.

Until I wasn't.

As we stood to leave our final bar, I felt it: a brief, unmistakable warm trickle down my leg. Panic hit. I grabbed Chris's arm and whispered, "Dude, I just... " as I gestured downward.

Without missing a beat, he told me to sit back down. Then, in a stroke of late-night genius, he grabbed a half-full beer and dumped it down the front of my shirt.

Crisis averted. What could've been humiliating became a mythical drinking story. That's not just quick thinking; that's brotherhood. In that moment, Chris didn't hesitate. He didn't flinch. He just had my back, like he always did.

Back at Chris's place, I bolted to the bathroom for another Austin Powers–style evacuation. I pushed and pushed and pushed . . . and pushed some more. It felt like I was holding every drop of liquid from the past week. The truth was clear: I'd exceeded the limit. Denial might get me through the night, but it always came with a cost.

That night wasn't just a party. It was a wake-up call. If I wanted anything close to a "normal" life, I had to play within my new limitations.

Still, no regrets.

Austin was absolutely the right call. It was wild, ridiculous, and weirdly empowering. I'd crossed another threshold. Not just into legal adulthood, but into a version of myself that was learning, with every high and every hiccup, how to live in a way that worked for me.

WEST OF RECOVERY

With summer just ahead, everything felt a little clearer, like I'd leveled up. Sure, I'd gotten a birthday wake-up call from my bladder, but I'd also pulled off a wild weekend, navigated a solo flight, and proven to myself that I could still claim milestones without bending to expectation. That spring semester was now in the books, and with a few more credits under my belt, I wasn't just surviving college; I was actually gaining momentum.

I decided to stay in Lubbock over the summer to keep that forward motion alive. It helped that Brad, my younger brother, had just graduated from high school and was heading to Tech for summer school too. He was living on campus while I scrambled to find a new place after another round of the roommate shuffle. Kevin had graduated and returned to Dallas, and Brad Smith only had one semester left and needed a shorter lease. Lucky for me, I reconnected with a high school friend who needed a summer roommate. It was a bit of a walk to campus, but it worked, and with Brad in town, I had good company.

Being away from our parents gave Brad and me a new kind of brotherhood. We weren't just siblings anymore; we were adults, wingmen, co-conspirators. I introduced him to the beats of college life, and we both started to learn what made the other tick. We bonded that summer in a way we hadn't before, and we both came out of it with solid grades and a new appreciation for each other. It was a very meaningful success.

The bonus win, though? I got a cell phone. I wanted the flexibility, the freedom, the ability to make last-minute changes without relying on a landline or someone else's schedule. Aunt Judy swooped in to help make it happen financially, and just like that, I was the proud owner of a Nokia 6110. That little phone was my lifeline to autonomy. I could call friends, set up rides, and make plans on the fly, and I felt like I was finally keeping pace with the world around me.

With the fall semester just around the corner, two more high school friends, RJ and Joey, were also searching for a place to call home. We found a house to rent right across the street from campus, and it was exactly what I needed. Walking distance to class, stores, bars, and restaurants? Check. Roommates who were already part of my social circle? Check. My confidence? Growing by the day.

With my cell phone in hand and campus at my doorstep, I could finally imagine what it might feel like to finish college by my own design. It wasn't just about catching up anymore. It was about building something.

Around this time, another thought had been creeping back into my mind—Jenn. For months, I'd felt this low hum of regret, wondering if I'd made a mistake by ending things. Then one night, while out with friends at a long, crowded table, someone leaned in and casually whispered, "Hey, Jenn is down at the other end of the table."

Of course I hadn't seen her, but apparently she was there. It was one of those dimly lit bar scenes where the lights were low, the music was loud, and every table was buzzing with overlapping conversations. As fate would have it, Jenn and I were seated at opposite ends of the same table—just close enough to share the same space but far enough that a conversation would take some maneuvering.

As people came and went—grabbing drinks, switching seats, chasing conversations—I gradually worked my way down, moving one seat closer at a time until I found myself right beside her. When I finally made it, I leaned in, close enough to be heard over the noise, and dove right in. I told her everything I'd been holding onto: that I'd made a mistake, that I was overwhelmed and scared back then, that I hadn't known how to be in a relationship when I didn't even know how to be myself. I apologized for the way I ended things, for my words, my delivery, my timing. And I told her I wanted to try again.

Jenn listened quietly. She didn't interrupt. She didn't get up or cut me off. She heard me out. And when I finally stopped talking, she was polite but clear; she was seeing someone else now and had moved on. There wasn't going to be a second chance.

I told her I understood and respected her decision. Before we parted, I added that I hoped she could forgive me for the way I'd acted.

Later, I found out the guy she was dating would become her husband. Some things just aren't meant to be, and this was one of them.

Our new living arrangement was chaotic but perfect. RJ had converted an old refrigerator into a kegerator, which lived on our back porch and was practically a campus landmark by week two. Between the steady flow of fraternity brothers, friends, and random passersby, our place became a revolving door of social energy. You never knew who was going to walk through it, but you could bet someone would soon.

Location-wise, we hit the jackpot. We were just steps away from several stores, bars, and restaurants, which meant I could get almost anywhere I needed to go on foot. For someone who hated relying on others for rides, this was everything. My independence was no longer hypothetical; it was walkable.

With everything so accessible, I hit my stride. School was going well, and socially, I was loosening up. I even started dipping my toes back into dating. I wasn't ready for anything physical, but I didn't always know how to explain that. So I moved slow (sometimes too slow) and more than once found myself playing hard to get against my own will.

One of the bright spots that semester was Heather. She was smart, kind, and sharp as a tack in our business classes. Turned out she'd gone to my high school and graduated a year ahead of me, but our paths had never crossed. She was also close friends with RJ and quickly fit right in with our crew. Amazingly, we were almost on the exact same degree path. We studied together, shared notes, and over time, she became not just a classmate but a real friend. I didn't feel like I had to perform around her. I could just be me.

Our go-to hangout became Cricket's, a bar whose name I always figured was a nod to Buddy Holly's band. Whether it was that or just a Lubbock quirk, it became our Cheers. For me, it was more than a watering hole—it was a logistical bonus. When I needed to run home to handle bathroom duties, I could be back in fifteen minutes, no questions asked. Most people didn't even realize I was gone. They had no idea I was making pit stops for bladder management. By the end of most nights, RJ and I would race home like it was the one-hundred-yard dash. To everyone else, it was hilarious. To me, it was getting home as fast as I could to relieve the pressure.

Life was clicking. I was in a groove academically, socially, even emotionally. But just when I felt most comfortable, life reminded me that comfort doesn't mean invincible.

With new roommates came new energy . . . and new people. Most of them were great. But one weekend night, someone brought along a cousin who clearly hadn't gotten the memo on how to behave like a decent human being.

We had a good crowd hanging out in the front yard, the usual mix of lawn chairs, plastic cups, and laughs drifting into the night. I was leaning back in a chair, relaxed and mid-conversation, when I heard a familiar voice behind me: one of our friends, joining the festivities. I reached out my hand to greet him.

But it wasn't him who took it.

Instead, his cousin, whom we barely knew, grabbed my hand and yanked me back so hard that I lost my balance and tumbled backward, drink flying, landing flat in the grass. Before I could react, I heard him laughing and saying something about my lack of vision being the reason I fell.

Time slowed. I was on the ground, soaked, stunned, and humiliated, my disability the punchline of his joke. I didn't move right away. I couldn't. A few friends rushed over to check on me while others made a beeline for the cousin. They got him out of there fast, making it clear he wouldn't be welcome back.

I stood up, dusted off, and gave the usual *I'm fine* head nod. But I wasn't fine. Not even close.

I made my way inside through the side door and straight into my room. I locked the door, sat on the edge of the bed, and let it all out. I hadn't cried like that since the night with MacKenzie more than a year earlier. This wasn't just about falling or being embarrassed; it was about someone seeing my vulnerability and mocking it. It cut deep.

Heather found me not long after. She knocked gently, and I let her in. She didn't try to fix it. She just sat with me, let me breathe, and reminded me that people like him weren't worth my energy. That moment of support meant more than she probably knew.

The rest of the night blurred into quiet. But the sting of that moment stayed with me, less like a scar and more like a bookmark. A page I didn't choose but one I wouldn't forget. I'd worked hard to build confidence again, to rejoin life with my own blueprint. And while that night shook me, it didn't break me. It reminded me that I could still fall, but I could get back up, too.

RHYTHMS OF THE ROAD

After the emotional highs and lows of that fall semester, life didn't slow down; it just shifted into a different kind of gear. I had a regular crew, a robust class schedule, a house full of energy and convenience, and I was done drifting; I was dancing. Not without setbacks, but with more steady wins than losses. What I called my version of the Texas two-step: two steps forward, one step back, just like Dad and I had talked about. I wasn't winning many style points, but I'd found a rhythm.

And with that rhythm came ideas. Possibly crazy ones. Possibly brilliant. One of them: start a band.

I'd noticed something over the years: guys in bands got attention. A lot of attention. From girls, mostly. But it wasn't just that. They had presence, identity, a built-in reason to stand out. After spending so much time chipping away at my social anxiety and cobbling together some actual confidence, I figured, why not add "mysterious front man" to the résumé? I needed a little extra swagger. Also, yes. I wanted to get girls.

There was just one problem: I didn't play an instrument. At least not one that would help in this department. My saxophone days had ended with seventh-grade band. So I pivoted.

I decided I would learn the guitar. You know—overnight.

Even before I owned one, I pitched the idea to RJ and Zach with complete confidence. "We'll be called the John Grimes Band," Zach proclaimed. He was clearly in, and when RJ nodded without hesitation, that sealed it. Just like that, it was official: we were a band. No instruments, no rehearsal, but plenty of attitude.

Zach, ever the overachiever, took it seriously—so seriously he had shirts made. Shirts! With our band name. We hadn't played a note, but we were already doing street-team marketing. We wore them around campus with completely unearned pride, handing them out to friends like we'd just wrapped a summer tour.

We did eventually get guitars, though "play" might be too generous a word for what we did with them. Most of the time, we sat on the front porch drinking beer and strumming vaguely in time with each other, more sound therapy than music. But we embraced the spirit of The Front Porch Boys, a legendary band from College Station that included bona fide musicians Robert Earl Keen Jr. and Lyle Lovett. As far as anyone walking by knew, we were the second coming. And we encouraged the myth.

We never played a show. We barely rehearsed. But somehow, it felt real. It gave me a sense of identity I hadn't had in a while, something that was mine, even if it only existed in our heads (and on those amazing shirts). The John Grimes Band may have been more myth than reality, but it gave me one more thing to feel good about.

Off the porch and into the real world, I was learning a different kind of rhythm—the daily one, the independent one, the kind that required actual choreography. Because when you live across from campus but can't drive, the only way forward is on foot. And for me, that meant crossing University Boulevard.

There was a safer two-block detour, the main campus entrance, with a grand pedestrian crosswalk, blinking signals, and friendly chirps for the visually impaired. But it was the opposite direction from where I needed to go. So I crossed at a regular intersection. No pedestrian signals, no chirps, just raw traffic lights and instinct.

Over time, I developed a system. I memorized the light cycle by sound. The louder the street, the better. Noise was my ally. I tuned in early, often from half a block away, tracking the patterns of engines, the shifting hum of acceleration and idle, the cadence of a city in motion. If the light was about to flip in my favor, I picked up the pace. If not, I slowed down just enough to hit the green.

I would joke, "I can see just enough to be dangerous," and nowhere was that more true than crossing that intersection. I'd breeze through confidently, sometimes even while talking on my cell phone. "If you hear screeching tires followed by a thud," I'd tell whoever was on the line, "just call 911—I've been hit."

The real risk came during quiet stretches, when sound cues disappeared. In those moments, I was guessing. No cars meant no data, and I had to decide: wait or go? And when the jaywalking temptation won out, I moved like a deer in headlights—fast, twitchy, praying.

But I always made it across. And every safe crossing reinforced the same message: I could do this. No help. No ride. Just me, my instincts, and the sounds of the road.

Dodging traffic was its own sport, but it couldn't compete with tailgates and touchdown Saturdays.

In Texas, football is more than a game. It's sacred. And Texas Tech's program held its own. I'd always loved the energy: the student section, the flying tortillas, the red-and-black waves of school spirit.

But after meningitis, the experience changed. I was disconnected from the action. The bleachers felt steeper. The crowd felt louder. And the game, visually, was gone.

I tried going, but it felt like I was faking it. I quickly got bored because I couldn't follow the plays, couldn't track the ball. Relying on the stadium announcer's delayed commentary didn't help. So I stopped going. Watching at bars wasn't much better: tiny TVs with no sound turned it all into a blur. Most of the time, we watched from home, where at least I had play-by-play commentary and a nearby bathroom.

The night we upset our undefeated rival, top-ranked Texas A&M, was unforgettable. From home we could hear the approaching roar and stepped outside just in time to catch students carrying the goalposts down University Boulevard like a championship parade. What a night.

While football may have lost some magic, baseball was different.

Baseball had been my sport growing up. I loved its slower pace, the in-between moments, the way you could talk during the game, all the stats and the excitement of the crack of the bat. So when spring rolled around, I asked RJ and Joey if they wanted to catch a game. Tech's baseball stadium was walkable, the games were free with our IDs, and it felt like a good fit.

Our first game we sat in the student section way out in left field. I couldn't see a thing, but at least I felt safe from foul balls. Still, I wanted to be closer to the action. That's when RJ spotted a few open seats—front row, right between home plate and the visitors' dugout. Best of all, they were protected by a giant net, so I'd still be safe. It seemed too good to be true, and by the third inning, we kept waiting for someone to show up and claim them. But no one did.

"Let's make our move," I said, already halfway to standing. "Worst case, someone shows up and I'll just say I'm blind and thought these were mine. What are they gonna do, argue with that?"

They never did. We returned for the next game. And the next. And the next. Sooner or later, they became our seats. We got to know the regulars, including a squad of hecklers who could roast a visiting team like it was their full-time job.

To take it up a notch, I brought my Walkman and listened to the live radio feed through one earbud. It gave me the play-by-play I couldn't see and let me narrate to my friends like a semi-legit color commentator. Baseball on the radio is its own kind of magic. The announcers are vividly descriptive because they have to be. No one listening can see the action, so every crack of the bat, every slide into second, gets painted with words. Suddenly, I wasn't just spectating; I was contributing. I was, once again, connected to the game.

I made it to almost every home game that season, and we had a crew of six regulars by the end. Those afternoons at the ballpark reminded me that I hadn't lost everything. Even in a world where so much had changed, I could still find my way back to the things I loved.

MILLENNIUM
CLARITY

B y the time the new year showed up, I was cruising in class, in social circles, and technically in a band, though no one expected an album. Life still threw in the occasional speed bump, but I felt like I was riding the wave instead of paddling against it. Fall gave me rhythm. Winter gave me lift.

And right on cue, the rest of the world was gearing up for disaster.

Over the past year, Y2K had been looming, and by Christmas break, it reached a fever pitch. It was all anyone could talk about. The "Millennium Bug" sounded downright apocalyptic: computers crashing, planes falling from the sky, bank accounts disappearing into the ether, all because programmers from the '60s and '70s had saved space by using two-digit years. Come January 1, 2000, the fear was that systems might think it was 1900 and trigger a digital meltdown.

Spoiler alert: it didn't. The bug was squashed, and the world rang in the new millennium with no catastrophes. The most exciting part for me? Being right in the center of a massive crowd in downtown Dallas, everyone partying Prince-style because it literally was the end of 1999, suddenly falling silent and holding their collective breath at midnight, only to exhale when utterly nothing happened. It was the perfect metaphor for life: the buildup is almost always scarier than the actual event.

With the Y2K scare behind us, the year 2000 brought some big strides for me. I started feeling the itch to wrap up my college life. Many of the friends I'd come to school with were now graduating and moving on. Sure, I was still enjoying the lifestyle, but I couldn't shake the feeling that I was approaching my expiration date on campus. If I wasn't careful, I'd age out. So I turned my focus to getting serious. It was time to ratchet up my schedule. By then, I had systems in place to tackle my schoolwork efficiently, and I was excelling in class while enjoying a rebounding social life, thanks in no small part to the John Grimes Band.

One of the highlights of the year was taking a couple of classes with Brad. It was great to share that experience with him, and everything seemed to be clicking on all cylinders. Our brotherly bond deepened in those classrooms; we studied together, joked our way through lectures, and knocked out some electives that made the load a little lighter for us both.

I also found myself involved in something new and exciting. Texas Tech had a student-run newspaper, which at the time was called the University Daily. Before losing my sight, I would check it out when I was on campus, but now, accessing it wasn't so simple. One day, while chatting with Margaret in the library, we were discussing a controversial article that had recently appeared in the UD. Neither of us had read it because the paper was only available in print. That's when it hit me: this is the year 2000. Why wasn't the UD online?

My rudimentary HTML skills could make that happen. I went to the journalism school to inquire, and as it turned out, they were just beginning the process of taking the paper digital. They had set up a very basic online presence on the campus intranet and asked me to help by uploading the articles. So that's what I did. I didn't receive any metrics on the online readership, but I know Margaret and I both appreciated being able to access the paper. It was my first foray into accessibility, and it felt good to contribute to something that benefited not just me but others as well.

I even struck up a relationship with LeeAnn, which lasted a few months. She happened to be a sorority sister of Jenn—a Kappa Delta—which certainly had the potential for salacious intrigue. Coincidentally, my roommate Joey met and started dating a KD sister. This meant that she and a few of her close sisters, including LeeAnn, were often hanging out at our place. Like most sororities, the KD house was big and had its own internal cliques. While Jenn and LeeAnn were friendly, they ran in different circles. I don't think either of us meant anything nefarious, but the optics were . . . complicated. That said, Jenn and I had moved on, and this just kind of happened.

Our relationship was mostly platonic but meaningful. LeeAnn was a great companion, and I opened up to her about my meningitis experience, vision loss, and bladder challenges. I kept the details vague, but to her credit, she was completely unfazed. We had a great time together, but unfortunately, the relationship came to an end when she graduated and moved on.

Despite all the progress I was making, I still struggled to find a good way to describe my usable vision to people. The term "legally blind" didn't help much. It sounded official but didn't match what most people saw when they looked at me. It wasn't easy to explain, but I wanted a shorthand that captured the gray zone I lived in, where I could see some things but missed a lot of others. In the end, I landed on Ambiguously Blind. It didn't exactly clarify anything, but that was kind of the point. It lived in the same blurry middle space I did. And at the very least, it made people stop, squint, and go, "Wait . . . what?"

The ambiguity led to some funny and awkward moments, too. At LeeAnn's graduation, I sat with her sister and family during the ceremony and joined them for lunch afterward. On the ride over, I found myself alone in the truck with her father, a rancher from West Texas. It likely wasn't a coincidence that we ended up together for that ride. He was probably trying to size me up as his daughter's boyfriend. He seemed like a great guy, but based on one of his questions, he hadn't gotten the full download on me. As we chatted, he asked, "What kind of car do you drive?" With his cowboy hat, big truck, and charming West Texas drawl, I quickly realized I wasn't going to have an answer that impressed him. So I decided to just go for it.

"I actually don't drive," I said. "I had a run-in with bacterial meningitis about two years ago that left me mostly blind. It's hard to explain, but I can see just enough to be dangerous." I chuckled, trying to lighten the mood. Then, just to keep the conversation moving, I added, "But when I did drive, it was a Honda Accord." Neither answer seemed to resonate much with him, and the conversation fizzled. By the time we reached the restaurant—a fittingly named place called Cattle Baron—I just chalked it up as a draw. LeeAnn asked how the ride went; I smiled and said, "Well, your dad and I probably won't be starting a carpool anytime soon."

Another memorable moment was when Heather and I were sitting in a packed marketing lecture and our professor, someone I'd taken multiple classes with and who knew me well, was talking about naming conventions for cologne. He put a slide on the screen with several ridiculous options and called on me. "John, if you were the marketing director, which one would you choose?" he asked. I froze. He knew I couldn't see the screen, right? My stammering must've jogged his memory, and thankfully, Heather jumped in with an answer. He apologized profusely after class for embarrassing me, but honestly, I was more surprised than upset. It was a reminder that even people who knew me well often didn't realize just how little I could see.

With another semester behind me and more friends moving on, my focus intensified. Joey fell in love and moved out to live closer to his girlfriend, leaving a vacancy in the house. My brother Brad, fresh off his first-year dorm experience, was more than happy to move in with RJ and me. Brad had already spent a lot of time at our place, so the transition was seamless.

In a surprise twist, Chris relocated from Austin to attend Texas Tech. He felt like he needed a fresh start and a change of scenery to reignite his college journey, and Lubbock offered exactly that. While he didn't live with us, he found a place nearby and fit right into our social circle. It was great having him back in the mix, and we picked up right where we'd left off. He even joined the band and made many of those uncoordinated, late-night dashes back from Cricket's.

As I reflected on the year, it struck me how far things had come. What started with the madness and uncertainty of Y2K had ended on a high note, with everything falling into place. My friends, my studies, my social life . . . it all seemed to be clicking. The year 2000 may have entered with a collective holding of breath, but for me, it ended with a sense of excitement and optimism for the future.

ON AIR AND ALMOST OUT

With the turn of the calendar once again, graduation was finally within reach, and for the first time, it started to feel real. In the past twelve months, I had taken thirty-six hours' worth of class credits, the most I'd ever tackled in a year. It was a heavy lift, but somehow, I kept pace. I'd successfully adapted to a new learning style along the way, transforming from a traditional student into an almost entirely auditory one. I knocked out several critical courses and was inching closer to my goal.

One unexpected highlight came from spending so much time in the journalism building, thanks to my work helping to put the UD online. Every day, I passed by KTXT, the campus radio station, and ultimately, the pull was too strong to resist. I decided to go for it.

A few DJ spots opened up that spring, and I jumped at the chance. The station wasn't exactly designed with accessibility in mind. That's when Brad stepped in. Together, we were given the highly coveted

6:00 to 8:00 a.m. midweek slot and launched what we affectionately called the *Wednesday Hump Day Spectacular.*

Yes, it was early, but it was spectacular in its own way. Brad handled most of the logistics: queuing up CDs, finding songs, and loading tracks. I brought the on-air personality, complete with over-the-top fake voices inspired by a Dallas sports radio station I loved. It was an incredible experience, and while Brad had fun, he was mostly there to support me.

We were only allowed to break from the preprogrammed playlist once an hour, so we chose our two must-play tracks with great care. Our debut track? "Shimmer" by Fuel. A great song, and a great memory. That opening riff hit like a spark, and for a few minutes, we weren't just playing music, we were living it. Loud, raw, and real. Because, yeah, all that shimmers might fade, but we sure made it shine while it lasted.

Talking into that mic, knowing my voice was out there for anyone to hear, was exhilarating. It brought me back to those early uncertain days after returning to school, sitting in my bedroom, tuning in to that same station, wondering what came next. Now, there I was, the one behind the mic, sharing some interesting sounds of my own and hopefully connecting with someone like me on the other end.

That semester, I also corrected one of my earlier academic missteps, the infamous literature class I had dropped during my first semester back. This time, I was ready. Audiobooks had become more available, and for the ones that weren't, Chris and RJ helped out. Both of them needed the same class, so we took it together. But the real highlight turned out to be the professor herself. She was young by professor standards, hailed from Ohio, had a Spanish name, and spoke with a mysterious British accent. Her pronunciation of words like *aluminum* and *advertisement* had us stifling laughter on more than one occasion. Clearly, she took her role as a British literature professor very seriously.

In a genius scheduling move, Chris, RJ, and I also signed up for an intro guitar class for a single elective credit. It was perfect: fun, low-pressure, and maybe even a chance to expand the John Grimes Band's nonexistent repertoire. Each week, we brought in popular songs we wanted to learn, and our instructor, a grad student, total guitar savant and pretty cool guy, did his best to teach us the chords and techniques. While none of us became rock stars, we definitely got better and had an absolute blast along the way.

Getting to that finish line involved more than just showing up to class; it meant adapting every part of the academic experience, including test-taking.

Instead of heading to the regular classroom on exam days, I went to a centralized testing center designed to accommodate all kinds of learning differences. Normally, my professors would send the paper test ahead of time, sealed in an envelope. Once I got there, someone would read it aloud, and I'd dictate my answers to be written down. After that, it went right back in another sealed envelope. Pretty straightforward. At least in theory.

Over the years, I got very comfortable with the process and even worked with a few orators who understood my style almost intuitively. One standout orator had a way of reading that synced perfectly with how I processed information. She repeated things before I even asked, adjusted on the fly, and made the whole experience feel seamless.

Of course, occasionally, there were hiccups. One particularly memorable hiccup happened during a British literature exam.

I arrived at the testing center on time, but my test wasn't there. After some searching, the staff called the professor, who sheepishly admitted she'd forgotten to send it over. So off I went across campus to retrieve it myself.

She handed me a stack of papers with a theatrical sigh, saying, "I'm so sorry. I forgot to send your bloody test to the center," sprinkling in yet another one of her oddly random British terms. I couldn't help but chuckle at her commitment to the role and began the walk back.

Just a few steps outside the building, I heard familiar voices. Chris and RJ had just finished their tests. As we walked across campus together, they naturally started reading the questions aloud, and before long, we were talking through answers.

Now, is this cheating? Probably. But I prefer to think of it as another example of taking advantage of a disadvantage. I was well prepared for the test anyway, and it wasn't exactly a make-or-break moment in my academic career. Sometimes, life hands you an unexpected assist. And I wasn't about to turn it down.

By the time summer rolled around, I had just one class left between me and graduation. It felt surreal. After all the challenges, the setbacks, and the triumphs, it was finally happening. But as the reality of the end sank in, I found myself wanting to savor the college lifestyle just a little more.

The campus radio station had more openings over the summer, and this time RJ wanted in on the action. We knew that if we wanted total control over the playlist, we'd have to create a specialty show with a clear theme. So we got to work. After kicking around a few ideas, we landed on one that felt like a perfect blend of creativity and loophole exploitation.

Inspired by Oingo Boingo's "Dead Man's Party" from the Rodney Dangerfield movie *Back to School*, we pitched a show called—you guessed it—*Dead Man's Party*. (For the uninitiated: *Back to School* is a comedy about an older man enrolling in college to support his son, complete with a wild '80s soundtrack.) Our show's premise was simple but brilliant: every song we played had to have appeared in a movie. And let's be honest, at some point, every song has shown up in a movie, right?

So each week, with a little help from the internet, we created fresh playlists that technically fit the theme, sometimes obviously, sometimes questionably. The result? A specialty show that gave us complete creative freedom and a whole lot of fun.

The station loved it, and we landed an evening weeknight slot, right before the psychedelic show hosted by guys who looked like they'd taken a wrong turn at Woodstock and decided to ride it out behind a microphone.

The show developed a bit of a cult following. Friends and random listeners would call in, requesting songs and trying to challenge us on whether our picks actually appeared in a movie. It became a full-on game. Some were easy, others required a bit of explanation, and every now and then we had to cite our movie source to prove a track passed the test. The back-and-forth with our audience was electric.

Dead Man's Party wasn't just a show; it was a celebration. And for me, it was the perfect way to close out the summer and, with it, a life-changing college experience.

And then came the final test.

I remember the moment clearly. I'd just finished my last exam, a business management course, and walked across campus with a head full of disbelief. Was that it? Had I really done it?

I made my way to the student union and found the bench where Brad Smith and I had met on that tumultuous first day back. I let the wide-open, blue West Texas sky settle over me like a punctuation mark.

Can this really be the end? Did I actually finish everything? Am I really going to graduate?

I thought about the journey that brought me here, about how much I had changed. I came into college a much different person than the one leaving it. But then again, isn't that what college is supposed to do?

My path was anything but typical. I had finished in just over five years what most do in four, but what should have happened certainly didn't. I should be proud of this, I reminded myself.

After a few minutes of reflection, I pulled out my phone and called my dad.

"Dad," I said, smiling as I spoke the words, "it's all over. I'm done with college."

The pride in his voice made it feel official.

THE WALK

Graduation day marked almost exactly five years since I first stepped foot on Texas Tech's campus. It felt surreal to be donning a cap and gown, preparing to walk across that stage. My time at Tech had been transformative in ways I never could have anticipated, shaped by challenges I didn't choose but had to face head-on. I was no longer just a college student; I was a survivor and a graduate, someone who had found a way to move forward.

As I waited for my name to be called, memories from the past five years swirled. I went back to the beginning—moving into the dorm with Ryan as a freshman, wide-eyed and excited to be on my own. That first year was the start of an incredible adventure. The momentum continued as I moved into an apartment and began carving out a life that felt like it was unfolding the way it was supposed to. There was a cadence to it all, a sense that I was on the right track.

Then, meningitis rudely interrupted life, and everything changed.

The excitement gave way to uncertainty, and I found myself grappling with questions I hadn't been prepared for.

Answers came slowly, revealed through every step I took, sometimes tentative, sometimes fueled by stubborn determination. The journey wasn't linear. It moved like a two-step: one part rhythm, one part misstep, full of trial and error, made possible by people willing to help me find my way.

My family sat in the audience, their unwavering support reflected in proud smiles. My parents were there, as was my brother Brad, who had become not just family but a steadfast ally through every phase. My four grandparents and Judy and Wilbur were there too, beaming with love. And then there were the Finnells, divinely placed in our lives when we needed guidance most. They were our shepherds through the storm, steadying us when everything else felt uncertain. Their presence that day felt like more than support; it felt like grace. So many friends filled the seats as well, each one a reminder that I didn't get here alone. It truly had taken a village.

When my name was finally announced, I crossed the stage, taking careful but confident steps to receive my diploma. The applause was deafening—or at least it felt that way to me. Walking across that stage wasn't just about completing a degree. It was a declaration: I had done it. Against many odds, I took the detour life threw at me and still made it to the finish line.

Afterward, at my favorite restaurant, Stella's, there were photos, stories, and laughter with everyone. My friends joined in, many of them expressing disbelief. "We had to see it to believe it, man!" Kevin joked. And he wasn't wrong. The road had been anything but smooth, yet there I was, diploma in hand, reflecting on the whirlwind that brought me to this moment.

Chris, sitting right next to me—just like he had since the eighth grade—was essential to the journey. From his visit to my ICU room, when my vitals jumped at the sound of his voice and hope slipped into a terrifying unknown, to the countless moments of laughter, late-night honesty, and brotherly backup, including my birthday adventure on 6th Street, he was there when it counted. And one presence loomed especially large: Brad Smith, who had shown up at my apartment that fateful day. His visit wasn't just timely; it was divine. Without it, my story would have ended right there, alone, face-down on the floor of that bedroom. Everything that followed—this stage, this ceremony, this future—was possible because of that intervention. Standing on the cusp of what was next, I couldn't help but marvel at how far I'd come from that moment.

Mindy and Heather crossed my mind—both brilliant, both patient, both integral in helping me adapt to new study methods. Their dedication played a crucial role in my academic success and reminded me of the importance of having the right people in your corner.

Jenn's memory surfaced as well. Although things hadn't ended well between us and we had both moved on, I remained grateful for what she did for me during some of my darkest days. Her presence during my illness and recovery meant more than I could express, even if I hadn't always shown it. While our paths had diverged, I respected what we had shared and carried that gratitude with me. I hoped I could express it someday and mend what I still perceived to be a broken fence.

Each challenge—adapting to a new learning style, relying on sound to move through a bustling campus and cross hectic intersections, finding new ways to connect socially—shaped the person I was becoming. I had been the "lost ball in tall weeds," unsure how to navigate this new world. Yet here I was. Through persistence, I found myself quite literally in the dark. I could see just enough to be dangerous, but what I lacked in clinical acuity sharpened into something quietly commanding, clear enough to take on life with resilience, humor, and determination.

I took a deep breath, letting the moment sink in. I had graduated. Not everyone in my freshman class could say the same. I remembered the obligatory line at orientation: "Look to your right, look to your left. One of you won't be here in two years." That almost applied to me. Meningitis had nearly taken me out, but here I was, proving that even the steepest obstacles could be overcome.

Surrounded by loved ones and friends, I felt that spark of optimism again—and the stubborn conviction that possibility is always a possibility. Meningitis forced me to navigate the world in a new way, and through that process, I discovered a sense of identity I hadn't known before. This wasn't just a chapter closing; it was a whole new story beginning.

I boarded a flight back to Dallas, for good this time. I couldn't help but wonder: what will my future bring? What's in store for me? The truth is, the future of my education would go far beyond college or anything academic. At nineteen years old, I didn't understand what life could be. Now, with the experience of this journey, I knew I was becoming something I could never have dreamed of, not even in a coma.

—SECTION VI—
My So-Called Adult Life

HELLO, REAL WORLD

The boxes were stacked neatly in the corner of my old upstairs bedroom, a mix of college relics and remnants from the life I thought I'd outgrown. Moving back home felt both familiar and foreign. The furniture was the same, and the sheets on the bed carried the nostalgic April Fresh fabric softener scent my mom always used in the laundry. Everything else, though, had changed; or maybe it was just me. Brad wasn't there; he was still doing the college thing, and for the first time ever, the house felt quiet, like an echo of itself.

It was strange to think about how far I'd come, especially when I thought back to the summer of 1998. It had only been three years since I'd been in this same house, recovering from meningitis, working to piece together the fragments of my life. Now I was a college graduate, standing at another crossroads. I'd proven to myself and everyone else that I could adapt, persevere, and finish what I started, but here I was, right back under my parents' roof.

Being back in my old bedroom brought up memories of every version of myself that had lived there before. The middle school me, obsessed with collecting sports cards and talking on the phone with friends. The high school me, jamming out to music, chasing girls, and dreaming of freedom and independence. The college me, excited to explore a bigger world. And perhaps most defining, the meningitis recovery me. Now I was the "adult me," whatever that meant. It felt more like a question than a statement. Was I really an adult if I was back living with my parents?

For the time being, it was okay. I knew I needed a soft landing before diving into the uncertainty ahead. Most of my friends had already graduated and moved into the real world. I'd heard about their jobs, their moves to new cities, their engagements, and their promotions. I was happy for them, but it was hard not to feel like I was still playing catch-up. I had no clear answers about what came next, but one thing was certain: staying here too long wasn't an option. I was itching for independence again, but I also recognized the practicalities of regrouping before taking my next steps.

Of course, Mom convened a graduation party. It was a well-attended affair. Friends and neighbors came over to congratulate me, offering warm handshakes and the inevitable question, "What's next, John?" I smiled, deflecting with vague answers like, "Taking it one step at a time." Truthfully, I didn't know. It wasn't that I lacked ambition; I just hadn't figured out where to channel it yet.

I stayed busy where I could. I was still doing web design, a side gig that had carried me through college and gave me a sense of purpose. My HTML skills had come a long way since those early days in the College Park neighborhood of GeoCities, and I'd continued to refine my flagship project, johnbgrimes.com, ever since. I was also doing occasional work for small businesses: tweaking layouts, updating pages, or helping them create a web presence from scratch. It wasn't enough to build a career on, but it kept me connected to the digital world where I felt most competent. Outside the digital world, I spent time on the road with my dad visiting insurance agencies across Texas.

One trip stood out. A drive to Houston to visit Warren, one of my dad's colleagues. I had met him earlier that summer at a convention, where my dad introduced us. Warren and my dad had known each other for years, and we'd had a brief but engaging conversation during that initial meeting. Apparently, I'd made a good impression, because when we met this time, Warren didn't beat around the bush. He asked me directly to come work for him.

Warren was building something incredible, a dynamic, fast-growing operation with a clear vision and huge potential. I admired his confidence, his business savvy, and his belief in me. He explained how I could be a part of his growing empire and even floated the idea of my heading back to Lubbock to open a branch office.

I really liked Warren and was in awe of what he was building, but I wasn't convinced insurance was what I wanted to do. My dad had carved out a successful career on the corporate side of the industry, and Warren was one of the company's brightest agency stars. But something about the whole setup felt like I was trying on someone else's suit: sharp, well-tailored, but not quite mine. And then there was Lubbock. As much as I'd grown during my time there, I had no desire to return. That chapter felt closed.

Still, the encounter stayed with me, a reminder that people saw potential in me, even when I wasn't sure where to direct it myself.

And then, just as I was getting used to my quiet postgrad rhythm, the world changed.

On the morning of September 11, 2001, I was jolted awake by a call from Mom. She rarely called that early, and I answered groggily, unsure what to expect. Her voice carried a mix of urgency and confusion.

"Hey, turn on the TV. Something's happening in New York City," she said from school.

I rubbed my eyes, stumbled out of bed, and flipped on the TV, just in time to see the second tower get hit. Smoke, fire, chaos. I tried to describe the scene to Mom, but I could barely process what I was seeing myself.

I stayed glued to the screen for hours, watching the same haunting footage play on repeat. Hysteria broke loose on live TV. Reports came in nonstop. The towers collapsed. Another plane went down in Pennsylvania. The Pentagon was hit. The news anchors seemed as lost as the rest of us, scrambling to piece it all together. My brain couldn't process it fast enough. Were we under attack? Was this a war?

It had been exactly one month since I walked across the stage to receive my college diploma. That celebration suddenly felt unbelievably distant.

At some point, Dad called from Austin. "Everything's shut down here. I'm driving home now," he said. His calm voice helped steady me, but the unease lingered. It felt like the ground had shifted beneath us. The skies went quiet. Businesses closed. It felt like the country was unplugged and no one knew when to plug it back in.

As the days passed, we learned more, but understanding didn't make it easier. It was a strange, heavy time, the kind that divides your life into a before and an after.

I couldn't help but reflect on my own "before and after." I knew what it felt like to have your world flip in a day.

I was lucky; I wasn't working yet or traveling much, so my life wasn't directly disrupted. But the collective grief, the fear in the air, and the eerie silence in the skies all left their mark.

As the world slowly steadied, my thoughts returned to the more personal unknown: what was I going to do when I grew up?

I'd had a lot of those conversations with Dad. His long and respected run in the insurance industry made it seem like the obvious next step for me. But I wasn't sold. A career in insurance didn't really appeal to me, plus it required licensing, and licensing meant more tests—and I didn't want to take any more tests. I wanted something of my own. Something that felt like me.

I felt the itch for entrepreneurship, but I didn't have a clear calling yet. So I kept circling the question, trying to find a direction. Nights at the bar with old friends often turned into brainstorming sessions, half serious, half beer-fueled nonsense. Open a bar? Start a tech company? Launch a blog? One idea that stuck was writing a book about my meningitis experience. My friends even had a working title: *The Life and Times of Johnny Grimes*. Sure to be a bestseller. And a blockbuster movie, of course.

But the timing wasn't right for my book. My story wasn't close to complete or ready to share with the world. I didn't realize it at the time, but there were so many new people, experiences, and things that would shape it into something more meaningful. I tried to write, but the words wouldn't come. I'd sit at my computer, staring at a blinking cursor or a sea of rambling sentences that didn't even make sense to me. It was maddening, like trying to tune a radio that only played static.

In quieter moments, I reflected on the uncertainty ahead. College had provided structure—a clear path from start to finish—but now that framework was gone. The independence it gave me felt both empowering and daunting. For the first time, there wasn't a syllabus guiding my next move, and I had to figure out what success looked like on my terms. It was exciting, sure, but also a little overwhelming.

And so, I took small steps. I said yes to opportunities that came my way and allowed myself the grace to admit that I didn't have all the answers yet.

I interviewed with Dad's insurance company for a claims role. No spark. I met with a financial services company that intrigued me, but the opportunity was far away and just didn't feel right.

With no clear path emerging, I enrolled in insurance licensing classes—not because I was passionate about it, but because I didn't know what else to do.

Then came the accessibility issue. The exams were computerized but not built with visually impaired people like me in mind. I had to advocate. After weeks of explaining, negotiating, and staying politely persistent, they allowed me to take the test with an orator, just like I had done in college. Apparently, I was the first person who'd ever needed that accommodation. I passed on the first try. A few weeks later, I passed the second one, too. Boom. Done.

Despite the challenges, I felt a dubious sense of accomplishment. I was stepping into something I hadn't been sure I wanted but was going to give it a go. It wasn't the dream. It wasn't writing. It wasn't some bold entrepreneurial leap. But it was a step forward—clunky, maybe, but mine. I just had to keep moving, even if the dance didn't come with music yet.

GOOD ON PAPER

Once I was licensed, I interviewed with a nearby insurance agency. My dad knew the owner well, and I actually knew her, too. Back in high school, thanks to Dad's connections, I'd done some light office work in agency settings, so I was already somewhat familiar with the environment. She had followed my story for years and knew what I'd been through. It felt like a good starting point.

The agency focused on personal insurance—home, auto, life—and from day one, the sales part came naturally. Talking to people, breaking down coverage options, closing deals over the phone—I was good at it. I was immediately recognized as one of the top producers in the office. But being kind of blind and doing paperwork? That was a nightmare.

Paperwork quickly became my nemesis. Computers helped, but not enough; more than half the business was still done in person and on paper. I needed a specialized setup to help level the playing field, and thankfully, my employer bent over backward to help. My desk had a massive brand-new monitor and a dedicated printer and fax machine—accommodations my coworkers envied but that just made the job possible for me.

To anyone with normal eyesight, my screen probably looked like a Monet painting zoomed in on a single pixel. But for me, it was clarity. It let me not just function, but excel. The digital side of the job was second nature.

But once the information left the screen and entered the physical world? Game over.

In-person appointments were the hardest. I was supposed to instill confidence, guide clients through policies that protected their families and financial futures. That's hard to do when you can't always make eye contact or visually walk someone through a document. It's one thing for people not to know what you're pointing at; it's especially weird when you don't know what you're pointing at!

Coworkers often jumped in to help collect signatures and finalize deals. Sometimes even Dad would swing by to close things out. I appreciated the help, but it felt strange—like I was capable but constantly needed backup. I started to wonder, "Why am I even here?" The job was working, technically. But I wasn't happy.

I leaned into what I was good at. My computer skills made me the unofficial IT guy: fixing networks, solving printer issues, and creating better, more accessible documents for the team. Initially, I made them for myself, but soon the whole office adopted them. They were just better. My lack of sight forced people to rethink old systems, and it often led to more efficient ones for everyone.

Still, even with those small victories, the frustrations lingered. I was swimming against a tide of paperwork and awkward client interactions, trying to make a system work that wasn't built for someone like me. I'd proven over and over that I could adapt, but this wasn't the environment where I could thrive.

After a couple of months on the job, I had some money in my pocket and was raring to get out on my own. I quickly found a strategically located apartment halfway between my parents' house and the office. Moving out felt like the next obvious step toward independence.

The apartment was brand new and really nice—my first place entirely on my own. Friends came by often, and I even bought my own washer and dryer, which, as mundane as it sounds, felt like peak adulthood at the time. For the first time in years, I didn't have to tiptoe around roommates or anyone else's schedule. The location was perfect for work, but the area was barely developed—no stores or restaurants within walking distance unless you packed a lunch for the journey. I was independent, technically speaking, but only about halfway. I still needed rides for just about everything, so while the space was great, it wasn't exactly freedom on demand.

Financially, things were going well. I was outperforming expectations, which made the idea of upgrading even more tempting. I daydreamed about a bigger apartment, or maybe even buying a house. There was one for sale within walking distance of the office, and I couldn't stop picturing how convenient that would be. I ran the numbers and even talked to a realtor. But then reality set in.

I didn't love my job. The thought of locking myself into a mortgage while feeling stuck in work I didn't enjoy? That seemed foolish. I didn't have a next step in mind yet, but I knew I wanted something different. The daydreams faded, replaced by something louder: the growing urge to leave.

On rides home with Dad, I vented. The job wasn't hard. I liked the people. But every day felt like a reminder that my disability made everything harder than it needed to be. I had good ideas about improving the business, but no platform to implement them. I felt like I was stuck on a treadmill, working hard and going nowhere.

As my twelve-month lease neared its end, it became clear: it was time to move on. I'd been there about a year and a half, and nothing about the job was trending in the right direction.

So I made the call. With mixed emotions, I turned in my notice. My coworkers were surprised. The owner made a couple of offers to keep me. But I was resolute.

I packed up the apartment, ended the lease, and moved back home—again.

It felt like a setback, like I was rewinding instead of moving forward. But as frustrating as it was, it didn't compare to the frustration of doing a job I wasn't built for. I needed to regroup, to reset. I'd figured out how to survive, but I wanted more than that. I wanted to build a life I could be proud of.

Looking back, it was a false start. But even false starts get you out of the gate. This one gave me clarity. I needed to be more methodical with my decisions and far more patient than I was pretending to be. I needed to live somewhere with actual nearby options, not just future construction sites and wishful thinking. Most of all, I needed to stop contorting myself to fit into places that clearly weren't built for me. If I was going to keep adapting, I had to start by removing obstacles, not collecting them like they were refrigerator magnets.

Suddenly, I had downtime; a lot of it. I had space to rethink my next steps. So I headed back to the digital world—it had always been a lifeline for me—and found Audible.com. It was incredible to discover a treasure trove of books that were not only accessible but easy to find and consume. Best of all, I could access popular titles I'd always been curious about, seemingly without limits. My wish list grew quickly, filled with classics, contemporary favorites, and topics I'd always wanted to explore.

I also discovered something surprising: reading for pleasure was actually enjoyable, far more rewarding than reading because I had to in high school or college. Without the pressure of assignments or exams, I could immerse myself in topics that genuinely interested me. One of the first books I listened to was *When Bad Things Happen to Good People* by Harold S. Kushner. As a Christian, it resonated with me deeply as Rabbi Kushner discussed questions I had been wondering about myself. It encouraged me to explore my faith further. For years, I had been so busy going, going, going that I hadn't had time to think about these bigger questions. Now the stillness allowed me to face them.

Mom, ever perceptive, noticed the wheels spinning in my head. One day, she suggested I consider talking with a counselor. At first, I wasn't sure. I had tried counseling back in Lubbock, but it hadn't been a good fit. Yet the more I thought about it, the more it made sense. I realized I had things to unpack, things I couldn't comfortably share with friends or family, despite having a strong support system. Before long, I decided to give counseling another shot.

Every Friday, I met with my counselor, Cathy, and this time, the experience was transformative. I couldn't wait to get there. It was incredible to finally say things out loud. For years, I had carried so much inside, unsure of where to put it all. The act of speaking openly—of being heard—felt like a release I hadn't known I needed.

One of the most transformative realizations was understanding that I was still navigating the grieving process. Sure, I'd heard about the stages of grief, but I hadn't recognized how they applied to me— or that they weren't linear. Being able to pinpoint certain markers helped me make sense of my emotions and experiences.

The biggest topic we tackled was my sexuality. I had just turned twenty-four, and I felt like I had been castrated for five years, some of the most formative years of my manhood. It wasn't that I thought college was one endless opportunity for intimacy (though that's the stereotype), but I had completely removed myself from anything resembling romantic or physical connection. My fear of embarrassment had kept me from even trying.

In college, my hormones were screaming at me, but I suppressed them like I was constantly tightening a pressure valve. The desire to connect and explore was ever-present, but I didn't know how to channel it in a way that didn't feel overwhelming. Counseling gave me a chance to work through these feelings without judgment. It was the first time I had opened up about that enormous issue, and I felt the pressure being released.

Week after week, we dug into the layers of frustration, embarrassment, and longing that had built up over the years. It turned out to be much easier than I'd feared. I realized there were no quick fixes, but just having someone to talk to helped me begin to piece things together. This time, I was ready to face the hard truths I'd been avoiding.

LEGACY IN MOTION

During the downtime, Dad and I had a lot of discussions about what went right and wrong with my stint in the insurance agency office. We worked through the logistics and brainstormed how things could operate more effectively. These conversations weren't just about problem-solving; they reflected the unique bond we shared. Dad and I had always been close, and this new chapter gave us the opportunity to collaborate as partners. He had a grand plan in mind, one that included going into business with his sons. For him, this wasn't just about building an agency; it was about creating a legacy.

My dad brought a wealth of experience to the table. About twenty years earlier, he had started as an agent and found quick success. That success led to an opportunity to cross over from the agency world into the corporate side of the insurance industry, where he was tasked with hiring and mentoring people to become agents of their own. He excelled in that role, too.

In the early '90s, Dad was asked to relocate to Texas and replicate his success on a larger scale. The move was a great opportunity for our entire family. Our transition from Ohio to Texas brought new experiences, new opportunities, and a fresh start in a rapidly growing area. Now, after decades in the corporate insurance world, Dad was considering retirement. But before he stepped away, he decided to make one final hire—himself. He wanted to bring his insurance career full circle by opening a brand-new agency, and he wanted me and Brad to be part of it.

After several months of planning, the Grimes Group Agency was formed, and we were off and running. The main office was a scratch operation located near my parents' house in the burgeoning city of Frisco. We recruited a couple of team members, designed and built out a brand-new office space, and officially opened our doors in late October 2003. It was an amazing time, and I loved everything about creating, building, and developing business plans, setting goals, and recruiting people to work with us.

From the very start, Dad and I worked incredibly well together. His expertise and industry knowledge paired seamlessly with my ability to modernize our technology and streamline processes. I used my skills to ensure the office was fully operational: networked, connected, and equipped with the latest tools to optimize workflows. The technology was a game changer for everyone, but it was especially helpful for me. It allowed me to overcome some of the challenges I'd faced in my previous role, making my work not only manageable but highly efficient. It was a win-win for the entire team, creating a more productive environment for everyone. Together, Dad and I created an operation that balanced his traditional strengths with my forward-thinking solutions. It was a true partnership, and the results spoke for themselves.

The insurance portion of the business came naturally to me, which made the transition easier. But what I truly enjoyed was being in a leadership role. This time, I no longer felt awkward about delegating tasks. My visual impairment and my old nemesis, paperwork, became much less of an issue. Sure, there were still some challenges, but they were minor and easily solved by assigning the right person to the right task. My role shifted from grappling with personal logistical hurdles to focusing on strategy and growth.

We experienced remarkable success from the start, not just because of Dad's expertise or my technological contributions, but because of how well we complemented each other. Our shared vision and collaborative dynamic laid the foundation for the agency's rapid growth. I was proud to be not just part of the team, but instrumental in making it thrive.

In the summer of 2004, Brad joined us after triumphantly receiving his MBA. He was a natural fit, and his energy, fresh perspective, and enthusiasm took us to the next level. He picked things up quickly, seamlessly fitting into the team and elevating what we had already built. Together, Dad, Brad, and I formed a tremendous trio. Occasionally, we had disagreements, but we never faced an issue we couldn't easily work through. I guess you could say we were pretty weird in that way. For Dad, this was the dream: building something meaningful with his sons. It wasn't just a family business; it was a shared vision that brought out the best in all of us.

Thanksgiving week was shaping up to be a low-key but productive time. Our office was closed for the holiday, and Chris came by to lend a helping hand with a project. We were installing new audio/video equipment in our conference room. Once the job was done, we agreed it was time to unwind. Chris's dad was also free, so the five of us decided to head out and relax together for a bit.

Naturally, we landed on Hooters, a spot Chris and I had frequented since high school. The wings were good, the beer was cold, and the waitresses had a certain charm, if you know what I mean. It was the perfect place for a group of guys to hang out and catch up.

We grabbed a table with a good view of a basketball game and ordered a platter of wings for the group. When the waitress came back to take our drink order, we decided on a pitcher of beer. That's when things took an unexpected turn.

The waitress asked to see our IDs, which seemed a bit odd considering Chris and I were twenty-six and Brad was just shy of his twenty-fourth birthday. Still, we handed them over without a second thought. Chris and Brad's Texas driver's licenses passed inspection quickly. Then she got to mine, a Texas identification card. She looked at it, paused, and asked, "This isn't a driver's license?"

I explained, as I often did, that I didn't have a driver's license because I'm visually impaired and legally unable to drive. Instead, I have a state-issued ID. She nodded and said, "Let me check something," before walking off with my card.

A few minutes later, she returned with my ID and our wings. "I'm sorry," she said, "but we can't serve you alcohol without a valid driver's license."

At first, I thought it was a misunderstanding. Surely, once we explained the situation, they'd reconsider. I appealed to her common sense: I'm twenty-six, well over the legal drinking age of twenty-one, and my lack of a driver's license has nothing to do with my age. Dad chimed in as well, reiterating my point and adding that this was a family gathering of dads and their adult sons, not exactly the kind of group looking to break the law. I also pointed out that I'd been served beer at this very location numerous times before.

She went to check again, and I figured that common sense would prevail. But instead of the waitress, the manager returned, and things only got worse. The manager reiterated the policy: no valid driver's license, no beer. Then he said something that floored me: "We can still serve everyone else at the table, but not you."

Now I was more than a little embarrassed. I was frustrated, defensive, and completely bewildered by their lack of flexibility. Everyone at our table pushed back as well, politely but firmly, pointing out the absurdity of the policy. You have to be able to drive to drink alcohol here? Isn't that ironic? But the manager wouldn't budge.

Defeated, we asked for the bill, paid without touching our food, and walked out the door. We headed to a sports bar down the street, where we had the same wings, the same beer, and—most importantly—the same group of guys laughing and catching up. But the Hooters incident lingered. It stung in a way that felt like a personal attack on my dignity.

Over the next few days, my frustration grew. I did my research and became convinced I'd been discriminated against. I contacted every state agency I could think of, as well as the franchise owner of the Hooters location and the Hooters corporate office. I fired off strongly worded letters, demanding answers.

Hooters' response was underwhelming. They issued a half-hearted apology and enclosed some gift cards. They also included the logic behind their policy and agreed that this was an unfortunate incident, but they had no intention of making any changes. Furious, I sent the gift cards back and made it clear I had no plans to return to their establishments.

Weeks later, as the anger subsided, I had time to reflect. I realized that, legally, they hadn't done anything wrong. They were a private business with policies designed to curb underage drinking. From their perspective, a fake ID was easier to obtain than a fake driver's license. I wasn't faking anything, of course, but I could see how I'd inadvertently fallen into their policy's blind spot.

As a business owner myself, I could understand their desire to protect themselves. Still, I couldn't help but think they'd missed the bigger picture. Policies are important, but so is the ability to apply them with a little common sense and humanity.

The experience taught me something important about life with a disability: you will encounter roadblocks that aren't always fair. Some you can work around, some you can fight, and some you simply have to accept. It's not always about winning the battle; sometimes it's about learning how to navigate the battlefield.

More than twenty years later, none of us at that table has ever returned to a Hooters. The wings might have been good, but some lessons leave a bitter taste that no amount of hot sauce can cover up.

Thankfully, not everything in that season left a bitter aftertaste. Brad and I had found the perfect setup, an apartment complex right next to our office building. Moving in together felt like an ideal arrangement. I could walk to the office, giving me a renewed feeling of independence. Most of the time, I rode with Brad since our schedules usually aligned, but having the option to come and go on my own was liberating.

Rooming with Brad again was something I genuinely enjoyed. We hadn't shared a place since our college days in Lubbock, and it felt good to have that camaraderie back. We'd always gotten along well, and our rhythm made daily life feel effortless. Whether we were watching a game, grabbing dinner, or playing poker with friends, it was comforting to have him there—not just as a roommate, but as a brother.

In addition to the convenience of the office, the area offered some nearby shops and restaurants. They were across a busy street, requiring a longer journey by foot to safely cross at a traffic light, but I didn't mind. I frequently visited the area and appreciated the accessibility.

Brad and his girlfriend, Rachel, had known each other since their early college days and started dating during their last semester. Over the past year, their relationship became more serious. Rachel was incredible, and we were all thrilled about the idea of her joining our family. She had a natural ease about her and fit in so well with all of us. It was hard to imagine Brad without her.

Before the wedding bells started ringing, I figured it was probably time for me to pack up and give the happy couple their space. Just a couple of miles down the road from our office was an area that had everything I needed within walking distance . . . except the office. Mom encouraged me to consider the move. While I was a bit torn about losing the ability to walk to work, she reminded me that work wasn't everything. The new location would provide access to fun, popular places and offer more opportunities to meet new people.

So, with a nudge from Mom and a growing itch for more autonomy, I moved into The Shops at Legacy, a high-end area brimming with shops, bars, and restaurants. For the first time in years, I was truly on my own again. I had total say over what was going on: what to eat, where to go, how to spend my time. It was a great feeling, and I relished the independence.

As I settled into my new place, I couldn't ignore the growing feeling that it was time to put myself out there in the dating scene. Watching Brad and Rachel prepare for their future together made me realize how much I desired to find my own partner. Living in a vibrant area surrounded by new faces gave me hope that the right person might be closer than I thought.

The bustling social environment felt like a fresh start, and my new location broadened my social network significantly. I also had friends living nearby, and we often caroused together, making the most of the exciting nightlife the area offered. It felt good to have that balance of fun and exploration while also keeping an eye on the future.

Starbucks became a regular hangout spot for me. There was a group of locals who gathered there regularly, and I quickly became part of the crew. I loved getting there early to spend time with them, making it a cornerstone of my routine. Often, Brad or one of my parents would join us for a while before we headed to the office.

By this time, Mom had retired from teaching and joined us at the family business. Our family dynamic was unique in the sense that we seemed to blur the lines between family time and work time with ease. Whether it was at the office or over coffee, we had an easy camaraderie that others often commented on.

In many ways, this move felt like the perfect step forward, balancing my professional life, my independence, and a new, ever-expanding social circle, while also holding space for the possibility of finding the person who would complete my own story.

BACK IN THE MIX

Things at work were going well. Our agency continued to grow, and we'd opened additional office locations across Texas. It was an exciting time, but I realized I'd been so focused on the business that I hadn't taken much time to relax and disconnect from work. It felt like life was passing me by while I was glued to the grindstone. I remembered my mom's sage advice: *Work isn't everything.* That thought lingered in my mind and pushed me to carve out time for myself. Over the next couple of years, I made an effort to step away and reconnect with friends, taking several trips that left me with unforgettable memories.

Among those trips, a weekend in Philadelphia with childhood friends Ryan and Drew and back-to-back visits to the Kentucky Derby stand out. But the one that lingers most vividly in my mind is the Chicago trip with Chris.

It was the weekend before Martin Luther King Jr. Day, and Chris and I were looking for a place to get away. Somehow, we settled on Chicago, despite it being the dead of winter. It was also the weekend before Barack Obama's inauguration as the forty-fourth president of the United States, and the city was alive with energy. As a senator from Illinois, Obama had deep ties to Chicago, and we could feel the buzz of anticipation in the air.

Chris and I stayed downtown, bundled up for the freezing temperatures. It was bitterly cold, so cold my face and ears felt frozen solid the moment we stepped outside. My Texas winter gear, while decent, wasn't quite up to the challenge of a Chicago winter. Each breath felt like a shock to the system, but the chill only added to the sense of adventure. We walked just about everywhere, taking in the sights and sounds of the city.

We indulged in one of Chicago's iconic deep-dish pizzas, tossed back drinks on the one-hundredth floor of the John Hancock Building, and traipsed up and down the snow-covered sidewalks of Michigan Avenue for two days. Each afternoon, we ducked into a Starbucks to warm up, settling into chairs in front of a roaring fireplace. Over cups of coffee, we reminisced about the glory days: college adventures, mutual friends, and the moments that had shaped our paths. Our conversations were effortless, filled with movie and TV quotes, song lyrics, and inside jokes flying back and forth like a championship match at Wimbledon. We had an uncanny ability to keep things going endlessly, each one of us playfully trying to land the perfect line like it was match point. It was the kind of friendship that made everything else in life feel a little lighter—even if your face was half frozen.

The towering buildings, brisk air, and lively streets made everything feel exhilarating. It was one of those weekends when time seemed to stand still, and the moments felt bigger than they were. Chris and I laughed a lot and resolved to make trips like this a tradition.

Maybe it was the lingering cheese from the deep-dish pizza or the fact that I narrowly avoided frostbite, but something about Chicago left a mark. It felt like a city where big things could happen. I came home different. Recharged. Hopeful. It was time to stop waiting and put myself back in the mix.

For quite some time, I had the itch to start dating again, but I kept suppressing it. In addition to my social insecurities stemming from meningitis, I felt a strange discomfort about not being able to drive. It was one of those unspoken expectations, something that, for better or worse, had always felt intrinsically tied to masculinity. The idea of meeting someone new and asking her to pick me up didn't sit right. My lack of perceived masculinity was something I'd been working on with my counselor over the course of many sessions. Still, I wasn't ready to test those waters just yet.

Until that point, I hadn't lived in an area where I could sidestep that awkward first-date logistics issue. Having my mom drop me off or pick me up wasn't exactly a confidence booster. But now, I had a chance to meet dates at a popular coffee shop or restaurant nearby without the need for carpool arrangements.

I wasn't embarrassed about explaining my circumstances once we'd met. In fact, I was comfortable sharing my story with most new people. But leading with it? That would almost certainly ensure no first date. At the time, online dating sites were just starting to gain traction, and I was on them all. I wanted to navigate this on my own, without relying on well-meaning friends to play matchmaker. I needed to prove, to myself and others, that I could hold my own. My approach worked better than I expected. I made connections, went on many first dates, a handful of second dates, but very few thirds.

The few third dates that did happen often came with red flags. I'd find myself excited at first, only to feel uneasy after learning more about their stories. Something always felt a little off. But then

I wondered if they felt the same way about me. It was a frustrating cycle of doubt that I couldn't quite shake.

Then I met someone who seemed different. We clicked.

She was understanding of my visual impairment and seemed genuinely curious about my experiences. To my surprise, we discovered we had overlapping circles from our high school years—she'd even gone to my rival school. We bonded over a shared love of music, diving into deep conversations about our favorite bands and trading mix CDs (yes, still CDs). From the start, we had that rare conversational spark, the kind that makes you forget to check the time.

Over the next few months, we went to concerts, spent time together, and grew closer. She met Brad and Rachel over lunch one day, and they seemed to like her. I was even planning to meet her brother. Things were going well, except for the one thing I hadn't figured out how to navigate.

Although our relationship had progressed in many ways, the physical side was noticeably off track. Over the course of our dates, she had shown clear interest in advancing our physical interactions. It killed me not to respond to those signals. I wanted to. I was frustrated—frustrated with myself and the situation. But I couldn't bring myself to cross that threshold without addressing the underlying issue. And I wanted to keep the good times rolling.

One night, after an incredible concert experience, we headed back to my apartment. The writing was on the wall: the scenario was perfect, the timing felt right, except to me. The entire ride home, I rehearsed what I'd say, my mind racing through every possible outcome. When we got back to my apartment, I knew I couldn't avoid it any longer.

We sat in the living room, and I began cautiously. She already knew the outline of my meningitis story—my sight loss, my time in the hospital, and how it had changed my life. But now I had to address the part I'd avoided. I explained that another one of the complications from meningitis had left me unable to perform in the way she might expect. I emphasized how much I valued the connection we'd built and shared my frustration with this part of my life. I also told her I had been researching ways to overcome it— alternative ways to navigate intimacy—but I knew it wasn't the same.

She listened quietly, her expression seemingly sympathetic—or maybe disappointed. The rest of the evening played out as usual, but it felt like we were both avoiding the elephant in the room. When it was time for her to leave, I walked her to her car. We were cordial, but I could feel the unspoken weight between us. As her taillights disappeared around the bend, I couldn't help but wonder if I'd just sabotaged something meaningful or if I'd finally freed myself from the fear of hiding this part of my story.

REMIX IN PROGRESS

Well, as it turned out, that was our last date. A couple of days went by with no communication, which was unusual. Deep down, I knew. This wasn't a coincidence. It had taken me more than a decade to build up the confidence to have that conversation about my deepest, darkest insecurity. I thought I'd worked through it in counseling, but when the moment came, I realized I didn't really have a plan, just the hope that she'd understand.

It felt like she checked all the boxes. We had so much in common, and everything seemed to flow naturally. For the first time in years, I thought I'd found someone who could see beyond the surface, someone who could accept me, flaws and all. Before meningitis, I would have eagerly welcomed her forward advances toward a more physical relationship. But now, postmeningitis, it left me on my heels, backed into a corner where I had no choice but to divulge the truth— my inadequacy.

I'd done my homework, read the books, explored alternatives, and tried to convince myself there were ways to navigate this. But the research was murky at best, filled with weird advice and methods that felt anything but practical. Still, I clung to those ideas as my potential way forward, doing everything I could to make the best of my situation.

And then it came, just a couple of days before my thirty-first birthday, an email. After weeks of talking daily, sharing so much of ourselves, that's how it ended. I didn't see it right away, but as soon as I did, I opened it. My heart sank. It wasn't long, but every word cut deeper than the last.

She explained she'd been thinking about our conversation and had come to a decision. She couldn't continue with me. She said she had ended her last relationship because the guy wasn't physically attentive enough to meet her needs, and I was, in her words, "far less than that." She couldn't go through that again. She needed more. She was moving on.

I reread the email, each sentence a dagger. This was exactly why I'd kept this part of my life locked away for so long. This was my worst-case scenario. Everything I feared would happen had just unfolded, and now it was staring at me in plain text. I slumped in my chair, staring blankly into the distance. How do you even begin to process something like this?

I replayed every moment we'd shared over the past three months, every conversation, every laugh. I went back over it all, looking for signs I might have missed. Was I fooling myself the whole time? Was she never as invested as I thought she was? Was this inevitable? And then a darker thought crept in: was everyone on these dating sites just as broken as me? Were we all just circling the same drain, pretending we weren't?

And an email? Come on. It felt so cold, so impersonal. But then the irony hit me. Our relationship had started online, so maybe it was only fitting that it ended there. That didn't make it hurt any less.

I took the email to my next counseling session. It was all we talked about. Actually, it was all we talked about for several sessions. Counseling was the only place I could say these things out loud. There was no other outlet. The only other person who knew even a fraction of what I was going through was Chris. He checked in on me constantly, but even that wasn't the same. This wasn't something a friend could fix with a laugh or a distraction. It was something I had to work through.

The sessions didn't fix everything either, but they gave me space to vent, sort through the mess, and start picking up the pieces. I wasn't okay, not by a long shot, but at least I had a place to begin.

One of the things that carried me through the breakup trauma was music. Counseling helped, of course, but there was something about music that felt even more powerful. It had a way of reaching the parts of me I couldn't articulate. I didn't involve many of my friends in what I was going through. A few asked where she was, but most got the standard "It just didn't work out" answer. I wasn't ready to share the deeper truth yet.

Amid the wreckage, I needed a distraction, something creative, something just for me. That's when I discovered podcasts, a brand-new medium back then. There were some music podcasts I followed and thoroughly enjoyed. With the internet, it felt like an endless sea of undiscovered music waiting for someone to curate it. I dove in deep, exploring bands, unique sounds, and independent artists. After compiling a lengthy list of tracks I loved, I thought, *Why not share these discoveries?* And just like that, the Indie Jack Podcast was born.

I taught myself basic audio editing, quickly threw together the inaugural episode, and sent it out onto the internet. The response was amazing; almost immediate. I was hooked. Every two weeks, I released a new episode featuring songs I'd unearthed. The podcast opened doors I hadn't anticipated. I connected with local venues as a member of the media, attended live shows, and built relationships with bands and indie record labels. It was a ton of fun and gave me a creative outlet I hadn't realized I was missing.

Around this same time, I received a long-overdue software update for ZoomText, the program that allowed me to use my computer. While going through the process, I stumbled upon an unexpected opportunity: a resource in Dallas called Ester's Place, operated by the American Foundation for the Blind. It was a showroom designed to display adaptive technology and solutions for people who were blind or visually impaired. I decided to check it out with Mom.

Neva, who managed Ester's Place, gave us the tour. Neva was totally blind and navigated with the help of her guide dog, who was as much a part of the showroom as she was. Ester's Place was designed like a mock home, with a bedroom, bathroom, kitchen, living room, and more, all outfitted with adaptive equipment. While most of the technology wasn't new to me, there was one moment that changed everything.

As we toured, I asked Neva about cell phones. I explained my frustration with being left out of the texting and mobile email world. My flip phone's tiny screen was useless to me, and I'd dismissed the uber-popular BlackBerrys for the same reason. The iPhone had also recently hit the market, and while it was making waves, it offered no accessibility for visually impaired users like me. "Oh! You've got to check this out," Neva said, leading us to her office. She turned up the volume on her Motorola Q9 and let me hear the phone talk. The phone had a screen reader, just like my computer software. I was floored. "When did you get this? Where did you get this? How do I get one of these?" I peppered her with questions.

The very next day, Mom and I went to our cell phone store. There it was—the Motorola Q9, a smartphone running on the Windows Mobile operating system. It wasn't a BlackBerry or an iPhone, but it didn't matter. For the first time, I had a device that worked for me. Getting the adaptive software installed was a bit of a process, but within forty-eight hours of meeting Neva, I had a fully functional phone.

What a game changer. I was texting nonstop. I had a backlog of conversations to make up for. Then I added my personal email account and marveled at how easily I could access it. It was like stepping into a world everyone else had been living in for years. How had I, the self-proclaimed tech guy, missed this? Other than ZoomText, this was the best piece of technology I'd ever experienced. Still, part of me couldn't help but wish I could use something as sleek—and as universally hyped—as the BlackBerry or iPhone.

This new phone didn't just further connect me to the world; it reminded me that there was always more to discover, more ways to adapt, and more reasons to be optimistic. Life, like technology, is always evolving. And sometimes, when you least expect it, the next big thing changes everything.

Then, meningitis rudely interrupted life, and everything changed.

—SECTION VII—
Erin

INBOX DESTINY

I was sitting at my desk at work, halfheartedly going through my inbox, when it appeared. The subject line read: Friend of Your Mom's. I didn't recognize the sender, but curiosity quickly got the better of me. Clicking it open, I had no idea what to expect.

John,

Hi, you do not know me, but your mom (and her group) from church feed the homeless with my group every 4th Sunday. They are so sweet. Anyway, while serving, your mother and I visit about everything. She said you and your brother graduated from Tech!! My husband and I (so far 3 out of our 4 kids) did too, and our senior in high school is only applying to Tech.

This is a little awkward, but I work with a wonderful, sweet, darling girl who teaches 3rd grade. She graduated from Texas A&M, but is not a typical Aggie. She said she would love to meet you. I have never really played matchmaker before, but really think the two of you would hit it off from all the nice things your mom and her friends have said about you. I have her email (she has your name) so if you want to contact her, please let me know. Her name is Erin, by the way.

Match-maker Raider!
Kerrie

I leaned back in my chair, rereading the email. A setup? Really? After weeks of untangling my emotions and trying to rebuild my confidence, the last thing I expected was an email from a stranger suggesting I meet someone new. The idea felt absurd, and yet Kerrie's enthusiasm was oddly infectious.

I couldn't help but wonder *is this woman crazy?* Of course a mom would make a great character reference for her son. But let's be real; what's a mom going to say? "Oh, don't bother; he's a total wreck"? No, she's going to paint her son as a saint, someone perfect in every way.

But as I sat there, contemplating the ifs, another thought crept in. I'd always considered myself an eternal optimist. Sure, I was skeptical, but there was a part of me that couldn't help but wonder if maybe, just maybe, this could turn into something good.

After a few minutes of internal debate, I decided why not?

Sure thing, Kerrie! I'd like to chat with and meet Erin, even if she's an Aggie. :) We'll see what happens. How can I contact her? Thanks!

Kerrie quickly replied with Erin's email address. I stared at the screen. Something about it felt…different.

I spent the rest of the afternoon mulling over whether I should really act on this setup. The optimist in me kept whispering, "What's the worst that can happen?" but I still hesitated. Did I really want to put myself out there again? The thought of trying felt exhausting and terrifying.

It had only been a few weeks, and I hadn't fully shaken the sting of rejection. Even though talking with my counselor was helping, I wasn't sure I was ready to dive back in. But then I reminded myself I'd already been at rock bottom and survived. And there was that infectious excitement from Kerrie . . .

With all of that in mind, I decided to roll the dice and send an email to Erin.

Subject: Greetings.

Hey Erin,

Kerrie and a group of women that included my mother (which is kind of weird), told me I should look you up. So, here I am sending greetings and salutations on what should be your first day of summer vacation. Maybe? So far, I know you're a teacher and an Aggie.

Huh, well, I'm a Red Raider, so we could be diametrically opposed. But perhaps since we are adults now, I guess I shouldn't hold being an Aggie against you. :D

John

I hit send, half expecting silence. It wasn't the smoothest opener, but it was me—quirky and honest.

I was pleasantly surprised when Erin responded about twenty-four hours later. Maybe she was busy, or maybe she waited intentionally so she wouldn't seem overzealous. Either way, I was excited to read it.

Hi John,

It sounds like Kerrie has been busy with this new project of hers. It was good to get an email from you yesterday. Monday was officially my first day of summer, and I had a very busy day. I worked out, had lunch with a friend, went to some of my students' baseball games, and had dinner with another friend. Today has pretty much been just as busy. I am on the leadership team at my school, and we had a meeting this afternoon. I think things will slow down a little after today. I am very excited about my summer vacation! It is so nice to have 2 1/2 months off to do whatever I want.

You mentioned you knew that I was a teacher and an Aggie. I was told that we are about the same age, that you work in the insurance business, and that you went to Tech. You and I were thinking the same thing; I don't think that I can hold it against you that you chose to go to that university ;) I know I can educate you on why A&M is so great!!!

A little about myself...I am the youngest in my family (I have 2 older brothers). In my free time, I love to work out, mostly running. I am pretty laid-back ...so if I am not working out, I am hanging out with friends, going to the movies, dinner, sporting events, traveling when I can, etc. What about you? What do you like to do when you are not working?

Erin

Her email sounded genuine, and I couldn't help but smile as I read it. Here was someone who seemed to have her life together but also didn't take herself too seriously. I found myself rereading her words, letting the curiosity grow. I felt a spark.

Over the next five days, Erin and I exchanged a steady stream of emails—dozens of them, sometimes fired off within seconds—that felt like the written version of a long, engaging conversation. Each message revealed a little more about who we were, and the rapid back-and-forth kept me energized and captivated by how easily we seemed to connect.

Both our attempts at internet "stalking" the other didn't yield much. Erin had recently deactivated her Facebook account and wasn't on any other social media platforms. The teacher photo on her school website was taken from quite a distance and didn't reveal much. With the help of her friend Amanda, she managed to find me on Facebook, but since I was pretty well locked down, she could only see my profile picture. Unfortunately for her—or maybe fortunately—it didn't exactly clarify things. In the picture, I was wearing a crazy wig, sticking my finger in my ear, and sporting a shirt that she couldn't quite read. "Does it say 'John Grimes Band'? What?" she wrote in one email. Her inquisitiveness made me laugh, and I teased her about needing to get back on Facebook to see more.

We bonded quickly over shared interests like music and movies, even poking fun at our differences—she loved running, while I leaned more toward a good cup of coffee. There was plenty of good-natured ribbing about our respective alma maters, too. Somehow, it made the emails feel less like a setup and more like an organic connection.

As the days passed, I found myself opening up quicker than I had expected. I shared some of my meningitis story: how it had changed my life, how I'd fought my way back through college, and how I'd learned to adapt to living with vision loss. I wasn't sure how she'd react, but her response was nothing short of kind and supportive.

At one point, I mentioned that at six feet four inches, I was tall for my age, and for some reason, she thought I was joking. Her disbelief cracked me up, and it became one more thing we teased each other about as the emails went on. Her curiosity added to the playfulness, and I enjoyed how natural it felt.

During a flurry of emails that stretched into the early morning hours of the fifth day, I gave Erin my phone number and encouraged her to call. It was about 1:00 a.m. when I sent it, and she quickly responded with a one-word question: "Now?" Her email made me laugh, and I replied with a simple "Yep." A couple of minutes later, our email conversation seamlessly continued by phone.

We chatted for over two hours, covering many of the same topics from our emails, but now there was a new dimension—voice. Adding her voice to our text exchange only deepened the intrigue and gave the conversation a richer, more personal feel with a hint of Texas twang. It was also much easier for Erin to tell when I was joking, which revealed her endearing and contagious laugh.

By the end of our call, we had done more than just matching voices to our words; we'd matched schedules. After tossing around ideas, we settled on meeting at a popular Mexican restaurant near me. The plan was set, and the anticipation for our first date was almost tangible. Just a couple of days away, it felt like the perfect mix of excitement and nervous energy. What would it be like to meet Erin after all those emails and that incredible call? I couldn't stop wondering if the spark we'd built through words and voices would carry over into real life or crumble like a bag of old tortilla chips.

BEYOND THE INBOX

The day arrived: June 16, 2009. I was nervous, for sure. We had agreed to meet outside Mi Cocina, a popular Mexican restaurant within walking distance for me and still very close for Erin. The area was lively, with Mi Cocina perfectly situated on the corner.

Just like my nerves, I also liked to arrive fashionably early. Since losing my sight, it had become my go-to move; it gave me time to get a feel for the layout of new places or, in this case, to let people find me. Because of my visual impairment, I typically couldn't identify others easily; faces, outfits, even familiar gestures were often out of reach. It was simply easier and far less awkward if people approached me first. Roaming around asking strangers if they were Erin seemed far less appealing than my early arrival strategy, and frankly, not the way I wanted our first date to begin. I had a better plan.

I realized I didn't know what Erin would be wearing or what she looked like at all. Not that it would've made much of a difference anyway. And since I wasn't wearing a crazy wig like in my Facebook photo, she didn't really know what I looked like either. She was still skeptical about my six-foot-four claim, too. It hit me: this was a blind date in more ways than one.

I figured the best approach would be to sit on a bench and act like I was staring down at my phone. A common enough pose in the smartphone era, but my intention was to let her approach me. The idea of unknowingly looking directly at her without realizing it was painfully awkward to me. Plus, I had an icebreaker in mind. So I sat there, seemingly glued to my phone, but I was listening for everything and watching the ground in front of me for feet.

I noticed someone approaching, though it had happened a couple of times already and they walked right past. This time was different; the person slowed down and stopped in front of me. I kept looking at my phone, pretending to be oblivious.

Then she spoke: "John?"

I knew it was Erin immediately—her voice gave it away.

I slowly looked up from my phone in an attempt to make eye contact with her. Shaking my head, I said, "No," then looked back down at my phone.

She started to turn away, and I quickly stood up, gently grabbed her arm, and said, "Yes, I'm John Grimes," with a big smile and a chuckle.

She let out a gigantic sigh and immediately responded, "John Grimes, you're never going to live that one down!"

The icebreaker worked.

We had a good laugh, and from that moment on, everything flowed smoothly. We walked inside and were seated in a booth next to a window. Any lingering worries vanished within seconds. Erin was funny, easygoing, and carried herself with such a natural charm and grace. Our conversation picked up right where we'd left off on the phone. The spark wasn't just there; it was beginning to ignite.

After dinner, neither of us wanted the evening to end. We decided to keep it going by heading to the Starbucks next door. Drinks in hand, we continued talking . . . about life, about family, about everything. Erin now believed my claim of being six foot four, especially when she realized, standing next to me, that I was a full foot taller than her.

When our drinks were empty, we still weren't ready to part ways. Erin hadn't spent much time in the area, so I gave her a tour, pointing out my favorite restaurants, shops, and places to hang out. We passed by my apartment building, and I showed her where I lived. Then we took a stroll around the pond at the center of the Shops at Legacy. The pond was serene, reflecting the soft glow of the surrounding lights, and the calm water mirrored the ease of our conversation. We'd come full circle, literally, and the spark was now a flame neither of us wanted to put out.

We ended up at a nearby bar, where we grabbed one more drink. She ordered wine; I got a beer. We sat and talked about the music playing, laughing and exchanging stories like we'd known each other for years. Before we knew it, the bar was closing, and we realized the date had lasted almost four hours.

Walking to her car in a nearby parking garage, I felt both calm and excited, like things were exactly as they should be. We said our goodbyes, ending with a hug. Before she drove off, we both agreed we should definitely do this again.

Over the next couple of months, our relationship continued to develop. Erin's summer break gave her the freedom to travel, and she made the most of it, visiting family and friends around Texas and even making a trip to see her good friend Melissa in Tennessee. Despite the miles between us during her travels, we stayed connected through regular phone calls and emails. When Erin was back in town, we made it a point to meet up. Each date felt like a building block, steadily strengthening our connection.

Our third date was one I'll never forget. Erin suggested we go to Abuelo's, a Mexican restaurant she loved that was outside my usual stomping grounds. It wasn't within walking distance for me, so Erin picked me up. During the drive, she casually mentioned how much she liked driving. While that wasn't a requirement for dating someone, in my case, it was a definite bonus.

After being seated, the conversation flowed as it always did, easy and natural. At some point, the topic moved to my meningitis story. I mentioned that we hadn't talked about it much since our initial emails and that if she wanted to know more, all she had to do was ask—no questions were off-limits. Once the door was open, I found myself sharing more than I ever had with anyone outside of my family or close friends.

I told Erin almost everything: the onset of symptoms, miraculously being found unconscious on the floor of my bedroom, the fight for survival, and the long road of recovery that followed. I shared the Elevator Angel story and explained how it was a transformative moment for my parents, a glimmer of light in their darkest hours, and a critical turning point in my journey. Letting Erin in on this felt significant, like I was opening a door to a deeply personal chapter of my life that few people knew about. She seemed genuinely moved.

We also talked at length about my sight loss. I did my best to explain legal blindness, describing what I could and couldn't see and how it affected my daily life. Erin had already been around me enough to pick up on some of it, but this conversation seemed to make things click for her. She listened intently and asked questions that showed she sincerely wanted to understand. Her curiosity wasn't invasive; it was compassionate. I found myself sharing details I hadn't planned to because they were too complicated to explain. But with Erin, it felt natural and seemed to make sense. It was cathartic, finally putting those words out there and having them met with nothing but kindness and understanding.

On the drive back, the conversation lightened, and we laughed about some of the funny parts of the evening—the overzealous waiter, my inability to stop eating tortilla chips, and the fact that we were so entrenched in conversation we drove right by my apartment building.

By the time she dropped me off, I felt a shift in our relationship. It wasn't just about the fun or the chemistry anymore. Erin had seen a deeper part of me and didn't back away. That night, I realized she wasn't just someone I enjoyed spending time with; she was someone I could trust. The experience gave me a glimpse into the depth of her heart—the quiet strength, the genuine compassion, the steady kindness, the way she leaned in when others might have pulled away. It made me feel like this was something rare, something real.

ON THE FAMILY PLAN

U p to this point, my parents were in the dark about my relationship with Erin. I had mentioned her in passing to my mom one day at the office, casually saying I'd been out with "Erin—the girl you and your friends suggested I meet." Mom's ears perked up immediately, and she peppered me with questions, clearly very interested in the details. But I played it coy, giving her very little insight.

I still thought the setup process was a little weird. The whole thing felt orchestrated in a way that I wasn't fully comfortable with yet. And while things with Erin felt steady and full of promise, deep down, I feared that exposing my hidden struggle would collapse everything we'd built. I wasn't ready to explain all of this to my mom. Our family was very close and got along well, but there were some parts of my life I felt needed to remain private, at least for now.

My brother was a different story. He was aware of Erin and, based on what I'd told him, eager to meet her. So we made plans to see a popular local band play at a lounge-style venue. Erin and I arrived first and found a table near the stage.

I'd told Erin just about everything there was to know about Brad and Rachel, so she knew what to expect. Understandably, she was a little nervous because the real headliner that night wasn't the band; it was Erin, making her debut for my family. She obviously wanted to make a good impression.

When Brad and Rachel arrived, everyone hit it off immediately. The conversation flowed smoothly, as I knew it would. Rachel, pregnant with their second child, was tasked as the driver for the evening, leaving Brad free to cut loose. His first order of business: a round of tequila shots for the three of us. A move that was slightly out of character for him but one that was well received by the table. The night was filled with laughter, good music, and an overall great time.

Brad and Rachel left a bit early to pick up their toddler, Will, from my parents' house. Not more than five minutes after they left, Erin's phone buzzed with a notification, a friend request from Brad. Though she had been off Facebook when we met, I'd talked her into getting back on a few weeks earlier. Brad wasted no time signaling his approval. Erin accepted the request with a smile and maybe a little amusement at how fast the Grimes welcome wagon rolled in.

I'm not sure what Brad and Rachel reported back to my parents, but whatever it was must have been good. Mom's birthday was the following week, and during one of our office conversations, she politely insisted that I invite Erin to the family lunch we had planned to celebrate. When I asked Erin, she said yes, though she admitted to feeling a little nervous about meeting my parents. But with her new Facebook friend Brad now officially in her corner, she felt optimistic about how things might go.

We went to my mom's favorite restaurant for lunch, and as we walked in, I was surprised that my mom's best friend, Linda, and her husband, Robert, were seated at the table. Whoa. Mom was pulling out all the stops. Suddenly, this wasn't just a casual family meal; it seemed like the welcome wagon was rolling at full speed.

All nine of us squeezed into a circular booth that was definitely too small for our group. Cozy family gatherings were nothing new for us, but with Erin in the mix, the stakes felt higher. Was she already being considered as a potential new member of the family? I had a feeling my mom thought so, even before officially meeting her.

Despite the close quarters and the extra audience, everything went swimmingly well. Erin charmed everyone with her warmth and humor, fitting in as though she'd been there all along. The conversation was lively, and the lunch flew by.

On the way home, Erin told me how much she enjoyed meeting my parents and how fantastic my family was. Hearing that made me feel proud, and I couldn't help but smile the rest of the ride. Maybe it was too early to say out loud, but a part of me was already picturing her at the next family gathering.

Her integration into my life was happening on multiple fronts—emotional, social, and soon, even technological.

For quite some time, I had been using my Motorola Q9 smartphone with remarkable success. It gave me access to texting and email but relied on Windows Mobile, an unstable operating system that required expensive third-party software called Mobile Speak Smartphone (MSS) to work for visually impaired users like me.

While it was a game changer in many ways, it came with its share of frustrations. The phone frequently froze and needed restarting. Once, I even got the dreaded Windows "blue screen of death," forcing me to reinstall the entire OS at the phone store—followed by MSS. The process was tedious, time-consuming, and maddening.

Still, the Q9-and-MSS combo had been an incredible leap forward. It wasn't perfect, but it gave me a level of independence I hadn't experienced before. I put up with the glitches and headaches because the alternative was being entirely left behind. That was just the reality of adaptive tech at the time.

There were rumors of a promising new screen reader being developed for BlackBerry devices—a hugely popular platform—but like many things in the accessibility world back then, it fizzled out.

Then, everything changed.

Rob, a couple of years older than me and also from Plano, was a technology genius. He'd been good friends with RJ growing up, and I'd met him in the twilight of my college days about ten years earlier. We instantly clicked over our shared love of all things tech, especially networking and digital media.

Over the years, Rob had helped me keep our business ahead of the curve with cutting-edge systems. He'd also been instrumental in converting my enormous CD library into digital format and organizing it for storage. A lifelong Windows expert, Rob had worked at Microsoft in Seattle before moving back to Plano. He was a brilliant teacher, and I trusted everything he said.

When the original iPhone launched, Rob jumped in early. It didn't take long before Apple's walled garden pulled him in, a surprising twist for someone who had once been all-in on Microsoft.

One day, he called with exciting news: "Hey, the iPhone just got an OS update that now includes VoiceOver, Apple's screen reader. It's built with visually impaired users in mind. You need to check it out." The latest version, the iPhone 3GS, now had VoiceOver built in.

I was more than intrigued. The idea of a mainstream product like the iPhone—including accessibility right out of the box—felt like a dream. No third-party software. No extra costs. And it wasn't just limited to text and email like my Q9. The iPhone had it all: web browsing, apps, multimedia, and GPS, and all of it accessible. Apple wasn't just checking a box; they were investing in accessibility. It was groundbreaking. For anyone blind or visually impaired, it was a revolution.

I quickly did some research, and everything I found confirmed it. Rob's ringing endorsement sealed the deal. I was in.

He offered to pick me up from my office and take me to the nearby AT&T store—still the only iPhone carrier at the time. I had about four months left on my Q9 contract with another carrier, but I wasn't about to let that stop me. Rather than cancel and pay the hefty termination fees, I started a new plan, got a new number, and walked out with an iPhone that day.

It was an abrupt decision, but having two phone numbers would only be a temporary inconvenience, and I was eager to get started.

When I got home, it felt like Christmas morning. The iPhone did everything I hoped it would—and more. It was sleek, intuitive, and, most importantly, accessible. Right out of the box.

It wasn't just a cool piece of tech; it was life-changing. Much like discovering ZoomText years earlier, this marked a whole new level of independence. But this was bigger. This was the world's most popular smartphone, and it worked for someone like me, no hacks required.

THE WAIT WAS OVER

I was really smitten with Erin. Everything about our relationship felt balanced, as if we'd been in step all along, with no red flags or awkward bumps. Still, a lingering doubt about my sense of masculinity followed me, a shadow I'd carried for years, and one that made me wonder if this steady progress with Erin could withstand my hidden struggle.

About a month prior, after another amazing date, I couldn't wait any longer to make the move. Our first kiss was a moment I'd wanted for a while. I didn't want Erin to think we were stuck in the friend zone. From that moment, physical affection became a natural part of our time together. We even started holding hands. While it may sound simple, holding Erin's hand meant so much more to me.

It wasn't just about connection; holding her hand gave me confidence. With her by my side, I felt more self-assured, especially when navigating unfamiliar spaces. Erin became a guide for me—helping me feel grounded and capable in every situation. Whether knowingly or unknowingly, she boosted my confidence in ways I hadn't experienced before.

Still, I was worried. Erin was a schoolteacher and had an incredible way with kids. She adored her nephews, and her maternal instincts were off the charts. Everything seemed perfect—except for the one thing I'd been holding back. I needed to tell her before the moment came when I'd have no choice. But what if this was the deal-breaker? What if she misinterpreted my hesitation for intimacy and thought I wasn't interested in her? The questions circled endlessly in my mind.

One Saturday afternoon, we were hanging out at my apartment, loosely planning our evening. My thoughts were consumed by the weight of what I needed to say. I waited for a natural segue—though for a topic like this, does such a thing even exist? As I debated internally, the conversation hit a break, and I realized it was now or never.

"Hey, there's something I've been meaning to talk to you about," I began, trying to steady my nerves. I joined her on the couch, sitting up straight and clasping my hands in an attempt to project some sense of confidence.

Erin already knew almost all of my meningitis story: my sight loss, my time in the hospital, the sheer gravity of what I'd been through. But this conversation would go deeper. I started by explaining how meningitis had disrupted my body in ways that weren't immediately visible—neurologic dysfunction that affected critical, intimate functions. I told her about my bladder condition and then broached the most sensitive part: one of the lingering complications had made it nearly impossible to meet the unspoken expectations that come with physical intimacy. That's why I'd been hesitant. Not because I didn't want her, but because I didn't want to disappoint her. This wasn't about attraction or timing; it was about vulnerability and the fear of falling short in a moment that's supposed to feel deeply connected and real.

As I talked, the frustration I'd carried for years began to pour out. I told her how maddening it was to feel like part of my identity had been stripped away, how much effort I'd poured into researching solutions only to come up empty-handed time and again. Every promising lead had turned out to be a dead end. I told her how this issue had forced me to confront parts of myself I wasn't ready to face, how it made me feel less than whole.

I tried to sprinkle in a bit of humor, my usual defense mechanism when things got too real. A few lines actually landed and Erin chuckled, which gave me just enough courage to keep going. But beneath the smiles, I laid it bare. I told her how nervous I was, how this conversation had been looming in my mind for weeks. I admitted how much I valued what we were building, and how terrified I was that this could unravel it. I didn't want pity. I didn't want to be seen as broken. I just wanted to be understood. The words poured out of me—unfiltered, slightly scattered, but honest. Somewhere in that flood of truth, I stopped. I'd said everything I could. And in the silence that followed, I held my breath, hoping I hadn't just undone the very thing I was trying to protect.

The silence was short-lived. Erin reached for my hand, her grip firm and warm, sniffling as she wiped away a tear. Her voice, when it came, was steady but full of feeling. "John," she said, "thank you for telling me this. I can't imagine how difficult it must have been to share something so personal." She paused, squeezing my hand just a little tighter. "I'm so sorry this happened to you. But this doesn't define who you are. It doesn't change how I feel about you or the connection we've built. You are so much more than this." She took a deep breath, her tone softening, and added with a small, reassuring smile, "John, it's not an issue. I like you just the way you are."

Her response was sincere and graceful, exactly as Erin had always been. My shoulders dropped, and I realized I was still holding my breath. There was no hesitation, no shift in her energy. She leaned into the moment with compassion and understanding, showing me once again why she was so different. She pressed in closer, offering the kind of acceptance that felt effortless yet profound.

Erin was beautiful—inside and out—a rare combination of kindness, strength, and grace. I had seen her heart before, on that unforgettable night at Abuelo's, when she listened to my story with a patience and empathy unlike any I had ever known. And here, once again, she was showing me the same unwavering grace.

In that moment, I felt another shift. It wasn't just about what we'd said or how she'd responded; it was the way she made me feel, like maybe I didn't need to keep waiting. Maybe waiting was just another form of doubt, one she had just helped me leave behind.

THE SEASON THAT STUCK

Introducing Erin to the people who mattered most in my life was a big deal, and few mattered more than Chris. Chris was my sounding board for just about everything, especially when it came to relationships. At the time, he was in law school in Louisville, Kentucky, but we talked by phone regularly. Chris knew Erin's story almost as well as I did, every detail, from our first date to her knack for making me feel confident and supported. He'd even spoken to her briefly on the phone a couple of times. But now, it was time for the real test.

Erin and I picked him up at the airport and headed straight to dinner at Maggiano's, a place that felt perfect for the occasion. The atmosphere was warm and inviting, and the conversation unfolded naturally. Over plates of gnocchi, drinks, and laughter, it became clear that Chris approved. We spent the rest of the weekend exploring, talking, and catching up. Along the way, we also introduced Erin to a couple of our high school and college friends, making the weekend even more special. By the end of Chris's visit, I had exactly what I'd hoped for: the thumbs up.

Word was getting around about Erin and my relationship. At my friend Alana's wedding in Chillicothe, I was met with a flurry of excitement from everyone. People kept coming up to me, asking, "Tell me about Erin!" and "When do we get to meet her?" It caught me off guard, and I couldn't help but think, *That's got Mom written all over it. Whoa! She must really like Erin.*

Erin's family started making appearances in our lives, too. Her oldest brother, Scott, came up from Houston for a Texas A&M football game. Erin and both of her brothers were proud Aggies, and—like most Aggies—their connection to their alma mater ran deep. Meeting Scott was great; he was personable, easygoing, and just as engaging as Erin. Then, a short time later, Erin's parents made the trip from San Antonio. We all went out to dinner at Abuelo's, and while I was a bit nervous about making a good impression, the evening couldn't have gone smoother. Conversation moved without a hitch, and Erin's parents were kind and welcoming. It just felt easy being around them.

During dinner, Erin's dad became enamored with our iPhones. He was intrigued by how instant access to sports scores and information was right at my fingertips. As I quickly pulled up the latest updates on his favorite teams, his enthusiasm was palpable. He leaned in closer, asking question after question, clearly fascinated by the technology. It was obvious he was hooked, and I had a feeling it wouldn't be long before there was another iPhone user in Erin's family.

Erin's parents weren't the only ones who showed they approved of us as a couple. One of the most meaningful interactions happened when my friend Drew came to town. Drew was a childhood friend from Chillicothe, now an ordained minister living in Philadelphia. He was in the Dallas area to officiate a wedding, and we made plans to meet up for dinner. Drew was someone whose opinion I deeply valued, like the big brother I never had. We'd shared countless conversations about life, faith, and relationships over the years, and his insight always meant a lot to me.

That Thursday night, Drew met Erin and me at my apartment before dinner. At one point, I stepped away for a minute, leaving the two of them alone in the living room. Several months later, Erin told me about their brief exchange. Drew had leaned in with a playful grin and asked, "So, you like John, huh?" Erin, without missing a beat, responded, "No. I love John!" Her smile was as big as her words. Drew replied, "Well, okay then!" with a knowing nod and a smile of his own.

When the night ended, Drew gave me a big hug and said, "Take care of that girl. She's a great one." Hearing that from Drew—someone who'd steered me through more than a few chapters of life—meant a lot. His words stuck with me.

During the holiday season, Erin and I found ourselves balancing our time between our families. For Thanksgiving and Christmas, she went to San Antonio to be with her family and I stayed in Plano with mine. But the day after Christmas, Erin returned and we exchanged gifts before heading over to my parents' house for dinner.

It was a quieter Christmas than usual. Brad and Rachel were away in Memphis celebrating with Rachel's family, and my grandparents and Judy and Wilbur were home in Chillicothe. My grandparents, always ahead of the curve when it came to technology, had embraced web cameras and Skype years earlier. Despite being in their eighties, they navigated video calls like pros. As usual, we spoke with everyone on the phone and made video calls with my grandparents, who were thrilled to meet Erin virtually.

Even with fewer people physically present, my parents went out of their way to make Erin feel welcome. To her amazement, everyone in my family had sent along a gift for her. My parents handed her the packages, thoughtful gifts from Judy and Wilbur, both sets of my grandparents, and even Brad and Rachel, who had left a gift for Erin before heading out of town. The joy on Erin's face was unforgettable. She kept telling everyone how thankful she was, her voice filled with genuine surprise and gratitude.

As I watched her interact with my family, I couldn't help but think, What's going on here? Is my family trying to send a message? Whatever it was, Erin clearly had made an impression.

The momentum didn't stop there.

Since our first trip to Chicago in January, Chris and I had been planning to do it again. Just like the prior year, we decided to go over the weekend before Martin Luther King Jr. Day, making it something of a tradition. But this time, with Erin in my life, I told him I wanted her to come along. Chris was on board, and we decided to make it a couples' weekend. Chris's date was a travel agent, and she handled all the planning. She found us an incredible boutique hotel just off Michigan Avenue, a perfect home base for exploring the city.

The weekend was a whirlwind of activity. We kicked things off with a Bulls game the first night, soaking up the electric atmosphere of a packed basketball arena. The next morning, we laced up skates for some ice skating in Millennium Park and, of course, stopped to marvel at the famous Bean sculpture. In spite of the bitter cold, Erin's excitement was contagious, and I found myself enjoying the city in a whole new way with her.

One of the highlights of the trip was our visit to the Sears Tower (now Willis Tower). After taking in the spectacular views from the observation deck, Erin and I nervously stepped into the glass-floored Skydeck Ledge. Standing 103 stories above the street and sidewalk below, it felt as though the city was miles away. My stomach did a flip as I gingerly stepped out, and I could tell Erin was equally nervous. But once we were both out there, the surreal sensation of floating above the city was exhilarating.

We walked almost everywhere, immersing ourselves in the true feel of a Chicago winter. The city's cold was unrelenting, but the allure of its snow-covered streets and busy sidewalks made it worthwhile. Along the way, we ducked into cozy bars, restaurants, and that same Starbucks Chris and I had visited the year before, where we thawed out by the roaring fireplace with warm drinks in hand. Those brief respites from the icy air became little pockets of comfort in an otherwise brisk adventure. We also hit up another iconic Chicago-style pizza restaurant, indulging in thick, cheesy slices that felt like a warm hug against the freezing cold. On a strong recommendation from the hotel concierge, we even checked out a mezzanine, enjoying drinks and the change of perspective it offered—but mostly just because it was fun to say mezzanine!

The fast pace of the trip added to the thrill. Every moment felt packed with excitement, and the city's energy kept us going despite the cold. Erin's enthusiasm for every stop—from the towering buildings to the bustling streets—was magnetic. Her love for the snowy landscape, paired with her adventurous spirit, made the trip feel even more special.

By the end of the weekend, it struck me just how naturally everything had fallen into place. The company, the city, and the memories we were creating... it was all perfect.

As Erin and I settled into our seats on the plane to head home, the woman sitting next to us couldn't help but comment. "You two are so cute together," she said with a smile. Then, as if she could see straight into the future, she asked, "When's the wedding?"

Erin and I exchanged a look and laughed it off, but I couldn't help wondering if the weekend had quietly set something in motion, something that might just lead to the question that woman had so casually asked.

CLOSER BY THE DAY

After Christmas and the Chicago trip, Erin and I were firmly in the thrill-of-the-new-relationship phase. The momentum from the fall family introductions, those holiday gatherings, and that unforgettable snowy weekend propelled us through the winter. We were growing closer with each passing day.

My second nephew, Sawyer, was born, and Erin was part of the festivities, her motherly instincts on full display. Aunt Judy came into town for the occasion, and she and Erin—already fast friends from calls and video chats—were instantly like two peas in a pod.

Around the same time, Micah's son, Asher, was born. Erin and I attended his bris together, an entirely new experience for both of us. It was one of many "firsts" we'd share.

We also started a new tradition of attending Highland Park United Methodist Church in Dallas on Sundays. I had a longstanding connection to Mark Craig, the minister there. About thirty years earlier, Mark had founded Custer Road United Methodist Church in Plano, where my family attended for years. Erin, who'd grown up Lutheran, was looking for a new church home, and with a close college friend already a member, HPUMC was a perfect fit.

Erin unknowingly nudged me toward a long-overdue health decision. For about ten years, I'd managed with my patented "hold and push" technique instead of using catheters. I avoided them because of the inconvenience, but with age (or maybe wisdom), I began to reconsider. More likely, Erin's presence and the way she helped me see things differently gave me the push I needed to make a change. I started using catheters again almost full-time. While still inconvenient, I realized it was a much better option than stressing my body by forcing my bladder empty.

That led me to my first urology appointment in years. It was unexpectedly enlightening. I'd always believed catheterization required near-surgical sterilization. At the appointment, the nurse handed me a catheter, plopped some lubricant on a paper towel, and sent me to the restroom—no gloves, no elaborate prep. When I asked, the doctor assured me this method was perfectly safe. That one appointment removed years of self-induced overcomplication.

Erin was, of course, supportive. I still wasn't ready to use them in public—too inconvenient—but at home and work, it became second nature. For the first time in a long time, I wasn't just getting by. I was starting to thrive.

By spring, Erin and I had nearly ten months of shared experiences behind us. Holidays, family integration, new traditions, and smaller moments were adding to the foundation.

But there was one moment that stood apart, marking a new chapter in our story.

It was a perfect spring day, warm enough to open the French doors to the faux balcony of my second-floor loft apartment. I moved an oversized loveseat in front of the opening and invited Erin to join me. The courtyard below buzzed with birdsong and blooming flowers. My finely curated '90s playlist poured softly through the speakers while we snacked on goat cheese and crackers.

I'd long teased Erin by calling her my "favorite girlfriend," but that day, the joking stopped.

"You know," I said, "I've told you you're my favorite girlfriend of the month, then the year, and now of all time—and that's true. But the more I think about it, you're even more than that. Erin, I love you."

Boom. I said it.

For a split second, time seemed to stand still. The rhythm of the music, the cool breeze through the open doors, the warmth of Erin beside me; it all seemed to sharpen, making the moment feel bigger than just the two of us.

And Erin didn't hesitate. "I love you too," she said, her voice bright with the kind of relief that comes from finally saying something you've been dying to share.

And just like that, we were in love. The words felt electric between us, and we couldn't stop smiling, thrilled to finally say it out loud to each other.

Newly in love, we entered our second summer eager to pack it with shared moments. We met more of each other's friends, tried new restaurants, and went to concerts.

We also joined my parents' group for their monthly meal service at The Bridge, the homeless shelter tied to our own origin story. It was my chance to finally meet Kerrie, the matchmaker whose email had set everything in motion. As my dad put it, Kerrie was "a party waiting to happen," and he was right! Her enthusiasm, which had first jumped off the screen in that email, was just as infectious in person, and any awkwardness melted away instantly.

After serving, both groups went out to dinner. Erin retold the story of our first meeting—how she'd asked, "Are you John?" and I'd deadpanned, "No" before grabbing her arm and admitting I was. She told everyone how mortified she'd been in that split second as she started to turn away, convinced she had just asked a random stranger and made a complete fool of herself. Her animated retelling had everyone doubled over, the kind of laughter that rolls around the table and makes it hard to catch your breath.

By the end of the night, we felt officially part of the group. Volunteering there became something we looked forward to, not just as community service, but as a way to celebrate where we'd been and where we were going.

As summer progressed, Erin's lease was coming up for renewal. We had been spending so much time together at the Shops near my apartment that I suggested she move there. To my delight, she was interested.

As it turned out, there was a unit available in my building that was more affordable than her current place. Fate.

We toured the unit, and as Erin walked through the space, I could tell she was already picturing herself there. It wasn't just the logistics that made it perfect; it was the feeling of taking this next step together, of Erin being closer, of our lives becoming even more intertwined. By the time we left the leasing office, Erin was beaming, and I was grinning ear to ear.

Over the next weeks, I helped Erin pack up. Thankfully, the movers did the real work, sparing Erin and me from testing our relationship with a sofa stuck in a doorway. The first night, we sat surrounded by boxes and takeout containers, holding our inaugural "box top dinner party." It certainly wasn't glamorous, but it was ours—a milestone.

The Shops at Legacy had always been a hub of activity and fun, but with Erin nearby, it felt different. It felt complete. This love thing was great, and it was getting better every day.

To close out the summer, we flew to North Carolina to visit her brother Ryan and his family. I was immediately tackled by her nephews, Taylor and Colin, their laughter mixing with Erin's as they tried to wrestle me to the ground. Watching Erin dote on her nephews was a joy in itself; she had this natural way of connecting with them, her laughter and affection making the whole room feel warmer.

We spent a lot of time outdoors, exploring the nearby mountains and soaking in the cooler summer temperatures—a welcome break from the Texas heat. One day, we ventured to a natural slide in the mountains—a spot where a stream had carved its way into the rocky terrain, creating a perfect slippery playground. Sliding down it was exhilarating, and the freezing cold water took my breath away. Erin's laughter was contagious, her joy lighting up the day as we splashed around. It was one of those moments that felt both timeless and fleeting, a memory that would stick with us forever.

Evenings were spent out back with Ryan and Tiffany after the boys had gone to bed. We'd sit on their patio, talking for hours under the stars, catching up on life and sharing family stories. There was a comfort in the way they welcomed me, making the trip feel more like a homecoming than a visit.

As the plane took off and the mountains disappeared from view, Erin leaned in and said, "That was a lot of fun." She was right, and I couldn't agree more.

A SEASON OF CHANGE

After the joy of our summer travels and the lightness of time spent with family and friends, life shifted. The seasons were literally beginning to change, but so too was the rhythm of my world.

Suddenly, it became evident that my dad's parents, Don and Dede, weren't doing as well as we had thought. Both in their mid-eighties, their decline wasn't entirely surprising, but it still caught me off guard. I'd visited them multiple times a year over the twenty years since we had moved to Texas. Sure, they had slowed down, but from my perspective, they were managing well. I spoke with them weekly—usually on Sunday afternoons—by phone or Skype. I had a close relationship with them and noticed, with amusement, how my dad, Brad, and I had picked up some of Grandpa's mannerisms over the years.

It began with Dede being hospitalized for congestive heart failure.

Though she had lived with the condition for years, a medication change required a brief hospital stay. Brad made the 1,000-mile drive to Chillicothe, following our usual route with a stop in Memphis, Tennessee—the natural halfway point—where his in-laws lived.

When Brad arrived, he quickly noticed they needed more help than they were letting on. They were still living at home, driving, and caring for each other, but something had clearly changed. Their independence had become a delicate balance that required intervention.

Brad urged my dad to visit and see for himself. The following weekend, Dad arrived in Chillicothe. After assessing the situation, he convinced Don and Dede to accept more help at home. Over the next couple of weeks, they tried several in-home care options, but nothing seemed sustainable. Surprisingly, Don agreed to move into a nearby independent senior living community. Dede, however, insisted she was fine at home. It wasn't long before she joined him, albeit begrudgingly. The transition was tough, but it was necessary.

While Erin and I were in North Carolina, Dad called from Chillicothe to update me on their situation. He encouraged me to visit soon. When we returned home, Erin and I made arrangements to travel to see them.

This would be our third trip as a couple and Erin's first time in Chillicothe. Though the circumstances were not ideal, Erin was excited to visit the place and meet the people I'd spoken of so fondly. Chillicothe, with its small-town charm, held so much history for me, a sixth-generation Ohioan, and for Ohio. It had been the state's first and third capital before Columbus, giving rise to the saying "A town so nice, it was the capital twice."

Once in Chillicothe, we dropped our bags at Aunt Judy's house and headed straight to see Don and Dede. Judy handed Erin the keys to her car, and with my direction, Erin navigated us through town.

The senior community where Don and Dede had transitioned exceeded my expectations. It was clean, modern, and well equipped to meet their needs. Dede, now in a wheelchair—a relief after years of struggling in their inaccessible home—was wheeled out by a nurse to join us, while Don, more mobile, met us in the common area. Erin and I greeted them with hugs, and we spent the next several hours talking over coffee and ice cream sandwiches. Though they had met Erin over Skype, this was their first time meeting her in person. Erin's presence put them at ease instantly, and it was clear to me that they adored her.

That evening, Erin and I met up with some of my friends from town. Erin had developed a bit of a mythical reputation in Chillicothe, and everyone was eager to meet her. She handled the attention with grace, and by the end of the night, it was obvious. She had captivated everyone she met.

The next day, we spent most of our time with Don and Dede. Erin, always thoughtful, asked if they wanted anything to eat. Don spoke up immediately, rattling off his order without hesitation: a chicken-fried steak, mashed potatoes with gravy, and green beans from Bob Evans, his favorite. Erin and I ran out to pick it up and returned a short while later with the bags in hand. As we sat around the table, Erin couldn't help but marvel at Don's precise and deliberate eating habits—cutting each bite carefully, wiping his knife clean with his fork, and savoring each mouthful as though it were the best meal of his life. His joy was radiant, and it was clear how much he appreciated the small treat.

That evening, we returned to Judy's house to visit with her, Wilbur, and Judy's parents, Kenny and Sharma. The conversation was lively, and I was thrilled to see Erin engaging so naturally with my family.

On our final morning, we visited the senior community one last time to say goodbye. It was difficult. I couldn't shake the feeling of how quickly things had changed, but I left comforted by the care Don and Dede were receiving. As we were leaving, I ran into a childhood friend, now an administrator at the facility. She assured me my grandparents were in good hands.

We headed to Columbus with Judy, Kenny, and Sharma, where we shared a late lunch before boarding our flight back to Dallas. On the plane, Erin took my hand and said, "Your grandparents are so sweet. I'm so glad I got to meet them. And Chillicothe is such a great place. I can't wait to come back."

On the flight home, I couldn't stop thinking about how rapidly my grandparents' lives had declined. The once-strong pillars of our family now needed so much care. The change felt heavy, but Erin's presence made it easier to carry.

It didn't take long for that heaviness to deepen.

Three weeks after Erin and I returned from Chillicothe, my dad received the call. On the day before his sixtieth birthday, the woman who brought him into the world had passed away.

Dad was at the office when the call came through. Mom, Brad, and I were there too, and we shared the weight of the somber moment.

Given our recent visit, the news wasn't entirely unexpected, but the speed and finality were hard to process. It felt surreal.

At thirty-two, this was the most significant loss I had experienced. I wasn't sure how to navigate it. I had been to funerals before, but never for someone so deeply woven into my life.

Mom and Dad quickly arranged flights for all eight of us—our entire Texas crew—to be there for the funeral. Four days later, Dad and Mom, Erin and I, Brad, Rachel, and their little ones, Will and Sawyer, were in Chillicothe.

Sitting next to Grandpa at the funeral, I could only imagine what was going through his mind. He stayed stoic, but the weight of his loss was unmistakable. He and Dede had been married for sixty-four years, a lifetime of shared moments, milestones, and memories. Now, his partner, his best friend, was gone.

The funeral brought an outpouring of family and friends, some of whom I hadn't seen in years. Even a few of my own friends came to pay their respects. It was a somber yet meaningful gathering, but leaving Grandpa behind afterward felt especially difficult. Though he seemed mostly well, I couldn't stop thinking about the loneliness he must have felt.

The morning after the funeral, before we left, Dad, Brad, and I took a picture with Grandpa—a photo of three generations of Grimes men. We didn't say it out loud, but we all knew it could be the last one.

Exactly one week later, Dad's phone rang again.

I remember it well. It was the evening of the fourth Sunday of October, and Erin, my parents, and I were volunteering with our group at The Bridge. Dad's phone buzzed, and he gave Mom a knowing nod as he stepped outside. She came over to me quietly and said, "Steve just called." I didn't need her to explain.

Dad's brother, Steve, and his son, Geoff, had been at Grandpa's side when it happened. Grandpa had passed away.

I was astounded at how quickly it all happened. We had just seen him last week. I had just spoken to him days ago. It felt impossible that, in just sixteen days, both Don and Dede were gone.

A chapter of my life had closed.

I had been so fortunate to have all four of my grandparents together and living well into their eighties. Perhaps that's where I got my sense of invincibility. They had always been there, steadfast and constant, a cornerstone of our family. Losing them so quickly, back-to-back, was staggering. I couldn't stop thinking about Grandpa's final days. I truly believe he succumbed to a broken heart. After more than six decades together, I can't imagine what life without Dede must have been like for him.

As I sat at Grandpa's funeral back in Chillicothe with all eight of us together again, my mind turned to the legacy my grandparents left behind. They certainly faced struggles, but they showed us the blueprint for a life well lived. Their devout Christian faith, their enduring commitment to each other, and their boundless love for us were lessons we will carry forever. The world is a better place because they were in it, and our family is stronger because of the foundation they built.

By the time the holiday season arrived, the grief was still fresh. Life, as it always does, kept moving forward—yet an unmistakable absence lingered.

Thanksgiving, in particular, felt strange and was tough for my parents, especially my dad. He and Mom had spent most of November in Chillicothe, navigating the process of settling the estate. While much of the work had been completed, it wasn't finished. Still, they made it back to Plano in time for our Thanksgiving traditions.

When they returned, Dad asked Brad and me to join him and Mom for lunch. This wasn't unusual for us; it was a routine we'd shared for years at the office. We piled into the car and headed to one of our go-to restaurants, not knowing this lunch would be anything but ordinary.

As we settled into our booth, the conversation quickly turned to

Don and Dede. They had been the focus of so many discussions in recent months, and this lunch was no different. Dad began talking about the estate, the legal processes, and the many details involved. Then, he paused and looked at Brad and me with a weight in his voice that made us lean in.

"Your grandparents loved you both so much," he began. "They were so proud of the men you've become." These were words we'd heard before, but something about hearing them now—after everything—felt different, deeper.

As Dad spoke, he reached into his shirt pocket and pulled out two folded index cards. Sliding one across the table to each of us, he said, "This is their way of continuing to support you, to propel you forward in life."

I unfolded my card to find a number written in bold black marker, clear enough for me to read right there at the table. Brad and I exchanged glances, both stunned. The number wasn't insignificant. This wasn't just a gift; it was a statement of love, trust, and belief in us.

I felt an overwhelming mix of gratitude and humility. Their legacy wasn't about money; it was about the life lessons they had instilled in us: the value of hard work, faith, family, and love. This gift was simply a tangible representation of their resolute support, a way for them to lift us even after they were gone.

That evening, over dinner, I shared the news with Erin. I told her how much the inheritance meant to me, not just for its monetary value but for the profound message behind it. I knew what to do. During our time off that week, Erin and I went to the bank together. I opened a new savings account, one I knew I'd use with intention and care, guided by the values my grandparents had passed down to me.

The day after Christmas, Erin and I drove to San Antonio to spend the holiday with her family. Her brothers, Scott and Ryan, were there, along with Ryan's family, who had traveled from North Carolina to also visit Tiffany's relatives nearby. We spent time with Tiffany's family, even joining them for a night out on the town.

During this visit, I found myself reflecting on how I fit into Erin's family. By now, I had been around them enough to feel comfortable, but this time, I saw things differently. I wasn't just Erin's boyfriend visiting. I was starting to see myself as a member of the family. I was focusing on just how seamlessly I could be part of their lives.

By this point, I knew Erin was the one. I can't pinpoint the exact moment I realized it, but I'd known for some time. Everything between us felt easy, natural, and right. Both of our families had embraced us, and there were no awkward moments, just a steady rhythm of connection and belonging.

People had started to comment, "When are you two tying the knot?" If I was hearing it, I knew Erin was hearing it even more. By Christmas, I had been seriously thinking about proposing. I knew I wanted to spend my life with her, but the timing didn't feel quite right.

Christmas felt too expected, especially with every other commercial on TV showcasing dazzling diamonds and cheesy proposals. Those ads had always made me roll my eyes, but that year, they gave me pause.

Several months earlier, Mom and I had passed each other in the hallway at the office. She gave me a gentle nudge and stopped me. "Hey, how are things with you and Erin?" she asked casually. "Things are great," I replied, thinking nothing of it. Then, in a way only a mother can, she added with stern conviction, "Don't let her get away."

Now, in the first week of the new year, as we passed each other in that same hallway, it was my turn to stop her. I gave her a gentle nudge and said, "Hey, it's time. I'm going to look at a ring for Erin. I'd like you to come along if you can keep it a secret."

Her face lit up, and without hesitation, she said, "Yes!"

THE PERFECT PLAN

After letting Brad and Dad in on the news, Mom and I visited Micah's office a few days later. Micah had been in his family's diamond business for many years, following in the footsteps of his father. This was an incredibly exciting moment, and I knew Micah was the perfect person to guide me.

After years of working in the insurance industry, I'd seen countless engagement ring appraisals and knew most of the terminology. I had a strong idea of what Erin would like after months of careful listening, but I wanted to be certain I was making the right choice. As I held the diamonds, running my fingers along their edges, I couldn't help but imagine Erin wearing one of them every day—a symbol of everything we'd built and everything we hoped to share in the future. With Micah's expertise and thoughtful input from Mom, Brad, and Drew, I carefully selected the perfect diamond. Only one detail remained: Erin's ring size. It seemed like a major hurdle, but it was essential and required some creativity.

Fortunately, the timing couldn't have been better. Erin's birthday was approaching, and her friend Melissa had planned a surprise visit from Tennessee to celebrate. Melissa reached out to me to coordinate the surprise, and I let her in on an even bigger secret. Nervous about trusting someone else, I knew Melissa could handle the delicate task of discovering Erin's ring size without giving anything away. She was thrilled to help and managed to get the information with clever subtlety. Erin never suspected a thing.

On February 13, Erin's birthday, we officially joined Highland Park United Methodist Church, introduced to the congregation by none other than Mark Craig himself. It felt symbolic: I had the ring, a brilliant proposal plan, and the perfect setting for our future wedding. But one critical step remained—I needed Erin's parents' blessing.

This was more than tradition; it was deeply personal to me. I wanted to honor them by asking for their permission to marry their daughter. A week before the visit, I called Erin's parents to arrange the meeting. "I have something important to discuss," I told them. "And Erin cannot know about this." It didn't need to be said. They knew exactly why I was coming.

To keep the visit disguised from Erin, I told her I had a day trip to Houston to meet with my mentor, Warren. She found this entirely plausible, as I'd made a similar trip recently. In truth, I was headed to San Antonio.

Early that morning, Dad drove me to Love Field for my flight and wished me luck. I carefully stored the ring in a secret compartment in my carry-on, and I was laser-focused as it went through the security checkpoint. I must have looked suspicious, nervously shifting my weight as I listened intently to the conveyor belt hum and the agents shuffle items around. I had never been so anxious about an airport security screening in my life. When I made it through, safe and sound,

I put the ring back in my pocket. On the short flight, I rehearsed what I would say—not because I doubted their answer, but because the moment carried so much weight. I wanted to use the perfect words.

I arrived at Erin's parents' home just before lunch. While the reason for my visit was obvious, I still took a moment to collect myself. I stepped into the restroom, carefully removed the ring from its box, and prepared for the conversation.

They were waiting for me in the living room. I walked in with a mix of confidence and nervous energy. True to form, I started with humor to break the ice. "Well," I said with a grin, "I suppose it's no secret why I'm here."

I shared a brief history of Erin and me and our time together, recounting how much she meant to me and how deeply I loved her. "I've never felt this way about anyone else," I said. "Erin is everything to me, and I know she feels the same. I promise to love, protect, and cherish her for the rest of our lives. It would be an honor to have your blessing to marry her."

Their response was everything I had hoped for. Erin's parents said yes without hesitation, their warmth and support evident in their voices as they hugged me. I showed them the ring and described my carefully crafted proposal plan. Then we toasted Erin's and my future over lunch at their favorite Italian restaurant.

While waiting at the airport for my flight home, I called Mom, Dad, Brad, my grandparents, and Aunt Judy to share the news. The excitement was almost overwhelming. Back in Plano, I could barely contain myself. For weeks, I had been stealthily orchestrating every detail: the perfect proposal, consulting with Erin's parents, finalizing the ring, and concealing it in my apartment. Now, the moment was so close I could hardly wait.

That evening, Erin shared some news of her own. She had just learned from Deb, one of her teaching partners, that Kathryn—her daughter and a good friend of Erin—was getting engaged. Kathryn's boyfriend, Joey, had just asked for permission and had a plan to pop the question that weekend. Erin was thrilled for her friend.

Her voice brimmed with excitement as she recounted the details of Joey's proposal plan. Little did she know I was planning the exact same thing for her.

As I sat there listening to her joy for Kathryn, the wait felt both thrilling and agonizing. Keeping the secret was one of the hardest things I'd ever done, but this time, I knew the wait would be worth it.

The plan was set. Everything had fallen perfectly into place. I knew exactly what I needed to do, and I wanted this to be very special for Erin, a moment she would always remember. All I had to do now was execute it.

Chris played a key role in the cover story. Our annual winter trip to Chicago with him provided the perfect excuse, and he was more than happy to help keep the real reason for the trip a secret. We even staged a couple of phone calls to make plans and relive our past Chicago adventures, making sure it all seemed normal. I was so nervous Erin might figure it out. I wanted this to be a surprise, and I was so excited about what was about to happen that I could barely contain myself.

We left very early on a Friday morning. Dad drove us to the airport, giving me a firm handshake and an extra squeeze goodbye, knowing what was about to unfold. My nerves were on high alert, especially as we went through security. The ring was snugly stored in my carry-on bag, but irrational fears swirled in my mind. What if my bag got flagged? What if Erin saw the ring? What if the surprise was ruined before it even began?

For a brief moment, I had the ridiculous thought that if this didn't go smoothly, I'd be proposing in the middle of the DFW Airport security line—just like every little girl dreams of. Fortunately, we made it through with the secret intact.

We met Erin's brother Ryan for breakfast before our flight, as he happened to be flying through Dallas on business. As we sat chatting, Erin stepped away to grab some napkins, leaving Ryan and me alone for a moment. For a split second, I considered telling him what I was about to do, but I held back, worried Erin might return and overhear. As we parted ways, I smiled and said, "I'm sure we'll talk to you again soon." It was an innocent enough statement, but it carried far more weight than Ryan or Erin realized.

The flight to Chicago went off without a hitch. I kept my carry-on bag within reach the entire time, the ring feeling like a ticking time bomb. When we arrived, we grabbed our luggage and hopped in a cab to the Ritz-Carlton. Staying at the Ritz was a bit out of character for us, and I worried it might tip Erin off, but I covered by saying, "We got a great deal on the rooms." That seemed to put her at ease, and the cover story held. As far as she knew, Chris and his date were staying at the Ritz too, though they wouldn't arrive until later that afternoon.

After checking in, we made a spa appointment for the next day and dropped our bags in the room. I recommended we go ice skating in Millennium Park, something I'd mentioned wanting to do again on the flight. I told Erin Chris didn't seem too enthusiastic about it, so we should go before he and his date arrived. Erin agreed, and we set off, walking briskly down Michigan Avenue through the freezing Chicago air.

The wind was biting, but adrenaline had me running hot. The ring was tucked safely in my front pocket, hidden beneath a sweater and heavy coat. We crossed over the Chicago River and made our way to the ice rink at Millennium Park. The rink was busy, and the festive atmosphere gave the space an electric energy.

We rented skates and hit the ice. As we began to skate, I clung to Erin for dear life; I was a terrible skater, wobbling with every step. Erin laughed as she helped me stay upright, her hand steadying me as we made our way around the rink. She spotted a group of Girl Scouts gliding around the ice. "Ahh, aren't they adorable?" she said, listening to their giggles and joyful chatter.

After a couple of laps, I motioned for us to move toward the center of the rink, saying I needed to adjust my skate. Once we stopped, I took off my gloves, knelt down, and pretended to fiddle with my laces. Slipping my hand into my pocket, I wrapped my fingers around the ring.

Erin was distracted, watching the Girl Scouts as their laughter floated on the chilly breeze. I called her name, and when she turned back, I was on one knee, holding the ring in front of me.

"Erin," I said, my voice steady despite my pounding heart. "I love you, and I'm ready to spend the rest of my life with you. Will you marry me?"

She froze, her hands flying to her mouth as tears began to stream down her cheeks. For what felt like an eternity, she didn't say anything. I couldn't see the joy on her face through her hands, and doubt started to creep in. Was she crying out of happiness—or something else?

Then, she hugged me so tightly she nearly knocked me over. Still on one knee, I steadied us both and asked, "Is that a yes?"

Through her tears and laughter, she wiped her face and said, "Yes! Of course—yes, yes, yes!"

Relief and joy washed over me. "I wasn't sure there for a moment," I said with a chuckle.

Our embrace was interrupted by a couple skating by who smiled and said, "Congratulations!" Then another couple passed, echoing the sentiment with a cheerful wave. Shortly after, the Girl Scouts skated by, giggling with excitement. "Congratulations!" one of their leaders said, stopping to offer to take our picture. I handed her my phone, and she captured the moment: Erin and me on skates, bundled up on the rink, with the Chicago skyline behind us. We were beaming. It was a photo we would cherish forever.

After our picture, we quickly returned our skates and sat on a nearby bench, still reeling from what had just happened. The first thing Erin and I talked about was how much we loved each other and how excited we both were. I told her about all the planning: the ring, the visit to her parents, and keeping the secret for so long. Erin couldn't stop smiling as she admired the ring on her finger. "I love it, and it fits perfectly! How did you get the size right?" she asked.

"Melissa helped with that," I said with a grin, explaining how her friend had been part of the plan.

Erin's eyes lit up with curiosity. "How many people knew about this?" she asked, laughing as she wiped away another happy tear. "Does Chris know?"

"Well, I had to tell a few people to make this all work. Yes—Chris knows. And he isn't coming," I said, smiling. "It's just you and me this weekend!"

She smiled and shook her head. "Of course!" she said, laughing at how perfectly everything had been planned.

We started making calls, one after another, to share the exciting news. Erin's parents, my parents, our siblings, grandparents, Aunt Judy, Melissa, Micah, Chris, Drew—it felt like the whole world was celebrating with us. Erin's joyful voice filled the air as she shared every detail of the moment. Each call was met with cheers, tears, and laughter on the other end of the line. When Erin called Ryan to share the news, he immediately connected the dots. "So that's what you meant by 'talk to you again soon,'" he said with a laugh.

Erin also called Deb to share the big news. Deb was with Kathryn and had been keeping her engagement a secret, as it was going to happen later that day. When she answered the phone with a whisper, Erin quickly assured her she wasn't calling about Kathryn. Instead, Erin shared our exciting news, and Deb was overjoyed. "What a weekend for you both!" she said, her excitement bursting through her hushed tone.

That night, we had dinner at the Ritz, where we toasted to our future with champagne—courtesy of Chris. We talked about everything. When and where we'd get married, who would be in the wedding, and how excited we were to start this new chapter together.

The next day, we relaxed at the spa, enjoyed some thoughtful activities I had planned, and soaked in the magic of being newly engaged. Everything felt brighter, more alive. The weekend couldn't have been more perfect.

As we boarded our flight back to Dallas, I reminded Erin of the woman from our previous Chicago trip who had asked, "When's the wedding?" Smiling, I said, "We have an answer for her. It's soon."

FOREVER IN THE MAKING

After returning home from Chicago, the excitement of our engagement lingered in the air, infusing everything with a newfound sense of joy and purpose. We retold our engagement story to friends, family, and coworkers, each recounting adding more depth to the magical moment. Erin's joy was unmistakable. Her eyes lit up every time she spoke about it, and her excitement was contagious. It was incredible to witness her happiness and to know I was part of it. I was so happy for her, for us, and for the life we were building together.

The first significant event of our engagement was bringing our parents together. While Erin and I each knew the other's parents well, this was the first time they would meet. Her parents made the five-hour car trip from San Antonio, a journey that would soon become a regular part of their lives as we planned the wedding. Though neither of us was nervous, there was a quiet anticipation on the way to my parents' house.

The evening couldn't have gone better. Conversation flowed easily, laughter filled the room, and by the time dessert was served, it felt as though our two families had known each other for years. It wasn't long before the conversation turned to wedding plans. Erin and I shared that we wanted to get married at Highland Park United Methodist Church, and both sets of parents agreed it was the perfect venue.

When it came to setting the date, our parents began comparing schedules. "How about next weekend?" I joked, earning a round of laughter. But the truth was, I had never been more certain about anything in my life. I was ready to make it official. While summer seemed ideal for its proximity, we took our parents' advice and considered fall dates as well. The following week, Erin and I checked the church's availability. A date in October stood out—a little more time to plan, but not so far away that we'd have to wait forever. Just two weeks after our engagement, we had our date set and church booked. Another milestone checked off. It was exhilarating to see our vision come to life.

Since Erin moved into my building, we were together almost all the time and were constantly walking around the ever-expanding Shops area. Now our walks began to feel different. The world we were building together was starting to take shape, and every conversation felt like a step toward our future. With Erin's trusty wedding binder in hand, filled with our growing guest list, color swatches, vendor brochures, and detailed notes, our walks now had purpose and direction. That binder became a constant companion, a symbol of the care and thought Erin poured into every detail of our wedding. Watching her during this time was nothing short of awe-inspiring.

She was radiant, her joy evident to anyone she encountered. I was overwhelmed with gratitude to be on this journey with her.

One evening, our walk took us past a section of new construction on the north edge of the Shops area. Townhomes were going up, and they immediately caught my eye. The idea of transitioning from apartment living—a hallmark of my single life—to a permanent home with Erin felt like a natural next step. These townhomes symbolized everything we were heading toward: permanence, partnership, and the life we were building together.

Over the next few weeks, we became regulars at the construction site, checking on the progress and imagining what life could look like there. The builder's sales rep greeted us warmly each time, eventually saying, "You two need to get a realtor and make this official." That was the push we needed. After touring other homes in the area with our trusted realtor, Vickie, we quickly returned to the townhome we'd been eyeing all along. Negotiations with the builder followed, and soon enough, we reached an agreement. Closing was just around the corner. We had found our new home together.

Wedding planning was in full swing by late spring, and Erin's energy was boundless. From the reception venue to the wine selection, from flowers to photography, Erin poured her heart into every detail. I mostly stayed out of the way, happy to jump in wherever I was needed. It was a tremendous ride. Watching her work her magic was incredible; her joy and dedication made every step feel significant. Even the smallest details, like chair covers for the reception, became memorable moments. I still remember joking with her, "Wait, people are going to be sitting on these, right?" She shot me a look that needed no words, and I wisely let her handle it. Of course, she was right. They tied everything together beautifully.

One responsibility Erin totally entrusted me with was choosing the music for our reception. I dove in with enthusiasm. I quickly narrowed down some options, and the best part was that Erin and I got to experience the bands in action. Over a series of fun nights out, we scouted different groups, watching them perform and imagining how their sound would fill the room on our big day. We finally found the perfect band, one with incredible energy and the ideal vibe for our celebration.

For the ceremony, we surrounded ourselves with the people who mattered most: eight on each side, a perfect blend of family and lifelong friends. Erin chose Amanda as matron of honor, her best friend since childhood and the one who had been there from the beginning, navigating emails and laughing at my crazy wig photo. For me, the best man choice was simple: my brother Brad, my lifelong best friend, constant supporter, and Erin's Facebook friend.

Choosing the minister was equally meaningful. For us, there was no question. We wanted Mark Craig. Though he was in high demand, we submitted our request with confidence, listing no second choice. Two days later, we received the news we'd hoped for: Mark said yes.

Looking back, it's hard to put into words just how perfectly everything was coming together. From the wedding plans to finding our home, every step felt like it was meant to be. The joy, love, and excitement of this time in our lives were unlike anything I had ever experienced. It was clear to me that a higher power was bringing everything into alignment, setting the stage for the incredible life we were about to begin together.

As summer kicked off, I closed on the townhouse. A huge milestone. My first home. It felt different from any place I'd lived before; more permanent, more stable. It was just outside the Shops area, still within walking distance of our favorite spots, but quieter.

It felt like the next step into adulthood. No more leases, no more temporary spaces. This was ours. A place to build our future.

Then, Erin found "the" dress. Probably the most important thing of all.

She had gone dress shopping with her mom and mine. She called me from the dressing room, her voice overflowing with excitement. I missed the call, but the voicemail she left is one I've saved for life. Fighting back tears of joy, she gushed about how fabulous the dress was, how much she loved it—and how much she loved me. It was an emotional moment, one that made everything feel even more real. I don't know if a guy is supposed to get emotional about a wedding dress, but knowing how much it meant to Erin brought tears to my eyes, too.

Erin and I agreed she wouldn't move in until after the wedding, honoring our values and keeping with tradition. Her lease would expire at the end of the summer, leaving a gap, but we had a plan. For now, we were separated by more than a few hallways, but being apart was a small price to pay knowing the permanence of what lay ahead.

With most of the big wedding decisions made and all the major events booked, we turned our focus inward, making sure we were fully prepared for everything ahead. We started with a full-day premarital class, where we worked through the essential topics of marriage— faith, family dynamics, finances, and children. It was reassuring to find that we were already aligned in so many ways. Religion had never been a question for us; we had built our relationship on shared beliefs. We had been transparent about money from the beginning, thanks in large part to Melissa's influence. She had introduced us both to *The Total Money Makeover* by Dave Ramsey, and we took its principles seriously. Even though our finances were completely separate at the time, we had full knowledge of each other's financial standing and were already planning for how we'd merge our lives after the wedding.

The family dynamic came easily. Our families already got along well, and any potential challenges seemed minimal at best. And when it came to children, Erin helped me see that the possibilities were far greater than I had ever imagined. Before our conversations, I had a pretty narrow view of how I might become a father, given my meningitis-related circumstances. But Erin opened my mind to so many other possibilities. Her heart for children was undeniable; between her profession, her nurturing spirit, and the way she instinctively cared for others, she was born to be a mom.

But despite everything going so smoothly, I had a nagging thought I couldn't get past. We had never had a fight. Not once. Not even a little disagreement. Marriage can't be this easy. Was I missing something? I had always heard that marriage takes work, but with Erin, everything felt effortless. We were so naturally in sync that I almost wondered if that was a red flag in itself.

So, we kept digging deeper.

After the premarital class, we started meeting weekly with a trusted minister at the church for more in-depth marital counseling, ensuring our relationship mirrored the values of a Christian marriage. Finally, we had a private meeting with Mark Craig. Mark challenged us to think beyond the wedding, beyond the excitement of the moment, and focus on the foundation we were building for a lifetime. He asked us to reflect on what marriage meant to us, to consider how we would navigate change, hardships, and the unknowns ahead. His words stuck with us. This wasn't just about a wedding day; it was about forever. And with each session, with every deep conversation, we only grew more certain that we were exactly where we were meant to be.

Prior to my own, I had never been a big fan of couples' wedding showers, probably because I had never actually been a couple at a wedding shower before. Luckily, I got the true experience! We had two as a couple. One was near home, hosted by Erin's teaching partner, Deb, and her daughter, Kathryn. The other was in Chillicothe, hosted by my dear friend Alana and her parents. That one was extra special.

We loaded up my parents and Erin's parents and flew to Ohio for the weekend. Seeing my grandparents, Judy and Wilbur, and so many of my childhood friends come together, celebrating not just me but Erin as well, was an incredible moment. And the highlight of the trip? Sneaking down onto the football field at Ohio State University. Mom, Judy, Erin, and I lined up on the 50-yard line, arms raised above our heads to spell out "O-H-I-O." Unfortunately, Judy and I somehow managed to invert our letters, so we ended up spelling "O-I-H-O" instead—a legendary blunder that will forever live on in photographic infamy. It was the perfect, hilarious punctuation to an unforgettable trip.

By the time we returned home, the wedding countdown was in full swing. The bachelor and bachelorette parties were unforgettable, and everyone came back with the same number of eyebrows, though there was a pink boa incident. The registry gifts were rolling in, and the townhouse was starting to fill with things that would soon become part of our everyday lives together.

When Erin's lease ended, she moved most of her belongings in with me but stayed with her good friend and teaching partner, Beth, for the final six weeks leading up to the wedding. The finish line was in sight. We had planned for this, prepared for it, and now, all that was left was to make it official.

AT LAST

The week leading up to our wedding was a blur of excitement, final touches, and joyful reunions as friends and family arrived from all over. Every moment was filled with anticipation—the feeling that something extraordinary was about to happen.

The rehearsal dinner wasn't just about the incredible food at Nobu, though that certainly didn't hurt. It was a celebration: a night filled with love, laughter, and toasts that ranged from heartfelt to hilarious. As we sat surrounded by the people who had shaped our lives, there was an overwhelming sense of gratitude. These were the people who had supported us, encouraged us, and in some cases, even conspired to bring us together. They were here to witness the next chapter of our story.

And then, before we knew it, the day had come. October 22, 2011.

The warm fall day couldn't have been better. The church was breathtaking. Every pew filled, every flower in place. The scent of fresh roses lingered in the air, mingling with the quiet hum of conversation as guests settled into their seats. A hushed anticipation hung over the room, a collective inhale waiting for the moment to begin.

I stood at the altar, hands clasped in front of me, heartbeat steady but fast. The weight of the moment pressed into me—not as nerves, but as something deeper. I could feel the presence of everyone around me, their energy palpable. My groomsmen stood beside me, their silent support anchoring me.

Then the music began.

A hush fell over the room, replacing soft murmurs with the organ's powerful chords. The doors at the back of the church swung open.

For a split second, there was stillness. One last held breath before everything changed.

And then, the air shifted.

Everyone turned.

The atmosphere transformed.

Erin stepped into the room.

Even without seeing every detail, I *felt* it. A wave of warmth and awe spread through the space as all eyes fixed on her. The collective energy turned electric, the quiet reverence giving way to an unspoken *there she is.*

Brad, standing beside me, leaned in and began narrating.

"She looks stunning, man. Absolutely beautiful. She's smiling so big, and…yep, she's tearing up. Her dad, too."

My heart swelled.

As Erin and her father made their way down the aisle, the emotion in the room was undeniable. It moved with them, growing stronger with each step. The closer she got, the more I could feel it—her excitement, her joy, her love.

Then, finally, she was in front of me.

Her father and I exchanged a look of quiet understanding, the kind of moment that didn't need words. I reached out and embraced him, and he placed Erin's hand in mine.

And in that instant, the energy transferred.

I felt it in her fingertips—her nervous excitement, her overwhelming happiness. It surged through me, steadying my heartbeat, filling me with a certainty I had always known but never so profoundly as in that moment.

I had tucked a handkerchief into my inside jacket pocket, knowing we would need it. Without hesitation, I handed it to Erin. She sniffled, gripping it tightly, tears spilling down her cheeks.

Mark Craig, standing before us, grinned and said just loud enough for everyone to hear, "I hope those are happy tears."

Laughter rippled through the church. Erin nodded, smiling through her tears.

As we began our vows, my mind raced. Not out of nerves, but because I wanted to remember every second of this.

I wasn't worried about the meaning of the words. The commitment had already been made in my heart. But in the back of my mind, I thought, *Do grooms ever mess these up? Will I be the first?*

Erin's voice, though thick with emotion, was steady. She was beaming through happy tears as she spoke. And when she said *I do*, I felt the truth of it settle deep in my chest.

Then, it was my turn.

"I do."

And just like that, the world clicked into place.

Mark pronounced us husband and wife. I leaned in, kissed her, and with that, everything else faded. The church, the guests, the months of planning…it all disappeared. It was just us.

Then we turned to face the people who had loved us through every chapter of our story.

For a brief moment, I paused. I wanted to bottle it all up—the cheers, the organ's rich, rising notes in the background, the pure, unfiltered joy radiating through the room.

My mind filled with memories.

The first email.

The crazy wig photo.

Our first date.

The night we said *I love you* to each other.

The ice rink.

The townhouse. The wedding planning. The nights spent dreaming about our future.

Everything had led us here.

Erin's hand squeezed mine, grounding me in the present. And then, hand in hand, we stepped forward—husband and wife.

My lonely days are over. It was time to dance. At last!

—SECTION VIII—
Love and Loss and Life

THE START OF EVERYTHING

The reception was unforgettable, a night filled with clinking glasses, packed dance floors, and the kind of joy that leaves your cheeks sore from smiling. Our first dance was to Etta James's "At Last"—a fitting choice, not just for the moment, but for everything it had taken to get there. The music, the love in the room, the way Erin and I held each other as if we were the only two people in the world; it was everything. That moment lit the fuse, and what followed was an explosion of love, life, and everything we'd been waiting for.

The toasts set the tone for the night: heartfelt, hilarious, and just questionable enough to keep things interesting. The kind that made us laugh while also leaving us wondering if our family and friends maybe knew us a little too well. Then came the dancing, the drinks, and the sort of unfiltered joy that only happens when a room full of people decides—together—to let go.

Perfect conditions for the Chillicothe contingent, a raucous, enthusiastic crew that had traveled with the clear intent of having a good time. They did not disappoint. They tore up the dance floor, drained the bar dry, and somehow convinced the band to extend their set. If you ever want to know what pure, uninhibited celebration looks like, just invite a crowd from Chillicothe, Ohio, to your wedding and stand back.

As if the night couldn't get any better, my dad—perhaps fueled by the energy of the room or maybe just seizing the moment— jumped on stage with the band and played the drums for a song. Reliving his teenage band days, he still had it. He didn't miss a beat, literally. The crowd went nuts. Someone snapped a perfect photo of him mid-action, drumsticks blurred, a huge grin stretched across his face. Proof that sometimes, dads are way cooler than we give them credit for.

Just before the final note was played, Erin and I made our grand exit to the elevator and out of sight. A few hours later, while most of our guests were still fast asleep, we slipped into the early morning darkness like honeymoon bandits stealing away with the night. The back seat of a black town car escorted us toward the airport, making us feel like VIPs, even though we were running on zero sleep and a questionable mix of champagne and wedding cake. By sunrise, we were halfway to Mexico.

For five incredible days, we lived in a perfect little bubble of sunshine, ocean waves, and uninterrupted time together. We let the rhythm of the surf set our schedule, indulged in every meal like it was a celebration, and let the warmth of the sun deepen our tans—just in time for the holiday season. No stress. No lists. No deadlines. Just us.

But honeymoons, like wedding days, eventually come to an end.

And when we touched back down at home, we weren't returning to "normal life." We were stepping into the next chapter.

First order of business? Moving Erin into the townhome.

They say marriage is about compromise, but what they don't warn you about is the deluge of stuff you suddenly inherit. We had her things, my things, and a mountain of wedding gifts. Our place looked less like a home and more like the aftermath of a department store explosion. But every box, every beautifully wrapped package, was a reminder of how loved and supported we were. Each dish, each towel, each carefully chosen gift represented someone who was cheering us on in this new beginning.

And we were still riding the newlywed high. Late at night, surrounded by stacks of thank-you notes and bubble wrap, we'd laugh and dream together about our first holiday season as husband and wife, our first lazy Saturday morning without a wedding to plan, our first Starbucks run as a married couple. Everything felt fresh, wide open, and full of possibility.

The future was ours, and we couldn't wait to see what it held.

The first big surprise of our marriage wasn't wrapped in wedding paper or written in any plan. It came with the force of a seismic miracle, something I never thought I'd experience again but one that would change everything.

Before meningitis, there were a lot of things I never had to think twice about: walking, seeing, eating a meal without needing a thickening agent, and certain other biological functions that had always worked the way they were supposed to.

Then meningitis came and rewrote the script. It left scars that weren't visible to the outside world, but I carried them every day. And one loss in particular cut deeper than I could ever admit out loud.

I'd accepted it as permanent and shouldered the weight of it into every relationship.

But when Erin came into my life, she accepted me fully and without hesitation. And that should have been enough to take the pressure off.

But pressure doesn't always come from the outside; it often comes from within. When you're told something is impossible long enough, you start to believe it. And when you believe it, hope begins to shrink, leaving little room for the audacity of change.

And then, against every prognosis and prediction, hope burst back to life.

No medical breakthrough. No new treatment. No explanation that science could give me. Just Erin—and something greater than either of us.

In a single moment, what I had grieved as permanently lost was suddenly alive again. For the first time since meningitis, I felt whole. A part of me I thought was buried forever had come rushing back, unexpected and undeniable. It wasn't just my body responding. It was my spirit. My identity, my sense of manhood, my hope for the future . . . all of it was restored in an instant. Our future had been rewritten in ways I had scarcely dared to imagine.

Medical science often lacks the ability to understand a man's heart. It can diagnose, categorize, and prescribe, but it cannot measure the quiet work of love, acceptance, and the mystery of human connection. By her presence, her beauty, her laugh, and some things that can only be described as the will of a higher power, Erin not only changed the destiny of my heart but also of my life.

Fatherhood, once a door I thought I'd never walk through, was suddenly right in front of me. Not as a workaround, but as a possibility. And though science may hold many wonderful discoveries in a laboratory, now our destiny could unfold the old-fashioned way.

Possibility is always a possibility.

And in my heart, I had always believed that. What I never expected was just how alive that belief would become. Against every odd and expectation, possibility wasn't just restored—it was thriving, reshaping how Erin and I stepped into our life together.

Over the next several months, Erin and I continued blending our lives into one. All the typical newlywed logistics—name changes, bank account mergers, insurance updates—were necessary and important, but they weren't exactly thrilling. The real fun was in living life together as husband and wife.

We joined a newlywed Sunday school class at church. We discovered new places to have brunch. We painted rooms in our new home, replacing the sea of builder beige with warm, inviting colors that actually felt like ours. We had friends over, breaking in all our shiny new wedding gifts—preparing elaborate meals with cookware we probably wouldn't have bought for ourselves, toasting wine, and soaking up the joy of that new season.

Life felt like one big adventure, filled with late-night laughs, long weekend getaways, and a sense of ease that only comes when you've married the right person. Everything just made sense, and our biggest challenge was deciding where to eat dinner.

And it was during one of those dinners that the conversation turned to family.

We had just come from the hospital, visiting my newborn nephew, Weston. Brad and Rachel had welcomed their third son, carrying on a long-standing Grimes tradition. For generations, the Grimes family had been overwhelmingly boy-heavy: girls usually had to marry into the clan. Brad was keeping the tradition alive with another perfect little addition.

Watching my brother beam with pride and feeling the weight of a newborn in my arms—it stirred something in me. But what really got me? Watching Erin hold him. There was something about the way she looked at him, the way she cradled him, spoke to him, and rocked him gently in her arms. It was so natural, so instinctual. I'd seen her motherly side in so many ways before, but this? This was different. It was as if, in that moment, I was catching a glimpse of something that had been there all along, just waiting for the right time.

Later that evening, as Erin and I sat across from each other at dinner, I brought it up. We had been married for almost a year, living in our newlywed bliss. Life was good—really good. But something inside me whispered *it's time*.

Erin listened, a twinkle in her eye as she let my words settle between us. And then, a smile. For a few weeks, the conversation continued.

She told me she had always known three things about herself: she wanted to be a teacher, a wife, and a mother. Teaching had been her calling, something she had poured her heart into. Becoming a wife had been a dream realized, and we were building something beautiful together. But motherhood? That was the dream still waiting to be fulfilled, the part of her story not yet written.

I had witnessed Erin's motherly instincts long before we had this conversation; it was just part of who she was. And, deep down, I knew she was born to be a mother, and when the time came, she would be nothing short of extraordinary.

And yet, I was still somewhat stunned that I could help fulfill the dream of parenthood for both of us. But here I was, sitting across from her, discussing the very real possibility of raising a child together.

We weren't getting any younger, and unlike many of our friends who had started their families years earlier, we were beginning this chapter later—making the question of timing impossible to ignore. My visual impairment already made certain aspects of life more challenging, and adding a child into the mix would only make things more interesting. But the more we talked, the more we prayed, the clearer the answer became.

We were ready. Or at least, we thought we were. Which is to say we were just as "ready" as every other first-time parent. Delightfully unaware of how unprepared we actually were.

But that didn't matter. We were doing this. Let the fun begin!

WE'RE HAVING A BABY

E rin shook me while I was sleeping. It was 3 a.m. and I was off in my usual deep slumber, completely unaware of what was happening. Erin, however, was wide awake. She had woken up with a feeling.

Since we had decided to start a family, we were fully stocked with pregnancy tests. The night before, Erin had sensed something different in her body. She had already done all the research. She knew the best brands, the best testing methods, and the best time of day to take them. Morning was ideal.

But morning was still hours away. She tried to go back to sleep, but she couldn't shake the feeling. Finally, she gave in. She grabbed a test on her way to the bathroom, heart pounding.

She followed the instructions, set the test on the floor, and paced around, stealing quick glances like a kid trying not to peek at Christmas presents before it was time. Her heart was racing, her thoughts a blur of excitement and nerves.

Then, finally, she looked.

She snatched up the test, bolted out of the bathroom, and sprinted back to the bedroom.

"John, John, John!" she said, shaking me awake.

I groggily came to, somewhat alarmed. "Are you okay?"

"I'm pregnant! John, I'm pregnant!"

I immediately shot up in bed.

"Really? Tremendous! Wow…that was fast."

We had only been trying for a couple of months. Erin, like most women, was incredibly in tune with her body, and she had been right.

She showed me the pregnancy test, and we both sat there in stunned, ecstatic disbelief. For the next hour, we talked about everything—all the things we needed to do, all the things we needed to get. Erin was ready to call her OB-GYN immediately, but the office wouldn't be open for hours.

Reality was setting in. We had created a life. I was stunned; completely at a loss for words. I couldn't believe this was actually happening.

While getting dressed and ready for the day, Erin and I were still buzzing with excitement, and we headed to Starbucks to keep the conversation going. There was so much to think about. I had no idea how pregnancy tests even worked.

While sipping my coffee, I suggested, "You should probably take another one," feeling like I was contributing something useful.

Erin nodded quickly, still caught up in the excitement. She didn't argue; she just smiled, agreed, and went along with it, but she already knew.

Later that morning, Erin called me from school. "I took another test," she said. "Still positive!"

She called her OB-GYN's office. They did the math and scheduled her first appointment in four weeks. At that point, she would be eight weeks pregnant. Four weeks felt like an eternity, but okay, we would be there.

I was riding the high of excitement and possibility, but Erin knew the risks. She understood how fragile early pregnancy could be. She had friends who had lost pregnancies. I, on the other hand, had no idea how common that was, how the first twelve weeks were a cautious waiting game. Erin didn't want to dampen the excitement, but I could sense the subtle tension in her voice.

We decided to only tell our parents at that point. We would break the big news that weekend—on the same day.

We started with Erin's parents. We FaceTimed them, and Erin casually asked, "What are you guys doing in October?" Puzzled, they responded that they hadn't planned that far ahead.

"Great," she said. "Because I'm pregnant! Due in October!"

Their excitement was instant and overwhelming. Cheers and an immediate flood of love.

Next, we went over to my parents' house. Trying to keep things casual, I made sure both of them were home before we stopped by. We did our usual small talk, but I couldn't hold it in for long.

I remember it like it was yesterday. The four of us were standing in the living room, and I started with something witty, but quickly got to the punchline.

"Erin's pregnant!"

Shocked is an understatement. They both looked at us, processing what they had just heard for a split second, then erupted in joy.

A big group hug followed, arms wrapping tightly around us, laughter spilling out as the shock turned into celebration. But beneath their excitement, I could tell my parents were confused. They knew my situation.

A few months before my wedding, Dad and I had gone to lunch, and he hesitantly asked, "Does Erin know about . . . ?"

With a quiet smile, I told him, "Yes. She knows. And she loves me—all of me."

And now? Despite everything they thought they knew, we were having a baby.

My mom's eyes lit up. After generations of Grimes boys, she dared to believe this might be the one to break the streak.

A couple of weeks later, I found myself in an OB-GYN office for the first time in my life. I wasn't sure what to expect. Bright, sterile walls. Baby magazine overload. A waiting room full of expectant mothers who all seemed to know exactly what they were doing. I sat there nervously looking around, scanning the room for other guys like me.

Surely, I wasn't the only one here, right? Were there secret dad-only appointment times I didn't know about? Did I just miss the weekly Dad Orientation meeting?

I wasn't sure if I should be leaning into my role as the supportive, doting husband or preparing for some kind of Dad Entrance Exam.

We were called back, and I met Dr. Roberts. He was the kind of guy you immediately trusted—not just because he had the usual "reassuring doctor" tone but because he had a presence that made you feel like he'd seen it all and nothing could rattle him.

Erin had known Dr. Roberts for many years. And she, of course, came prepared. She had a notebook full of questions, meticulously written out and ready to go. He didn't even flinch. He was used to this with first-time parents.

After going through Erin's list and getting answers to everything she had methodically researched, it was time for the moment we had been waiting for.

The room was dim, the screen flickering to life as the technician got everything in place. Erin reached over and grabbed my hand, her fingers lacing tightly with mine.

And then, the technician said, "There it is! There's your baby."

I couldn't see the sonogram screen. I could only imagine what was happening. But I could feel Erin's grip tighten.

Then, she gasped—soft, sharp, like she had just surfaced from deep underwater.

Tears welled up in her eyes, and the sound that followed was pure release—half sob, half sigh.

Her grip eased just slightly, as though her body had finally been granted permission to rest.

She didn't say a word. She didn't have to.

Her whole body seemed to release as she stared at the flickering heartbeat on the screen—exactly what she had been waiting to see, the proof that everything was okay.

Dr. Roberts gave us our official due date, October 4. He handed us a strip of sonogram film that showed our baby, still too small to fully comprehend, but undeniably real.

We left the appointment glowing, armed with stacks of pregnancy information, a list of next steps, and an appointment to come back in a month for the twelve-week checkup.

We were so excited. We told everyone. Family, friends, coworkers, and, honestly, just about anyone who happened to be standing near me at any given moment.

The reality of it all hadn't fully sunk in. Almost all my friends had already been married and had children. For years, I had been the guy showing up at baby showers and first birthday parties, smiling politely as I handed over tiny onesies without ever really connecting to what those moments meant. Fatherhood had always felt like something that belonged to other people. And now, here I was, finally catching up to normal adulthood. I was so full of pride.

I remember FaceTiming my grandparents to tell them. Instead of just saying it, I held the sonogram film up to the camera and asked, "Do you know what this is?"

Kenny and Sharma both leaned in, squinting at the screen, but they weren't quite sure. Maybe they had never seen one of these before, maybe there was a glare on the film, or maybe it just looked like a strange inkblot test to them. Whatever the case, they were clearly trying to figure it out.

So, I nudged Erin, and she said, "I'm pregnant! That's a picture of the tiny baby growing inside me."

After the call, Erin told me the look on Kenny's face was priceless—half amazement, half sheer delight. I don't know this for sure, but I suspect he and my grandma were aware of my situation and were trying to process this news with that in mind. But what was clear was their excitement for us.

Erin was feeling the same excitemen…but also, very nauseous. And not just morning sickness. All-day sickness. Something I couldn't comprehend at all.

It seemed like she was constantly on the verge of getting sick and often did. But she was a trouper and took it all in stride. I just tried to stay nearby with a bag.

At school, Erin had told her coworkers but was holding off on telling her students until necessity made that decision for her. After sprinting out of the classroom one too many times, the secret was out.

"Wow…how long does this last?" I asked.

From what Erin—and an endless number of internet searches—told me, it should mostly end by the end of the first trimester, the magical twelve-week mark.

"Okay, great! Just a few more weeks of this and it'll all be behind us."

Meanwhile, I had gone into extreme toxin-removal mode. I evaluated everything we were putting in and on our bodies—especially Erin's. We were already pretty mindful of what we used, but suddenly, I went deeper. Like, way deeper. I had always known that there were weird chemicals in shampoos and cleaning products, but now it wasn't just about us. We had someone more important to protect.

Cue endless late-night internet searches about which ingredients could be harmful. Okay, maybe I went a little too far. But a few changes actually made sense, so we kept those.

Going into the week of Easter, Erin was so glad to have Good Friday off. She had been dragging herself through work, running on exhaustion and nausea, and was ready for a break.

Then, something unexpected happened.

That weekend, her morning sickness quickly started tapering off. But instead of relief, Erin felt a creeping anxiety.

The progression was right, I told her. Our next appointment was just a couple of days away—the twelve-week mark.

"It's time for the sickness to go away," I reassured her. "This is a good thing."

Erin wasn't so sure.

She tried to keep a positive approach, but I could tell she was holding back her nerves. She didn't want to bother me with her worry, but it was there.

On Easter Sunday, after church, we met my parents for coffee.

Easter was about renewal, redemption, and the greatest hope we could ever hold onto. That year, it carried even more weight for us—new life, both spiritual and literal, felt closer than ever.

But Erin hadn't sensed any nausea for over a day.

When my mom asked her eagerly, "How are you feeling?" Erin hesitated, then admitted, "Actually . . . I feel fine."

I could hear the unease in her voice.

And me? A chip off Dad's optimistic block?

"This is a good sign," I told her. "Your body is adjusting. Everything is great!"

She forced a small smile and nodded.

Our appointment was the next day, Monday, April 1.

The timing wasn't lost on me. April Fools' Day. I even toyed with the idea of pulling a lighthearted prank on Erin, not because I thought it would be funny, but because after days of unease, I just wanted to hear her laugh again.

THE EXIT NO ONE WANTS TO TAKE

E rin had taken the day off, just as she had for the first appointment. She drove while I sat in the passenger seat, excited, optimistic, ready to hear our baby's heartbeat.

She was also excited, but something was different this time. The nausea was gone.

As we made our way to Dr. Roberts's office, I kept the conversation going, asking her about the questions she had for him, what we might hear today, and what we still needed to do to prepare.

She answered, but her voice was distant. Her fingers drummed the steering wheel, restless with nervous energy. Her grip would tighten, then relax, then tighten again, as if she were trying to quiet something inside her.

I could feel it—the worry weighing on her, pressing down in a way she wasn't saying out loud.

We checked in, and I settled into my now-familiar routine. Second visit to the OB-GYN's office. I was basically a pro now.

We were called back, and the nurse, Jacqueline, went through the usual steps: blood pressure, weight check, belly measurement. Everything looked normal.

Erin had her list of questions, just like last time, and Dr. Roberts patiently answered each one and tried to reassure her about the way she was feeling. Then, he set the clipboard down and smiled.

"Okay, let's listen to that heartbeat."

He pulled out the handheld Doppler, squeezed a layer of gel onto Erin's belly, and pressed the device gently against her skin.

The speaker crackled with static.

Dr. Roberts moved the probe, tilting it at different angles. More static. Nothing.

He didn't look concerned. "This happens sometimes," he said.

I nodded. Of course. The baby's probably just being uncooperative. Already taking after me.

But Erin's grip on my hand tightened.

"We'll just do a sonogram to get a better look," the doctor said easily.

We followed him down the hall to the same room where we had first seen our baby. The large screen flickered on. A sonogram I still couldn't see. I felt Erin's fingers lace through mine as the technician moved the wand over her stomach. Her grip tightened more.

Then, she started to cry. I smiled softly, imagining the happy tears on her face as she saw the tiny life inside her.

But something felt wrong. The technician's movements slowed. Erin's breathing grew uneven. Her fingers crushed mine. My mind raced. What do they see?

And then I heard something from Erin that I had never heard before. A sound that wasn't just crying—it was something deeper.

A wail, raw and unfiltered, tore from her throat as if her body were trying to expel the grief before her mind could even process it.

Then, without a word, the technician quickly wiped off Erin's belly, turned off the machine, and hurried out of the room.

Wait. What?

I sat there, frozen. Erin was shaking now, her body trembling as sobs turned into something primal, uncontrollable.

She squeezed my hand so hard it felt like she was clinging to something slipping away.

And that's when I knew for certain.

This wasn't joy.

This was pain.

A few minutes later, Jacqueline arrived and led us back down the hallway. Dr. Roberts was waiting for us in the exam room. Alone. No small talk. Just him and the weight of what he had to say.

He sat across from us and spoke in a voice that was warm, calm, and full of compassion. I didn't hear a single word he said. I could only hear Erin. I was focused on her.

She was sobbing, barely able to breathe, barely able to sit upright in the chair. I knelt in front of her, my hands on her knees, trying to steady her, trying to find something—anything—to say.

There weren't enough tissues in the entire hospital for this.

Her instincts had been right. Again.

Dr. Roberts told us to take our time. He stepped out, giving us the space to grieve, to process, to try to make sense of something that made no sense at all.

After several minutes, Erin began to collect herself, and I told her we needed to get home. I poked my head out the door, unsure of what to do next, unsure of how to even take the next step.

Jacqueline, as though standing guard, saw me immediately. She quickly walked over, and before saying anything, she bent down and wrapped Erin in an all-knowing wordless embrace.

When she pulled back, she looked Erin in the eyes and softly said, "I'm so sorry, Erin." Then she helped us gather our things. As we started stumbling toward the waiting room, she suddenly stepped in front of us.

"Oh no," she said quietly. "Let's go this way."

She turned down a different hallway, guiding us toward a separate door, a private exit that led directly to the parking lot.

They had planned for this.

This was a door meant for would-be parents who had walked in with hope but would walk out with heartbreak.

Erin didn't have to go back through the office. She didn't have to be in the waiting room with smiling expectant mothers or walk past newborn baby photos pinned to bulletin boards.

She didn't have to hear the laughter, the conversations, the life inside those walls.

We stepped into the parking lot, and the second we reached the car, Erin collapsed against me, sobbing all over again.

I held her. Then I gently helped her into the driver's seat and reclined the back slightly. I got into the passenger seat, reached over, and took her hand in mine.

She didn't say anything.

I slowly rubbed her leg, my fingers tracing gentle circles as she let it all out, her body shaking with grief.

This was the worst day of her life and all I could do was sit there beside her, holding her through it.

Erin pulled herself together just enough to get us home, her strength in that moment remarkable even as the weight around us felt unbearable.

As soon as we walked through the door, I was lost. There was no instinct for this, no reaction that felt right. I had never experienced pain like this. So deep it left me hollow.

For nearly two months, I had believed it. I was going to be a father. I had gone from wondering if it would ever be possible to discovering that it was to watching it happen to having it ripped away. It was a relentless, dizzying ride, one I never could have prepared for. And now? Now there was nothing.

The soonest Erin's D&C could be scheduled was three days later. Three days. Three days of waiting with the agonizing weight of what had happened.

Erin was shattered. She barely spoke. She didn't eat. She didn't sleep. She didn't want to see or talk to anyone.

I reached out to her school and let them know what happened and that she wouldn't be coming back for a while. I updated our family and some of our closest friends, but she wanted nothing to do with anyone.

I didn't know what to do with myself. I remember lying down on the floor, staring at the ceiling, then closing my eyes, just trying to exist in the silence.

Erin had just lost a part of herself. And as much as I was grieving, it wasn't the same. It didn't feel right for me to be as broken as she was, but I couldn't push away the sorrow.

I had no precedent for this. No manual, no guidebook. No words of wisdom for the man who had to watch the woman he loved unravel while knowing he couldn't put her back together.

My only outlet was prayer. Of course, none of this made sense, so the obvious prayer was *why?* But even in my grief, I knew the why wouldn't help. Even if I had an answer, it wouldn't change anything.

We didn't need explanations. We needed peace. We needed love. We needed hope. We needed comfort. We needed to know that God was with us.

This was yet another reminder of just how painful life can be and how little control we actually have.

Erin's parents came into town for support, and when the day of the procedure arrived, we all headed back to the hospital, the last place we wanted to be.

I stayed by Erin's side as long as I could before the surgery. She was visibly shaking. Her body, once a safe haven for the life we had created, was about to become empty.

Dr. Roberts was there to perform the procedure, as were several new nurses.

The anesthesiologist gave instructions, walking Erin through what would happen while I stood beside her, gripping her hand. She would be under for the procedure.

At the end of his explanation, he added something that struck both of us as strange.

"When the procedure is complete, I'm going to say, 'Open your eyes. Open your mouth.' That will be your signal to wake up," he said.

The way he said it—slow, overly deliberate, almost like a hypnosis command—felt unsettling.

Then, after a pause, he repeated it. "Open your eyes. Open your mouth." It was eerie, robotic, detached.

When he left the room, Erin and I looked at each other. "What was that?" she said through her tears, shaking her head.

It was weird. But at that moment, it was the least of our concerns.

Her body was still trembling, and I could feel her grip tightening like she was bracing for impact. One of the nurses noticed. She left the room for a moment, then returned and walked over to Erin, holding something in her hand.

A small white ceramic cross. She gently placed it in Erin's palm and wrapped her hands around it.

"A woman once held this same grief," she said softly. "She stood where you are now—broken, aching, wondering how she'd ever move forward. And through it all, she clung to this cross. A year later, the woman came back—but this time, she wasn't alone. She held her newborn in her arms, pressed this cross into my hand, and said, 'Give this to the next woman who needs to know that even in the darkest moments, hope is never lost.'"

Erin held the cross tightly and moved her hand under the sheets. I watched as some of the tension in her shoulders eased . . . just a little.

At a time when everything felt hopeless, here was a reminder that we weren't alone. That even in times like this, God was still with us.

And then, it was time. The OR nurses came to get her. We said our goodbyes, and I stood beside her gurney as long as I could.

Then, as they rounded the corner and she disappeared from my sight, I closed my eyes and prayed.

Giving thanks for the sign of hope. For peace. For comfort. For Erin and our unborn baby.

I made my way into the waiting room, where our parents sat. We did what people do in waiting rooms when the weight of grief is too heavy to hold. We talked about random things. Anything to pass the time.

An hour later, Dr. Roberts appeared and gave me the signal.

It was over.

He met with me briefly. His voice was gentle but heavy. "Erin made it through the procedure just fine. The remains will be cremated," he said. "They'll be sprinkled in a designated area of the hospital grounds."

I just nodded.

A nurse came in and led me back to Erin. She was still coming out of the anesthesia. And the second she saw me, she erupted into tears. Hysterical. Just like the moment she couldn't see the heartbeat. She sobbed uncontrollably, her body shaking, her grief as raw as it had ever been.

We had just removed everything she had ever lived for. She lay there in the hospital bed, crushed under the weight of it.

I held her, doing my best to console her. But I was failing miserably. This was the culmination of the worst week of Erin's life. For three days, she had carried the loss inside her, unable to do anything about it.

And now? Now it was really gone. The finality was unbearable.

As a man, I can only imagine the connection between a mother and her unborn child. From the moment she knows she's pregnant, she is changed. She is aware of every tiny shift, every flutter, every change in her body. She carries life—physically, emotionally, spiritually.

And Erin? Erin was born to be a mother. But now, it was over. After it had just barely begun. She had felt it developing inside her, and now she felt the emptiness. A hollow space where dreams had once been.

I held her as she sobbed. But nothing I did could fill that emptiness.

GOODBYE AGAIN

J ust weeks later, while we were still in the early stages of grieving the miscarriage, another wave of loss came crashing in. My grandmother, Sharma, was being placed under hospice care.

At eighty-seven, her body had finally lost its ability to fight off infections after years of battling breast cancer and enduring the grueling toll of chemotherapy and radiation. It wasn't a surprise, but the speed at which things shifted—from "everything's okay" to "it's time to say goodbye"—was staggering. One moment, she was still holding on; the next, we were preparing for the inevitable.

For several weeks, my mom had been making trips back and forth to Chillicothe, splitting her time between Texas and her childhood home to help care for her mother. She and Aunt Judy worked tirelessly alongside my grandfather, doing everything they could to love Sharma and keep her comfortable. But on May 11, after a long, hard-fought battle, she passed peacefully at home.

And so, Erin and I—now carrying our own fresh grief—and the rest of our Texas crew boarded flights to say goodbye.

At the funeral, Brad and I flanked our grandfather, watching as dozens of people passed by, offering their condolences.

Grandpa took it in stride, stoic as ever. But we all felt the weight of his loss. He and Sharma had been married for sixty-six years.

Sixty-six years.

Erin and I had been married for eighteen months. I couldn't begin to fathom what that kind of loss must have felt like.

I kept thinking about how amazingly lucky I was to have my grandparents for so long, to have their example of love, patience, and enduring commitment. They showed us how to live, how to love, and how to weather life's unpredictable twists and turns.

Sharma had been the heart of the family, the ultimate caregiver. Her touch was warm, her expressions gentle, her instincts always right. When we were sick, she knew exactly how to make us feel better, sometimes with medicine, but more often with something she whipped up in the kitchen. Even now, the recipes she passed down live on, filling our homes with the smells and flavors of the love she poured into every meal.

And Kenny—he was my hero. He was old-school, tough as nails, the definition of resilience. A self-made man who provided for his family, worked hard, and carried himself with quiet strength. But for all that toughness, he had the softest spot for his grandkids. I mean, this is the guy who had a phone line installed in his bedroom so he wouldn't miss my calls. That was the kind of man he was.

After the funeral, we stayed in town for a few more days. I did my best to lift Grandpa's spirits, and he seemed receptive. But deep down, I knew. He was hurting in a way that had no fix.

On the day we left, I hugged him a little longer, squeezed a little tighter, and as I did, I noticed the frailty of his shoulders.

"I'll call you when I get home," I told him. "We need to talk about the upcoming Buckeye football season. This could be the year!"

We loaded up and drove down the road. But even as my usual optimism tried to convince me I'd see him again, there was something else—an unease I couldn't put down, a question I didn't want to face: What if this was the last time?

The same feeling I had when we left my dad's father in Chillicothe, just two and a half years earlier.

And just like then, it wasn't wrong.

I did stay in touch with Grandpa. We talked a couple of times on the phone. We had gotten him an iPad for his eighty-eighth birthday— he was a whiz on that thing—so we were also able to text with him. But then, suddenly, my messages went unanswered.

Ten days after the funeral, Mom headed back to Chillicothe. Grandpa wasn't doing well.

Nearly a decade earlier, he had beaten esophageal cancer, a battle that required a complicated surgery and a complete reconstruction of his esophagus. And now, out of nowhere, complications from that surgery had resurfaced. He was hospitalized. My mom and Judy dropped everything to be by his side.

He was transferred to a more advanced facility in Columbus, but his body was failing. And on the evening of June 10, just two months shy of his eighty-ninth birthday, he went to be with Sharma.

Another flight. Another funeral. Another goodbye. Grief was becoming far too common.

And I couldn't help but see the pattern.

In both of my family lines, my grandmothers went first. And my grandfathers—men who had spent their entire adult lives by their sides—followed shortly after.

Maybe it was the weight of grief. Maybe it was the heartbreak. Or maybe, after a lifetime of being together, they simply couldn't bear to be apart.

And Grandpa was no stranger to defying the odds. Kenny served as a flight engineer on a B-24 bomber, nicknamed *The Flak Magnet*, with the 68th Squadron Bomb Group stationed in England, flying thirty-four documented missions in World War II, including two D-Day missions, one of which struck Omaha Beach just minutes before the full Allied invasion. He was awarded the Distinguished Flying Cross and the Air Medal with three oak leaf clusters for his service.

He had survived war, beaten cancer, and built a life filled with love, family, and unwavering resilience. But losing Sharma? That was the battle he couldn't fight.

And though his body had finally given out, I don't think it was the illness, the complications, or even his years. It was simply that his heart had been with her for almost seven decades, and he couldn't bear to stay behind.

As we said our final goodbyes, I thought about the weight of it all, the grief of losing our pregnancy, the heartbreak of losing both of my mom's parents in the span of a month. It felt like the hits just kept coming. I didn't know how much more we could take, but I knew we wouldn't be walking through it alone.

THE CRUELEST DÉJÀ VU

The holiday season was brutal. The heaviness of the year's losses pressed down on us, making it difficult to find the usual joy in the celebrations. The lights, the music, the laughter of others; it all felt like it was happening in another world, one we couldn't reach.

But as the new year arrived, we held on to hope. Maybe this year would be better than last. Maybe this year would bring something good. After many prayers and long, late-night conversations, Erin and I agreed: we still wanted to create a family.

And just like before, it didn't take long. The test was positive. Erin was pregnant. We were overjoyed, but cautious. We had been here before. We knew what could happen.

At our eight-week appointment, we sat in the same waiting room, in the same office, meeting with the same doctor. When Erin saw the tiny flicker of a heartbeat on the sonogram, she squeezed my hand. I finally exhaled, recognizing the tears of joy.

The due date? October 5. One year and one day after our first due date. A sign? A full-circle moment? A chance to rewrite the past? I didn't know, but I wanted to believe it would be different.

We approached everything differently this time. Instead of sharing the news with the world, we kept it close, telling only immediate family. The first time, we had told everyone. We had shouted it from the rooftops. And then, after the loss, we had to un-tell everyone—the worst news of our lives. We couldn't go through that again.

And, just like before, Erin was sick. Constantly nauseous. And though it made her life difficult, she welcomed it. The sickness meant things were progressing. It was a sign that everything was as it should be.

And then, just like before, it stopped. At ten weeks, the nausea was gone. I tried to stay positive. I told her every pregnancy was different, that it didn't mean what she thought it did. But Erin knew better. She always did.

We called, and Jacqueline got us in right away. No Doppler this time. We were taken straight to the ultrasound machine. We were in the same room. The same flickering screen appeared in front of us— the screen I couldn't see. I held my breath. Without a word, I felt Erin collapse inward. Her breath hitched. Her fingers crushed mine. And then, the sound. That deep, guttural, soul-shattering sound of Erin breaking.

It was just as painful as the first time. Maybe more. Because then, we weren't just grieving a pregnancy; we were grieving the dream. The hope. The belief that we could do it was vanishing. It felt like we couldn't.

And then came the walk of shame. That awful, familiar shuffle out of the doctor's office—through the private exit, away from the waiting room full of expectant mothers, away from the bulletin boards of ultrasound photos and baby announcements.

It was supposed to be a compassionate route, a way to shield grieving parents from painful reminders. But walking through that door again didn't shield us from the devastation. It just confirmed our worst fear. We were right back there again.

Erin's parents came to town again. I sat in the waiting room with them and my parents, making small talk while Erin lay in a hospital bed, enduring yet another D&C.

It was déjà vu, only worse. The same nurses. The same doctor. And, horrifyingly, the same anesthesiologist, delivering his eerie, robotic instructions.

"Open your eyes. Open your mouth."

We had fought so hard to move forward, to hope, to believe. And yet, here we were. Again.

Erin clutched the small white ceramic cross, the one given to her during the first loss, the one she had carried ever since. But even with that symbol of hope in her hands, she was unraveling.

I had never seen her like this. Her grief was beyond tears now. It was deeper, darker, heavier. It was in her body, in her bones, in every exhausted breath she took. She wasn't just mourning a baby. She was mourning motherhood itself.

When it was over and she woke up from anesthesia, she saw me and immediately broke down. The same scene. The same devastation. But this time, it wasn't just grief. It was fear. Because now, we had reason to believe this would never happen for us. This wasn't just a tragedy; it was a pattern. And it was starting to feel like a cruel joke.

People tried to console us. They meant well. But it was during this time that I learned how painful words could be.

People don't know what to say in moments like this. So they say things they think will help. But often, they don't.

They say, "At least you know you can get pregnant."

They say, "Everything happens for a reason."

They say, "Maybe it just wasn't meant to be."

And possibly the worst of all, they say, "Erin, how many times are you going to do this to yourself?"

Every one of those words, no matter how well-intended, was a fresh wound.

Erin and I now understood grief in a way we never had before. My experience with meningitis, as life-altering as it had been, paled in comparison to this.

This kind of grief was different. It was silent. Lonely. Misunderstood. But it also showed us something else. It showed us who our people were. The ones who didn't try to fix it. The ones who didn't try to make sense of it.

The ones who just showed up. The ones who knew that sometimes, the only thing to say was nothing at all.

Because when you're grieving, the most powerful thing someone can do is sit with you in it.

And even as we struggled to make sense of the loss, even as the pain threatened to consume us, there was still something holding us up.

Our people. And the hope from that small white cross. With those reminders, those anchors, I still believed. Even in the darkest hours, I could still see light.

Erin and I loved each other deeply, but our grief took different forms. I withdrew into myself, growing quiet, introspective. Erin's grief was outward, raw, and often overwhelming. She cried often. I didn't. But that didn't mean I wasn't broken.

One thing became painfully clear: grieving men had nowhere to go. For women, there were books, support groups, forums—spaces where they could speak openly about their pain. And rightfully so—women carry the entire burden of pregnancy, the physical and emotional toll no man can fully comprehend.

But for men? There was nothing. I had friends who had gone through this, but none of us ever talked about it. In fact, I didn't even know some of them had been through it until years later. That's how men operate; we keep things locked up, buried under layers of silence. We're not taught how to process this kind of pain, much less how to talk about it.

I dove deeper into faith, trying to make sense of it all. I read the Bible cover to cover, searching for wisdom, for clarity, for something to hold onto. I found comfort in Job's story—the suffering, the questioning, the feeling of being forsaken, and yet, the steadfast faith. Faith isn't about understanding; it's about trusting when nothing makes sense.

I thought about the souls we had created. I prayed they were safe in heaven. I wondered who they would have been. What they would have looked like. What our lives would have been like together.

For a time, I let myself go down that path, let my mind wander into the what-ifs—the alternate realities where those pregnancies had lasted, where we had made it to the delivery room, where I had felt the weight of our child in my arms.

But I knew staying there wasn't doing me any good. I was comforted by the belief they weren't alone. I was sure my grandparents had already met them, welcoming them into our family in a way I never could.

Although genetic testing had been completed on them after the D&C, I chose not to know the genders. Maybe it was a way to protect myself. Knowing would have made it too real, too tangible. I wasn't sure I could carry that weight.

I saw what the past year had done to Erin physically and emotionally. She had carried two pregnancies, endured two surgeries, and spent months cycling through the highest hopes and the deepest devastation. Each time, she lost a piece of her soul.

Maybe she needed a break—physically and emotionally. Maybe we needed to step back and reassess. But with each passing day, we were one step closer to running out of time. Erin was nearing the end of her birthing years, something women have to consider in a way men never do.

Was that the issue? Did we wait too long? Did we meet too late in life? Were we fighting against something that was already decided? We had no answers. Only questions.

And then there was the question neither of us wanted to ask but couldn't ignore: were we just doing the same thing over and over, expecting a different result, the very definition of insanity?

Had we crossed into that territory? Were we just setting ourselves up for more heartbreak?

We prayed. We talked. We questioned. We calculated.

And yet, in the depths of all that sorrow, all that uncertainty, I found myself back in familiar territory. At a crossroads: give up or keep going.

I mean, I am the perpetual optimist. After all life had thrown at me, I still kept getting back up. Because I always knew there was a way. I believed deep down that we could do it. And Erin? She believed it, too.

HEARTBEAT AFTER HEARTBEAT

Like clockwork, just three months after our second devastating loss, Erin was pregnant again. We were thrilled but terrified. I joked that the third time's the charm. Right?

But deep down, neither of us was ready to fully believe it yet. We had been here before—twice. We had seen the heartbeat. We had made plans. We had let ourselves dream. And both times, those dreams had been shattered.

As much as we wanted to celebrate, the shadow of loss kept us grounded. Hope was there, but it was cautious. Fragile.

Erin's nausea kicked in right on cue, and that was the first sign that things were on track.

Because of our history, Dr. Roberts was exceptionally accommodating. We weren't going to play the waiting game this time. Instead of the usual four-week gap between visits, he arranged more frequent checkups, with an ultrasound every time, giving us a little relief from the uncertainty that weighed on us.

At six weeks, we had our first appointment. After the routine checks and questions, Dr. Roberts gave us news that made our anxiety spike even higher. Erin had turned thirty-five. By the time she gave birth, she would be thirty-six. She had entered advanced maternal age. It was a label neither of us had heard before, but now it was unavoidable. The risks had increased. Instead of being 1 in 10,000, she was now 1 in 1,000—or less—for certain complications.

It was difficult to hear; another reminder that we weren't in control. Despite everything we had already endured, despite all the hope we carried, there were still unknowns, still battles we might have to face.

Then it was time for the ultrasound. And there it was: the tiny flicker. A heartbeat. Relief flooded through us, but only for a moment. We knew better than to exhale too soon. We were given a due date— April 5—and an appointment to come back in two weeks.

Then came the eight-week scan. We walked in on eggshells. But there it was again: the heartbeat, strong and steady.

At ten weeks, another check. Walked in, barely breathing. Walked out smiling, sonogram film in hand.

Every appointment, every scan, was a battlefield of emotions. We lived in a constant state of tension, waiting for the other shoe to drop. And yet, every time, we left through the front door, the normal way, without needing the private exit.

That alone felt like a victory.

Twelve weeks came, the biggest milestone yet. The appointment where we had lost both of our previous pregnancies. We braced ourselves.

But everything was still on track. We got an incredible look at our baby, our little miracle. We still didn't know the gender. That wasn't our focus. We just wanted a healthy baby.

There was a prenatal genetic test available, a simple blood draw from Erin that could identify any chromosomal abnormalities—and it would also reveal the gender. We decided to do it, and then we waited ten more agonizing days.

When Erin's phone rang, we were in the car. She put the call on speaker and pulled into a parking lot. It was Jacqueline. We could already tell from her tone that everything was okay.

Then she asked, "Would you like to know the gender?"

"Yes," Erin said, gripping the steering wheel.

Jacqueline's voice lifted with excitement. "It's a girl!"

A girl.

Erin and I looked at each other, stunned, speechless. We had prepared ourselves for bad news for so long, we had almost forgotten that good news was possible.

We happened to be driving past my parents' neighborhood. I called my mom. "Are you home?"

Minutes later, we pulled in front of the house. She met us at the front door, curious, expectant.

Erin smiled and said, "It's a healthy . . . " She paused, letting the suspense build. "Baby girl."

My mom lost it—screaming, crying, hugging us, overwhelmed with joy. This was the first girl between our families. Erin's brother, Ryan, and my brother, Brad, had five boys between them. This baby girl was breaking the pattern in more ways than one.

We spent the rest of the afternoon calling our immediate family, sharing the news. It was happening. This was real. And yet, the anxiety never fully left us.

Erin's nausea was still relentless, and though I felt terrible for her, she never complained. She carried a bag with her everywhere, ready for the worst, but she welcomed the sickness. It was her reassurance that things were still okay.

At fourteen weeks, we had another checkup. Still good.

At sixteen weeks, another. Still good.

By then, we were practically on the OB-GYN frequent flyer program. Everyone knew us by name; the front desk didn't even bother asking for Erin's date of birth anymore, and I could've given the waiting room orientation tour myself, right down to recommending the chair with prime armrest real estate.

Up next was the twenty-week mark. For the first time, we waited the normal four weeks between appointments, four weeks of holding our breath. Four weeks of not knowing. We were gaining confidence, but every appointment still carried the weight of the past. Everything looked good.

And then, a complication. At the twenty-four-week appointment, the sonogram revealed an abnormality with the umbilical cord. Dr. Roberts wasn't alarmed, but he wanted us to see a specialist for a more advanced diagnosis.

The tension was back.

Within days, we were in a specialist's office, staring at yet another sonogram screen. Thankfully, the issue wasn't serious, but we would need frequent monitoring.

But Erin could feel our baby girl moving now. That was the new reassurance. Even when the nausea started to fade, the tiny kicks told her she was still there—still okay.

Weeks 28 and 32 came and went. This was really happening.

We completed a baby registry. Now it was official. There was no turning back—this kid, whom we had nicknamed Petunia, had her name on more baby gear than I knew existed.

And with that came the baby showers, the gifts, the endless decisions. Crib shopping. Stroller shopping (why do baby strollers have more features than my first car?).

We even signed up for new parent classes at the hospital. We read all the books, absorbing as much as we could, preparing for the moment our lives would change forever.

At the thirty-six-week appointment—our last checkup before birth—the doctor gave us more good news. The umbilical cord issue had not progressed. Everything looked perfect. Then he gave us instructions. "The baby could come anytime now," he said. "Here's what to do when it happens."

And the timing couldn't have been better. Erin's spring break was the next week, and then she was on maternity leave for the rest of the school year. She was exhausted and increasingly uncomfortable. She had carried this baby with every ounce of strength she had, and now it was time to rest for the home stretch.

There was still so much to do: pack a bag for the hospital, install the car seat, childproof the house, and finish the nursery.

But Erin? She had one job now: to take it easy. Finish strong. Because the next time we walked into the hospital, we wouldn't be walking out alone. We would be walking out as parents.

THEN THERE WERE THREE

Erin was fully embracing the first weekend of her long-awaited spring break. Thirty-six weeks of pregnancy had taken its toll—beautifully, uncomfortably, and with the kind of exhaustion only a mom-to-be can truly understand. She had loved every minute of it, every rush to the bathroom, every kick, every flutter, every little sign of life growing inside her. But she was also relieved to finally be off her feet.

Not that she minded the discomfort. She welcomed it, knowing it meant she was so close to becoming a mother.

We had shared the gender with family and friends, but not the name. That was staying a secret until birth, partly because we liked the idea of a big reveal and partly because it had taken forever for us to agree on a name. Erin leaned toward trendy contemporary names. I liked old-fashioned, unique ones. We each had our lists and, shockingly, a few names overlapped.

We combed through family names, found some contenders, and then, miraculously, we both landed on "the" name.

Well, our own "the" name.

Erin had her number-one choice. I had mine. Instead of picking just one, we decided we'd use both—one as the first name, the other as the middle. We just needed to figure out which order sounded best. Until then, we stuck with Petunia.

After a restful first day off, Erin was ready to get back to her to-do list. We still had a few weeks until the due date, but Erin is a planner. She had everything mapped out. That morning, she started packing the hospital bag, making sure nothing was forgotten. Our house was overflowing with baby gear—bottles, onesies, diapers, wipes. Everywhere we looked were reminders that life was about to change.

It was a casual Sunday. I was at the stove making Erin's famous Southwestern Quinoa—a favorite in our house—when my parents stopped by just before lunch. We had been trying all week to coordinate installing the car seat in both our cars and theirs. It was finally time. I turned off the stove, and we all chatted for a few minutes. Erin and Mom disappeared into the nursery while Dad and I got to work outside.

They were only there about thirty minutes. As I walked them to the front door, Erin headed upstairs. As soon as the door shut, I heard her call from above.

"John, I need you up here."

I strolled toward the bedroom. "What's up?"

She called again from the bathroom. "John…I think my water just broke."

I stopped. "Huh?"

"I think my water just broke," she repeated, slower this time.

"That can't be right," I said. "We still have three weeks to go."

"Babies do come early, John," Erin shot back. Then, she stepped out of the bathroom. "Well, either I wet myself or my water broke."

I was still skeptical. "Are you sure?"

She grabbed her phone and searched for signs of labor. "Okay, here's a checklist," she said. "Yes. Yes. Yes. Yes. Yes." She looked up, eyes wide.

"John…my water broke. I'm going into labor!"

The relaxed Sunday morning? Over. The slow, peaceful start to spring break? Gone.

"Okay, okay…let's do this!" I said as I smacked my hands together and rubbed them with excitement.

Erin grabbed the baby folder with all our notes. "We need to call Dr. Roberts."

Since it was Sunday, the office was closed, but the answering service relayed the message. Moments later, the on-call doctor, Dr. Taylor, was on the phone with Erin. She only needed about a minute to confirm what Erin already knew.

"Head to the hospital immediately," Dr. Taylor said. "I'll let them know you're on the way and will meet you there."

I looked at Erin, my mind racing. "Well, good thing you packed that bag."

I hastily threw together a bag for myself, grabbed a few towels for the car, and helped Erin down the stairs. My packing strategy? Shove first, sort later. Hopefully, I remembered pants.

Then a realization. "Wait, how are we getting there?"

It would have been nice if this had happened, say, ten minutes ago while my parents were still here. But now? We hadn't exactly planned for this.

"Unless I call them to come back, you're going to have to drive."

"They're not far away," I added, already reaching for my phone.

"No," Erin said, shaking her head. "I can do it. Let's go."

I helped her carefully into the driver's seat—on top of a beach towel, just in case—while I loaded the bags. The hospital was only a few miles away, and, thankfully, traffic was light on that late Sunday morning.

She had some minor contractions on the drive, but she held it together—white-knuckling the steering wheel, focused, determined. All I could do was watch her in awe. We had never planned for this scenario, but somehow, she was handling it like it was no big deal.

The hospital was quiet, and we found a parking spot right out front. I jumped out, ran to her door, helped her out, grabbed the baby binder, and we hustled inside as fast as Erin could waddle.

We took the elevator up to Labor and Delivery, checked in, and were immediately escorted to a room. They were expecting us.

For the first time in the past hour, things calmed down a bit. The urgency settled. We had made it. Erin was in a hospital bed, hooked up to monitors, IVs, and who knows what else. I stepped back, taking it all in. This is really happening. We're having a baby. I said a prayer of thanks for our safe arrival and what was to come.

Then, introductions. Our nurse, Mary. She was warm, kind, and immediately reassuring. She could tell we were first-timers. "I've got you both," she said. "We're going to do this together."

"Woo-hoo, let's have a baby!"

Once Mary had Erin settled, I made my way back to the car to grab a couple of things we had forgotten in our rush. When I returned, Erin was in good shape, and the room was filled with the quiet hum of monitors tracking every moment of her labor—the steady beeps, the rhythmic gallop of Petunia's heartbeat.

Time to make the calls.

First, Erin's parents. Just as shocked as we were. I spoke with them briefly, then handed the phone to Erin. She barely got a few words out before hanging up.

"That was quick," I said.

"They're putting their bags in the car," she replied. "On their way now." Five hours, and they'd be here from San Antonio.

I shook my head in disbelief. "Wait, they were packed? Like, ready to go at a moment's notice? Figures. Must be genetic."

Erin let out a quiet chuckle.

I called my parents next. They were at my brother's house. "You guys just missed all the excitement," I told them. "We're at the hospital."

They shared the news with Brad and Rachel and headed our way. I called Erin's brothers, texted a few close friends, and told them to start spreading the word.

Then Dr. Taylor arrived. We had seen her before at the OB-GYN office but never met her. Quite the way to make introductions. She did a quick exam and confirmed what we already knew—Erin was in labor. This baby was coming.

She had more news. Dr. Roberts was on vacation. He wouldn't be back until the next day. A little unsettling, sure, but we felt comfortable. "Guess that's what we get for having a baby during spring break," I joked.

She told us everything was progressing as it should, but Erin wasn't dilated enough yet. They would keep monitoring her contractions and seeing how things developed.

And then, another surprise. The anesthesiologist walked in.

And guess who it was?

Yeah. The "open your eyes, open your mouth" guy. Of course. Of course it was.

Erin and I immediately recognized him. He, however, didn't seem to recognize us—which was just fine. Better he didn't remember us at all. The less déjà vu, the better.

He ran through the usual checks, letting us know he'd be available if Erin needed anything.

We settled in, watching the clock. Hours passed. The contractions got stronger, more frequent, but still not enough dilation to start delivery.

Mary continued checking on Erin, offering support, reassurance, and care. She was incredible.

Now it was just a matter of time. But it wouldn't be long.

The baby was coming—and with her, a whole new world.

LOVE AT FIRST CRY

As our family members arrived, each group came into the delivery room to see Erin—my parents first, followed by Brad and Rachel, and finally Erin's parents, who had just arrived. The room took on a surreal quality, casual conversations mingling with the quiet hum of monitors and the sharp antiseptic scent hanging in the air. It felt oddly normal, more like a holiday gathering than a hospital room where Erin was actively laboring. Sure, she wasn't gripping my hand until it went numb just yet, but labor was labor. Eventually, everyone politely shuffled out into the waiting area, giving Erin space to breathe.

We quickly learned that a birth plan is more of a suggestion than a guarantee. Labor dragged on hour after exhausting hour with frustratingly little progress. Dr. Taylor checked in regularly, and after yet another exam with no change, she gently recommended induction. Erin and I had hoped to avoid this, knowing induction often led to a C-section. We weren't opposed; it just wasn't our first choice. But labor had stalled completely, and it became clear this was our best next step.

From the moment the induction started, everything ramped up quickly—everything, that is, except dilation. The contractions grew sharper and closer together, pounding Erin like relentless waves hitting a dam that refused to give. Her pain was fierce, unyielding, and constant. Mary, our steady and compassionate nurse, reminded us softly that sometimes labor moved this way: fast in agony, slow in progress. Erin's dilation stubbornly lagged behind the storm of contractions, and soon it was clear: we needed the anesthesiologist.

Yep. Him again. Thankfully, this time his eerie script wasn't necessary. Erin wasn't going under general anesthesia; he was only there to administer an epidural.

By evening, Erin had been laboring for more than ten grueling hours. Her strength was remarkable, but the exhaustion was undeniable. We were both spent—though let's be honest, she was the one carrying the real load. Adrenaline was all that kept us upright, pushing us to cling to whatever reserves we had left. That was also when the nursing shift changed, and Mary's reassuring presence left with it. The new team was kind and attentive, but none quite matched her steady calm.

Brad and Rachel soon left. They needed to get their boys to bed. My parents followed shortly after, comforted by the fact that they were only fifteen minutes away and could return instantly if anything changed overnight. Erin's parents, however, politely but firmly refused every offer of a nearby bed. They weren't going anywhere until they met their granddaughter.

The overnight hours felt excruciatingly long. Occasionally, I dozed off in the stiff chair beside Erin's bed, jerking awake at the slightest movement or whispered voice of a nurse checking Erin's vitals. Time blurred together yet somehow dragged endlessly.

Then, morning arrived, and with it, Mary returned. She seemed surprised we were still there, though thrilled she would be the one to see us through. Soon after, Dr. Taylor came in for another exam—still no change—but this time, she brought welcome news.

Dr. Roberts was back in the office and would be taking over shortly. Relief washed over us instantly. Dr. Taylor had been wonderful, but Dr. Roberts was our doctor, the one we'd trusted from day one.

When Dr. Roberts arrived, he calmly reviewed Erin's chart and quietly conferred with the nurses before examining her. It didn't take long before he turned to us, his expression gentle but serious.

"Your dilation is not progressing. It's been almost twenty-four hours since your water broke, and the risks are increasing for both you and the baby." He paused briefly, letting the reality settle. "You came here to have a baby, right?"

We both nodded immediately.

"Then it's time to have a baby," he said warmly, turning his full attention to Erin. "Are you ready?"

"Yes," she answered, her voice confidently excited.

Within minutes, we were preparing for the operating room.

Mary, once again, was invaluable, guiding us expertly and calmly. She handed me a ridiculous ill-fitting scrub suit and surgical cap so I could accompany Erin. I squeezed Erin's hand tightly as they rolled her down the hallway toward surgery.

A storm of emotions swirled within her: excitement, fear, joy, anxiety—all competing for dominance. This was her moment, the fulfillment of a lifelong dream, and she bravely embraced every bit of it. Still, knowing a C-section was a possibility was far different from actually experiencing it. Together, we were stepping into unknown territory.

Entering the operating room heightened every sensation. The room was frigid, bright lights glaring harshly off stainless-steel surfaces, and a giant digital clock on the wall silently counted each passing second. Nurses bustled about, quiet yet swift, precise in their movements. A nurse saw my phone and offered to capture some photos, a kindness I gratefully accepted.

I took my place beside Erin, just behind her head, clasping her trembling hand as the surgical curtain rose, blocking our view of the procedure. Dr. Roberts moved into position, reviewing everything one last time.

"Are you ready?" Dr. Roberts asked again.

Erin squeezed my hand and nodded, eyes filling with tears.

We quietly whispered a prayer of gratitude, strength, and hope.

And then it began.

I stayed close, softly talking Erin through each moment, reminding her to breathe. Emotion overcame her almost immediately, tears streaming down her cheeks. This was it—the culmination of every feeling she'd ever experienced about motherhood. The years of longing, devastating heartbreaks, and losses she thought might break her all led to this moment.

Just minutes later, Dr. Roberts spoke again.

"Okay...here she comes."

And in the very next second—

that cry.

Piercing. Raw. Utterly brand-new.

The first sound of our daughter.

The nurses moved swiftly, placing her under warming lights, weighing her, measuring her, checking her vitals. I stepped away from Erin briefly to take my first real look at our daughter. My hands shook slightly as I cut the ceremonial umbilical cord. She wailed, restless, until Erin softly called out her name. I pressed my pointer finger into her tiny palm, and she instinctively squeezed fiercely, immediately quieting at our touch and Erin's voice.

The nurse swaddled her carefully, then turned toward me.

"Do you want to hold her, Dad?"

For a heartbeat, I froze. I had imagined this moment countless times, but nothing—no dream, no expectation—prepared me for the sudden overwhelming rush of emotion as I felt her tiny weight. She was impossibly small, warm, and delicate, bundled so tightly that only her sweet face peeked out, eyes squinting at the brightness of this unfamiliar world. My heart flooded, a tidal wave of gratitude, awe, and profound responsibility sweeping through me.

"Hi," I whispered, my voice breaking slightly. "Let's get you to Momma."

I carefully placed her on Erin's chest.

That's when the floodgates opened, tears pouring down Erin's cheeks. She barely noticed that she was still being stitched up. Nothing else mattered. Motherhood, her lifelong dream, lay quietly breathing against her.

For the first time in my life, time actually stopped.

People throw around the word "miracle," but in that instant, nothing else described it. She was somehow simultaneously three weeks early, fashionably late, and right on time; perfect in every way.

It was just us. Me, Erin, and our little miracle. In a room filled with people, it felt like we were completely alone, wrapped in wonder.

We whispered another quiet prayer of thanks. Before we knew it, we were rolling back to the original delivery room. Mary, of course, was already there, smiling gently as she coached Erin through their first feeding. I watched in awe as she instinctively latched on—something as natural as breathing, yet magical to witness.

It was finally time to share our news.

I kissed my girls softly on their foreheads, then hurried down the hall, my body humming with exhilaration, relief, and a gratitude too big to contain. Bursting through the double doors, I saw Erin's dad posted there like a sentry, eyes locked on me, waiting for any sign.

"She's here," I said, beaming uncontrollably. "Emma, your first granddaughter, has arrived and she is perfect, just like her mom. Erin and Emma are both doing well. We can't wait for you to meet her."

That was all it took. Tears welled in his eyes, and we embraced tightly, overcome with joy.

Together, shoulder to shoulder, we walked down the hall—ready to deliver the news that had just changed everything.

The next three days at the hospital were a hazy blend of exhaustion and exhilaration. Meaningful sleep was a distant memory, replaced by adrenaline, hospital coffee, and fleeting power naps in chairs clearly never intended for rest. Before becoming a dad, I thought I understood what "tired" meant—but after a couple of days of parenthood, I realized I knew nothing of true exhaustion. Visitors flowed steadily through the door, family and friends eager to meet Emma and share in our excitement. It was joyful chaos—tiring yet somehow revitalizing.

When the moment finally arrived to head home, excitement mixed uneasily with anxiety. At the hospital, help had always been just a button press away. But at home, there'd be no nurses, no immediate support team. Just us. First-time parent jitters rattled me a bit. Would we really figure this all out? Thankfully, Erin's parents stayed for a couple of weeks, smoothing our transition and enthusiastically embracing their new granddaughter.

Stepping back into our house with Emma felt surreal, like a triumphant homecoming. For years, those rooms had quietly held our sadness—echoes of pregnancy losses and dreams deferred. But now, the house overflowed with the glorious mayhem we'd always imagined. The transformation was powerful, the trials of our past victoriously eclipsed by this perfect little miracle.

Watching Erin immerse herself in motherhood was nothing short of extraordinary. She instinctively knew exactly what Emma needed often before Emma herself sensed it—when to soothe, when to feed, when to simply hold her close. Witnessing this effortless grace left me humbled, slightly intimidated, and overwhelmingly proud. Erin made motherhood look easy, as if she'd been practicing for this role her entire life.

Meanwhile, I did my best to keep up, though sleep deprivation eventually got the better of me. I have vivid memories of drifting off, rocking in the nursery chair, Emma's tiny body nestled against my chest, her precious breaths, her heartbeat a steady drumbeat of reassurance. Everything else faded away in those quiet hours. It was just us, perfectly still, wrapped in a newfound peace. Even in my sleepiest moments, I recognized that those were times I would cherish forever.

Mother's Day that year hit differently, a profound celebration layered with gratitude and quiet disbelief. Erin, glowing with pride, held Emma close as we soaked in the realization that this day was finally ours to celebrate. And when Father's Day arrived, it carried its own quiet power—a moment I once wondered if I'd ever know that was now made tangible in the weight of my daughter in my arms.

Emma was immediately surrounded by love. She was the seventh grandchild in our combined families—but, notably, the very first granddaughter. Just three months earlier, Brad and Rachel had welcomed their fourth son, John David, completing their family just as ours was beginning. Emma's arrival ended the all-boy era, providing a welcome contrast to our world of toy cars and superheroes with bows, dresses, and dolls, adding a dash of pink that brightened everything.

By late summer, life had settled into a comfortable rhythm. Erin had cherished four uninterrupted months with Emma before reluctantly returning to teaching in August. Leaving each morning was tough, but the sting was softened by knowing Emma was in loving hands. My mom eagerly stepped into her role as caretaker, just as she'd lovingly done years before with Brad and Rachel's firstborn, Will.

Our days quickly settled into comforting routines: kisses goodbye in the morning, evening walks around the neighborhood with Emma tucked cozily in her stroller, and weekend adventures captured in family photos we'd dreamed of taking for years.

Life had fallen perfectly into place. More beautifully than we'd dared imagine.

And as Erin and I watched Emma grow, a quiet yet unmistakable hope stirred within us, gently whispering that perhaps our family wasn't complete. Maybe Emma wouldn't be our only miracle after all.

AND THEN THERE
WERE FOUR

J ohn, John, John!" Erin whispered urgently, shaking me awake.
I jolted upright in a groggy panic. "What? Is everything okay?"
"I'm pregnant! John, I'm pregnant again!"
Instantly, I shot upright in bed. "Tremendous!" I exclaimed, suddenly wide awake. Another one of those unforgettable 3:00 a.m. wake-up calls Erin seemed to specialize in.

From the moment Emma arrived, Erin and I knew we wanted another child. Given Erin's age, we couldn't wait long. Once again, we found ourselves in familiar territory: simultaneously thrilled and terrified.

We quickly settled back into the recognizable rhythm of pregnancy. Right on cue, Erin plunged headfirst into morning sickness—a strangely comforting reassurance that everything was progressing as it should. Our modified appointment schedule at six, eight, and ten weeks confirmed each time that things were going smoothly.

Still, a lingering anxiety from our past experiences quietly persisted, especially as we approached the critical twelve-week appointment. Dr. Roberts had already gently reminded us of the increased risks associated with "advanced maternal age." Erin was thirty-six and would turn thirty-seven a few months before the due date. Thankfully, that milestone came and went without complications. When Jacqueline called with the genetic test results, her words brought the sweetest news we could have imagined: everything was perfect—and Emma was getting a sister.

We nicknamed her Sweet Pea, a placeholder that matched our growing excitement. This time, choosing a name was surprisingly easy. Erin and I revisited the lists we'd agonized over the first time, added a few fresh possibilities, and quickly settled on "the one." Like before, we happily kept the official name to ourselves, content with "Sweet Pea" until she arrived.

There was no guesswork about the delivery date this time. Since Emma had arrived by C-section, we knew this delivery would be a scheduled surgery on July 5, giving us comforting certainty.

The sixteen-, twenty-, and twenty-four-week appointments passed smoothly. Erin radiated confidence, strength, and a certain unmistakable glow, clearly in her element. As her nausea faded, Sweet Pea's presence became even more pronounced, tumbling and kicking energetically as if she were already trying to keep pace with her older sister.

Our veteran experience made the twenty-eight-, thirty-two-, and thirty-six-week appointments feel routine, each bringing further reassurance and excitement. Knowing the exact delivery date allowed us to coordinate carefully with Mary, our amazing labor and delivery nurse. She graciously adjusted her schedule, ensuring she'd be by our side for this special day.

July 5 arrived swiftly. Mary warmly welcomed us, expertly guiding Erin through preparations and handing me those familiar, ridiculously ill-fitting scrubs. And yes, just as before, our old buddy, the anesthesiologist, returned to administer Erin's epidural—mercifully free of any creepy robotic instructions.

Our family gathered excitedly in the waiting room, this time joined by a curious and eager fifteen-month-old Emma, buzzing with anticipation at meeting her baby sister.

Inside the operating room, everything went exactly as planned. Yet, no matter how familiar it felt, nothing could diminish the awe and wonder that rushed over me as I heard our daughter's first cries. Sweet Pea was finally here—and she was perfect. I made the ceremonial cut, my hands calmer this time.

From across the room, Erin softly called her name, and I reached down, pressing my pointer finger gently into her tiny palm. Just like her sister, she gripped it fiercely—strong, reassuring, ridiculously real. Calmed by our voices and touch, she settled. Carefully swaddled, she was placed gently in my waiting arms. For a moment, I just stared at her tiny face, speechless and humbled by the miracle I was holding.

"Hi," I whispered, taking a deep breath to steady myself. Carefully, I placed her onto Erin's chest.

Erin's tears arrived instantly, beautifully overwhelming. For a brief moment, time paused again as we soaked in the magic of meeting our second daughter. The three of us, together, our family expanding, hearts bursting with joy.

Before we knew it, Erin was wheeled back to our room, where Mary stood by patiently. She effortlessly helped Erin settle in, calmly guiding her through the first feeding. Watching Erin handle everything so naturally and gracefully reminded me once again how remarkable she was as a mother.

With a gentle kiss on each of their foreheads, my heart racing with pride, I quietly stepped away, ready to share the news. I hurried down the hallway toward the waiting room, grinning uncontrollably. Our family looked up immediately, anxiously searching my face for any sign.

"She's here!" I announced proudly. "Laurel has arrived—beautiful, healthy, and perfect. She and Erin are both doing great. We can't wait for you to meet her."

If you'd asked me back when we were sleeplessly caring for one tiny human, I'd have confidently claimed I knew bedlam. Then Laurel arrived, and Erin and I quickly realized one child had practically been a vacation compared with two under sixteen months. Our neatly structured routines flew right out the window, replaced by endless diaper changes, sleepless nights, bottles piling up in the sink, and laundry mountains multiplying like rabbits.

Initially, we were blissfully naïve, certain we had it all under control. I mean, how much harder could one more little human be? Answer: exponentially. It felt like our lives had abruptly shifted from gentle jazz to heavy metal, and we were just trying to keep pace with the relentless beat.

The reality sank in one evening as Erin and I stood dumbfounded in front of two cribs set up side by side in one nursery, blinking in disbelief at each other.

"Two cribs?" I asked, staring blankly.

"Two cribs," Erin nodded, equally stunned, her eyes wide as if she'd just realized we were running a baby dormitory.

Emma, perfectly content in her crib, was too young for the transition to a big-girl bed. And so there we stood, two cribs symbolizing the sweet, messy, overwhelming pandemonium we'd willingly invited into our lives.

As if managing two babies under two weren't ambitious enough, we decided this was also the ideal moment to move. Our cozy, beloved townhouse—once perfect for just Erin and me and even manageable with one little girl—suddenly felt cramped. We needed more space, not just for the explosion of pink bows, stuffed animals, diapers, and double strollers we'd accumulated practically overnight but for something more meaningful. We needed a yard, a grassy space where Emma and Laurel could run, play, have adventures, and make memories outdoors.

And so, with a bittersweet goodbye to our first home, we packed our increasingly cluttered lives into boxes and moved into a house very close to my brother, complete with a backyard ready-made for toddler adventures, cousin playdates, and outdoor birthday parties. Although leaving our townhouse felt like parting ways with an old friend, the first time Emma and I rolled around on the grass in our new backyard, giggling uncontrollably, any lingering sadness evaporated.

Amid these life-altering shifts, we faced another significant decision. Erin, ever the devoted teacher, wrestled with the difficult choice of stepping away from the classroom . . . at least temporarily. Though she deeply loved teaching and knew she'd eventually return, the pull toward home was undeniable, even if it meant tightening our belts to make it work. In that moment, her heart was calling her home, to storybooks rather than textbooks, nursery rhymes instead of lesson plans.

"I think I need to be home for now," Erin admitted softly one evening, glancing between the two sleeping baby monitors glowing gently before us.

I took a breath, nodded, and smiled. "I think you're right. It's exactly what our family needs."

Watching Erin embrace motherhood full-time was inspiring. She threw herself into this new role with the same dedication and passion she'd always shown in the classroom. Our home quickly filled with storytime, songs, giggles, and the kind of small but unforgettable moments—Emma's laughter mingling with Laurel's coos—that felt ordinary yet infinitely precious. Even during the toughest, most sleep-deprived moments, Erin brought a warmth and patience that amazed me. On countless late nights, we found ourselves side by side on the living room floor, laughing deliriously at how utterly exhausting yet wonderful our lives had become.

Gradually, life settled into a new rhythm, far from perfect but beautifully chaotic in ways we'd never trade. Bedtime routines slowly became more predictable, laundry mountains shrank to manageable hills, and bottles began giving way to sippy cups.

Through every messy, chaotic, noisy moment, Erin and I found ourselves incredibly exhausted yet endlessly grateful. Our days felt wild and overwhelming, but our hearts had never been fuller.

And yet, even as we finally caught our breath and glimpsed the possibility of a more stable routine, we couldn't shake the sense that our family wasn't quite complete. Two little girls had transformed our lives in every imaginable way, yet there remained an unmistakable whisper—a quiet, persistent question lingering in our hearts.

AND THEN THERE
WERE FIVE

I really shouldn't have been surprised when Erin called me at work, whisper-shouting excitedly into the phone, "John, we did it again!" By now, it had practically become an annual tradition—five pregnancies in five consecutive years meant we were unquestionably skilled at two things: collaborative biology and embracing chaos. Yet somehow, even expecting it, a delightful shock surged through me every single time. Woo-hoo! The streak was alive and well. Perhaps we really did need to find a hobby, though.

We knew the drill intimately by now. Within days, Erin's familiar nausea kicked in right on schedule. The early appointments at six, eight, and ten weeks brought us smiles, relief, and new strips of grainy sonogram pictures for the fridge each time. At the critical twelve-week milestone, our nerves were eased again when Dr. Roberts gave us the thumbs-up. Jacqueline soon called with the genetic testing results, confirming that everything was perfect. She asked if we wanted to know the gender right then, but this time we decided on a small twist. If life wasn't wild enough already, we figured we'd add just a dash of mystery.

At the sixteen-week appointment, we were handed a sealed envelope with the baby's gender hidden inside. Erin promptly delivered it to a local bakery, requesting cupcakes filled secretly with either pink or blue frosting.

On a sunny Saturday afternoon, our kitchen table was crowded with family. My parents, Brad and Rachel with their four boys, our two little girls, and Erin's parents, who'd made the trip, all waited eagerly. Propped on the table, iPhones connected us to Aunt Judy and Erin's brothers via FaceTime. We made our way around the table, tallying predictions. Eight confident votes for a boy, six determined predictions for another girl.

With Emma's tiny hand steadying hers, Erin carefully sliced into the cupcake. A burst of pink filling appeared, signaling the arrival of another little girl. Three daughters. Simply incredible. My mom summed it up best when she playfully announced, "Everyone must contribute to the wedding fund!"

As always, we kept the name under wraps until delivery, giving our new daughter the nickname Daisy. Erin and I dusted off our trusty lists of baby names, which hadn't had much time to accumulate dust. Surprisingly, we quickly agreed on the perfect name, though we debated a bit about its exact spelling. The very next morning, in a moment that felt like magic, I overheard a catchy song at our favorite coffee shop. Curious, I pulled out my phone to identify the artist, and astonishingly, her first name matched ours perfectly—even down to the exact spelling. Destiny seemed to approve.

The remaining appointments with Dr. Roberts passed smoothly, familiar and reassuring. This delivery would also be scheduled as a C-section, set for December 18, exactly one week before Christmas. Our third miracle was destined to arrive right in the middle of the holiday season, and of course, we ensured our beloved nurse Mary was there to share in another unforgettable day. "You're an old pro at this now," she teased me. Despite lingering nerves, I laughed.

On the morning of delivery, I donned the now-comfortably familiar, still ridiculous scrubs and surgical cap, just before Erin was calmly wheeled down the hall and into surgery. Despite our familiarity, every nerve and emotion heightened as we entered the operating room. We may have known what to expect, but this was still a serious surgery, and our hearts beat just as quickly as before.

I took my place beside Erin, squeezing her hand reassuringly as Dr. Roberts began. Moments later, we heard that unmistakable, awe-inspiring sound—a sharp, beautiful cry followed by tiny coos that instantly melted us. Erin softly called her name across the room while nurses took vitals and gently cleaned her up. I reached down and pressed my pointer finger into her tiny palm, her grip just as fierce and reassuring as her sisters' had been. I cut the ceremonial umbilical cord with confident hands, watching as the nurse swaddled her carefully, then placed her gently in my arms.

For a brief moment, I just stood quietly, amazed once more by this perfect tiny face staring back at me. "Hi there," I whispered, my heart overflowing with love. Carefully, I walked over to Erin and placed her onto Erin's chest. Erin's tears of joy came swiftly, overwhelming both of us as we welcomed our newest daughter into the world. No matter how many times we'd done this, each child's arrival felt just as miraculous and just as powerful as the first. The three of us huddled together, whispering a quiet prayer of gratitude.

Soon, we were rolling back toward recovery, Mary's calming presence awaiting us. Like both her sisters before her, our new little girl latched effortlessly, settling in as if she'd done it a hundred times. I kissed Erin and our beautiful baby on their foreheads, feeling immense pride and love as I stepped away to announce our news.

I hurried down the hall to our waiting family, smiling uncontrollably. Everyone immediately looked up, eager to hear the update.

"She's here!" I announced joyfully. "Corinne has arrived! She's healthy, beautiful, and perfect, just like her sisters and her mom. We can't wait for you to meet her."

In the span of just 1,008 days, Erin delivered our three beautiful girls. To call this period of our lives a whirlwind would be the understatement of a lifetime. It was more like standing in front of a hurricane armed only with a diaper bag and a slightly caffeinated sense of humor. Emma was two years and nine months old and Laurel was just seventeen months old when Corinne arrived, making it three individual births in less than three years. Whenever people hear this, I usually add with a grin, "I don't necessarily recommend it, but it was definitely a fun adventure!"

For several months, all three girls were in diapers simultaneously, which meant our household consumed more than 350 diapers every single month. It was as if we'd accidentally opened an infant daycare without realizing it. Our house was a constant stream of chaos, laughter, and exhaustion. Days and nights blurred together into one endless rotation of diaper changes, feedings, soothing lullabies, and sleep deprivation.

Piles of bottles stacked precariously high in the sink and mountains of laundry grew like their own geological formations, threatening to engulf our home. Stepping barefoot on forgotten toys in the middle of the night became an Olympic-level event, testing both reflexes and self-control.

Going out in public was its own spectacle. Trips to the grocery store were strategic missions planned with military precision. The double stroller and baby carrier attracted comments ranging from "Are they all yours?" to the more pointed "You certainly have your hands full!" Restaurant visits involved careful maneuvers to keep everyone entertained, fed, and quiet enough not to disturb neighboring diners. Any family outing inevitably included at least one tantrum, two diaper blowouts, and a lost shoe or pacifier.

Despite the chaos—or maybe because of it—life was exceptionally full. Erin handled motherhood with unmatched grace, patience, and an innate ability to find humor in even the toughest moments. She was truly in her element. Watching her navigate the chaos made me fall even more in love with her every day. Erin didn't just manage; she thrived. Her dreams of motherhood were not just fulfilled; they overflowed, radiating through every bedtime story, every kiss on scraped knees, and every gentle reminder that crayons belong on paper, not the walls.

Over time, something incredible started to happen. We gradually found our rhythm. The fog of sleepless nights began to clear and routines emerged. We discovered ways to juggle naps, mealtimes, baths, and bedtime stories without losing our sanity (some days). The girls grew a bit older, gaining tiny measures of independence, which in turn gave us small, cherished windows of breathing room. Erin and I learned to tag team through every challenge, from midnight fevers to toddler meltdowns.

Our home transformed into a hub of constant giggles, imaginative play, and unforgettable moments. Dance parties broke out in the kitchen, bedtime became a sacred ritual of stories and cuddles, and weekends turned into adventures exploring parks, playgrounds, and every kid-friendly spot within driving distance.

Eventually, we reached a mutual understanding: our family was complete. With Emma, our determined leader, Laurel, our fearless explorer, and Corinne, our gentle but strong-hearted youngest, our hearts and hands were perfectly full. Erin's vision of motherhood had become reality, and our family was exactly as it was meant to be.

Looking back, I can't help but smile at those wild early days. Yes, it was crazy town. Yes, it was exhausting. But the truth is we wouldn't have had it any other way. We were—and still are—immensely grateful for every sleepless night, every messy day, and every laugh and tear that came with the chaos.

DAD'S DRESS

One of the best stories that emerged from the formation of our family revolves around a little pink dress. My little pink dress, to be precise.

Back in 1978, when I was born, technology didn't offer expecting parents a window into the womb. There were no gender-reveal parties or sonograms posted on Facebook. Instead, mothers relied on intuition, gut feelings, or simply wishful thinking. In my mom's case, she genuinely believed—or maybe hoped—that I was destined to be a girl. Of course, she'd tell you she simply wanted a healthy baby, but deep down, having a daughter would've made her heart soar.

So, in anticipation of her "baby girl," Mom excitedly went shopping. At Schachne's Children's Store, a charming little boutique in our hometown of Chillicothe, she found the perfect dress. It was adorable: baby pink, delicately smocked—the sort of outfit you imagine a baby girl wearing home from the hospital in style. Mom purchased it with a heart full of dreams, ready for my arrival.

As fate would have it, I was decidedly not a girl. Her joy over my healthy birth was enormous, but that cute little pink dress quietly went untouched, placed gently aside—never worn, yet never forgotten. Mom tucked it away carefully, thinking perhaps next time would be different.

Two years later, my brother Brad was on his way. Mom brought the dress out again, hoping this was her moment. Once again, fate smiled differently. Another healthy boy. Immense joy filled our family, but no little pink dress was needed. Still, she packed it lovingly away, keeping it safe in storage just in case, patiently awaiting its day in the sun.

Thirty years passed. Brad married Rachel, and soon they were expecting their first child. Thanks to modern ultrasound technology, they knew early on—a boy. Mom didn't even bother unpacking the dress. Two years later came another boy, then another, and finally a fourth—Brad and Rachel seemingly cornered the market on little boys. At that point, Mom probably wondered if she'd ever get to remove that dress from its decades-long hibernation. Still, she kept it.

Then, after all my ups and downs—my journey through life, meningitis, finding Erin, and our own rollercoaster ride toward parenthood—we finally received the news we'd been waiting for: we were having a girl. On that unforgettable afternoon, standing on her front doorstep, Erin gave my mom the news she'd waited a lifetime to hear. Mom's first thought? "I've got the perfect dress."

After we left, she immediately pulled the dress from storage, miraculously preserved, still on its original hanger, wrapped protectively in its clear plastic garment bag, complete with the original price tag: $17.99. In 1978 dollars, that was quite the splurge! Yet despite three-and-a-half decades tucked away, the dress remained flawless, perfectly preserved for its moment.

Just days after coming home from the hospital, my high school friend and professional photographer, Carey, captured the priceless image of our first daughter, Emma, proudly wearing the dress initially intended for Mom's first daughter. It felt nothing short of destiny. Emma's features mirrored Mom's beautifully, as if somehow the dress had brought the two generations full circle.

We carefully packed the dress away once more, hoping its job wasn't yet complete. Fifteen months later, history repeated itself when Carey took another timeless photo, this time of Laurel proudly sporting that same pink dress, just as charming as ever. And seventeen months after Laurel, our youngest daughter, Corinne, continued the legacy, photographed by Carey in that beloved, storied gown.

As I like to say, my daughters' first dress originally belonged to their dad. Hopefully, they'll be prepared to carefully explain this family heirloom when their own kids inevitably ask, "Wait—why did Grandpa have a dress?"

That little pink dress, purchased on a hopeful whim in Ohio, ended up traveling more than three decades and a thousand miles to Texas just to fulfill its purpose. My mom's dreams of having a girl might have skipped a generation, but in the end, Mom—now better known as GiGi—got something even better: four handsome grandsons and three beautiful granddaughters to love.

The dress is more than fabric and thread. It's the embodiment of hope, patience, and serendipitous irony. It's proof that although action should never be postponed, the greatest joys sometimes find their own perfect timing.

AFTER ALL OF THAT

Almost a decade since our family became complete, I am surrounded by more pink than I ever imagined, and I would not trade a single shade of it. I have become a proud girl dad in every sense of the phrase, fluent in the language of hair ties, bedtime giggles, and glitter emergencies. Our days have their own rhythm, a soundtrack of squeals, questions, and little feet in motion. A chorus in the next room keeps time better than any metronome, proof that chaos can still carry a melody.

Writing this book asked me to walk back through rooms I had locked and to sit with scenes I would rather have skipped. In doing so, I found the kind of clarity most people do not get until the last chapter. I am not saving life for later anymore. Putting these pages into the world has turned my days toward purpose and intention and made me unafraid to speak about the hard and the supposedly taboo because this is my life, and I intend to live it out loud.

I used to think meaning lived inside the plans I drew on clean paper. I believed progress was a straight arrow, that a good life followed instructions. It turns out I was chasing a fantasy that never existed. Progress, I have learned, is more of a dance; sometimes you step back to keep the rhythm, but you are still moving forward. Surviving taught me that meaning shows up in smaller footprints. It lives in what you choose to notice: the kettle beginning to sing, laughter that starts soft and takes over the room, the way a child's hand finds yours like it has a map. Loss is real, and disability is not simple. A lifetime subscription to a catheter is not a prize anyone seeks, nor one most could easily afford. Yet the storm did what storms do. It stripped the branches and left what was durable. In the quiet that followed, I learned a new way to see. There is a steadiness that comes when you stop asking for the life you had and start building the life you have.

The compass has settled, and I have begun to find authentic meaning in my life, including the work that feels like mine. Advocacy, story, and connection have given me a rhythm I can keep. I have watched people find language for their own storms and then use that language like a key. I have seen faith inch forward, people quietly show up for one another, and meaning sneak back into the routines that once felt ordinary. That does something in you. It changes your energy. It puts fuel in the tank. It reminds you that progress rarely announces itself. It is one honest step, then another. One phone call made, one appointment kept, one page written before the house wakes up. If there is a secret, it is this: the next right thing is usually small, and you will never have perfect conditions to do it. Don't wait. Begin as you are. Adjust as you go. Keep moving toward the life that fits the person you are becoming.

Destiny is debatable, and the pen is in your hand. We do not get to choose every storm, but we do get to choose what we do after we come inside and towel off. The easy choice is seldom the right one, but the right one is almost always available. Take what you can carry. Set down what you cannot. Offer thanks where you can, ask for help where you need it, and keep writing the story you want to live, one messy line at a time. Because survival isn't the end of the journey—it's just the beginning.

THE STORY BEHIND
THE STORY

This book exists because survival did not write the end; it handed me a blank page. I wanted to tell the truth about what it takes to keep writing, line by line, every day—especially on the ordinary days when no one is cheering.

Writing asked me to uncover things I had kept buried and to put words to feelings I had spent years avoiding.

It was uncomfortable, sometimes embarrassing, often tender.

Yet giving language to those truths became its own kind of healing—a catharsis beyond anything the page alone could hold.

The past did not change, but my understanding of it did, and that has changed how I live now.

A note about how the story was built.

Memory is imperfect, and so am I.Dialogue is recalled to the best of my ability, timelines are compressed where it served the shape of the story, and a few names and identifying details have been changed to protect privacy. My standard was simple: to be faithful to the emotional truth of what happened and the people who lived it with me.

A note about medicine.

What you read here is my experience with bacterial meningitis, blindness, neurological dysfunction, and recovery. It is not medical advice. I am deeply grateful to the professionals who kept me alive and kept me going, and I recognize that every body, every case, and every outcome is different.

A note about meningitis.

In 1998, when I contracted the disease, I was never offered—nor was I aware of—any vaccine that could have prevented my case. Today, there *are* vaccines that can help protect against it. I encourage you to talk with your doctor or your child's pediatrician about vaccination, ask questions, and get the information you need to make an informed decision. Meningitis is rare, but this book illustrates how real the threat can be. No one expects it, but being better informed can make all the difference.

No one survives alone.

My faith, family, friends, caregivers, and a wider community of people living with vision loss, neurological dysfunction, and the aftermath of sudden illness helped hold me up.

Over time, this work has become about advocating for others, telling the truth through story, and staying connected in the hard places. Listening with intention, sharing what we have learned, and making space for honest conversations has given my life a steady rhythm that keeps me showing up, even when it would be easier to stay quiet.

If you are reading this, I hope it nudges you to notice what is already here—the breath you did not realize you were holding, how an ordinary moment can suddenly feel like grace, a small next step that fits inside the life you have. Meaning often slips in quietly, then waits for us to see it.

If you want to keep in touch or need a place to start, you can find resources for survivors and families, updates on my advocacy projects, details about my speaking engagements, and a glimpse at the next book taking shape—all at www.johnbgrimes.com. There is a growing community around this work, and there is room for you in it.

Thank you for spending time in these pages. I wrote them to make sense of my own storm and to offer whatever light they can to yours. If you are carrying a story, don't wait.

Tell it.

Even if it helps only one person, odds are that person is you.

ACKNOWLEDGMENTS

I t turns out survival takes a village, and in my case, it was a village stocked with faith, hope, humor, and a few people who refused to let me stay down for long. Writing this book reminded me just how many hands, hearts, and well-timed jokes helped me get here.

Trying to thank everyone feels a little like trying to fit the ocean into a coffee mug—it is not happening, no matter how strong the coffee. If I attempted to name every single person who shaped, supported, or saved me along the way, this book would be twice as long and half as readable.

So, consider this my blanket of gratitude: if your name has already appeared in these pages, know that it is my highest form of thanks, proof that your impact became part of my story. And if your name does not literally appear but you know in your heart I am talking about you, you are absolutely right. You are in here too, woven between the lines.

The Core of It All

My family did not just save my life; they reminded me what living looks like. There is no version of this story, or of me, without them at the center. Their love has carried me through moments when my body gave up, my faith cracked, and my hope needed CPR. They were there through it all, holding me up when I could not stand, believing for me when I could not see, and somehow finding ways to laugh when things were anything but funny.

My parents showed me what unconditional love looks like in its purest form—quiet, steady, and relentless. My brother has been my lifelong mirror, reminding me where I came from and keeping me grounded when I drift too far from center. My grandparents built the foundation we all stand on, and even though they are gone, their wisdom still finds its way into our family conversations.

Aunt Judy has always been a second mother, the kind of steady presence that makes you feel loved, known, and safe. Wilbur was part of that steady comfort too, always kind, always there, part of the rhythm of our family for decades.

And then there is Erin—my heart, my teammate, my proof that love can rebuild what life breaks. Her steady grace, patience, and laugh make the hard days lighter and the good days even better. Together, we have built a family that teaches me daily what resilience really means.

To my daughters: you are my light and my lesson. You have taught me that strength does not always look loud, and that love, real love, is the most powerful motivator there is. You are the reason I keep moving forward, and the reason this story exists at all.

Without this circle, there is no comeback, no second chance, no book. I am beyond blessed to have them as my core, the unshakable center of everything that matters.

The Lifelines

Some friends do not sit in the bleachers; they climb over the railing and carry you off the field. Brad Smith is one of those friends, the earthly reason this story can be told. Wayne and Emily Finnell are cut from that same selfless cloth, the quiet kind of faithful that shows up early, stays late, and never asks for credit. And Chris, equal parts ballast and spark, kept the lights on when I could not find the switch. You four are family, simple as that.

Beyond them is a wide circle that held me up when I could not hold myself. Friends who stood at the edge of a hospital bed and refused to let fear have the last word. Classmates who walked the maze of campus with me, counted steps, read the handouts, and turned hallways into safe routes. The ones who closed ranks around me until courage felt ordinary again.

Friendship, I learned, is both sacred and wonderfully ridiculous. Someone always knew where my keys and sunglasses were when I did not. Someone else always had a snack and a bad joke ready at exactly the right time. There were rides that became therapy sessions, study groups that turned into pep rallies, and more than a few moments when we laughed at the wrong time and somehow that made it the right time. If you showed up, if you walked beside me, if you kept me honest or kept me laughing, you are part of the reason I am still here and still dancing.

The Hands That Brought Me Back

To the doctors, nurses, therapists, and specialists who refused to see only a chart when a person was in front of them. You kept me alive, then taught me how to live again. You read the numbers, then read the room. You followed protocols, then trusted your gut. You taught me that strength shows up in many uniforms, sometimes in scrubs, sometimes with a clipboard, always with hope and compassion.

Thank you for being willing to believe in possibility, for the ability to speak cautiously in the hallway and still carry faith into the room. You took a shot on me when the odds were not impressive. You looked up from the metrics and saw a future worth fighting for.

There were teams who colored inside the lines and others who drew new ones. Both mattered. The science saved me. The imagination gave me back a future. If you ever chose hope over habit while caring for me, know you left a mark on these pages.

Mentors, Guides, and Teachers

To the mentors who entered my life after meningitis and stayed long enough to see what came next. You taught me that resilience is not a trait you have or do not have; it is a daily practice. You helped me trade performance for presence, certainty for curiosity, and you reminded me that progress is usually quiet.

To the pastors and faith leaders who held space for questions that did not have easy answers. You showed me that doubt is not the opposite of faith. You taught me to pray with my feet, to let gratitude be a habit, and to look for grace in ordinary rooms.

To the teachers who made learning possible when vision changed the way I met the world. You read what needed reading, adapted what needed adapting, and never made help feel like charity. You turned access into dignity. You opened paths I could not see on my own.

To the colleagues and professional mentors who taught me to bring the same care to my work that I bring to my home. You modeled integrity when no one was watching, encouraged me to speak plainly, and reminded me that leadership begins with listening.

To the writers who became companions, though we have never met. You do not know me, but your words helped me find my own. Suleika Jaouad and Ruthie Lindsey, whose memoirs gave me language for living after, for holding beauty and pain in the same hand, and for believing that a life can be rebuilt with honesty and hope. Ryan Holiday, whose work on Stoicism reminded me that obstacles can become the way forward when we choose how to respond. Your words kept me company at three in the morning and made the room feel less lonely.

I am shaped by all of you. If there is anything wise or useful in these pages, it is in part because you shared what you had and trusted me to carry it well.

Writing Team and Supporters

To everyone who helped shape these pages before they were ready for daylight: thank you. You read drafts that were more courage than craft and still showed up. Some chapters wandered like a GPS with no signal; you drew the map. Some sentences arrived half-assembled; you clicked the pieces into place. You asked honest questions, reminded me to keep going when the words would not cooperate, caught the countless typos my eyes missed, pushed for truth where I was still hiding, and celebrated each small win like it mattered. You did not give up on me; you encouraged me. Your care made this book better, and your faith made it possible.

By name, I want to thank the editors, early readers, coaches, and champions who lent their time and attention. Consider this my standing gratitude. If your name belongs here and I missed it, know that your fingerprints remain on these pages.

Margaret Black, Sierra Bodor, Debbie Burke, Jennifer Bushen, Bill Callejas, Kristina Conatser, Rachel Dawson, Christopher D. Elder,

Heather Entenmann, Chad E. Foster, Elizabeth Hamilton-Guarino, Gary and Teresa Klembara, Amy Lyle, Robert Sherrard, Linda Singerle, and Garrison Wynn.

To everyone who has ever faced an obstacle and chosen to move anyway, thank you. Destiny is debatable; what we do next is ours to decide. May we keep choosing the small, honest step that turns a life into a story worth living.

ABOUT THE AUTHOR

John B. Grimes is a writer, speaker, and meningitis survivor who learned the hard way that *survival is not the end of the story*. At nineteen, he was hospitalized with bacterial meningitis, spent eight days in a coma, and woke up with profound vision loss and lasting neurological damage. Learning to rebuild a life in the dark, he discovered that resilience lives in small, honest steps rather than dramatic comebacks.

Through his advocacy, speaking, and his podcast *Destiny Is Debatable,* John helps others facing illness, disability, or unexpected detours find language for their own storms and the courage to keep going. He is passionate about meningitis awareness, survivor support, and making the world more accessible for people with disabilities. John lives in Texas with his wife, Erin, and their three daughters, who supply an endless soundtrack of giggles, glitter, and reasons to keep moving forward. Learn more at www.johnbgrimes.com.